IN MEMORIAM

SO·THE·HEART·BE·RIGHT

Joanna Defrates
1945-2000

AN EGYPTIAN JOURNAL

BY THE SAME AUTHOR

Lord of the Flies
The Inheritors
Pincher Martin
Free Fall
The Spire
The Pyramid
The Scorpion God: Three Short Novels
Darkness Visible
Rites of Passage
The Paper Men
The Hot Gates, and other occasional pieces
A Moving Target
The Brass Butterfly: A Play in Three Acts

AN
EGYPTIAN
JOURNAL

WILLIAM
GOLDING

faber and faber

LONDON · BOSTON

Copyright © 1985 William Golding

First published in America in 1985 by
Faber and Faber Inc.,
50 Cross Street,
Winchester,
Massachusetts 01890

This book was designed and produced by
The Rainbird Publishing Group,
40 Park Street, London W1Y 4DE

Library of Congress Cataloging in Publication Data
Golding, William, 1911–
Egyptian journal.

1. Egypt—1945–   —Description and travel.
2. Nile River Valley—Description and travel.
3. Golding, William, 1911–   —Journeys—Egypt.
4. Novelists, English—20th century—Biography.   I. Title.
DT56.G54 1985   916.2   85-6777
ISBN 0-571-13593-5 (hc.)
ISBN 0-571-12547-6 (pbk.)

The text set by Tradespools Ltd., Frome, Somerset.
Colour originated by David Brin, London, England.
Cover art by David Biedrzycki, USA.
Cover design by Ken Silvia Design Group, USA.
Printed by Hazel Watson & Viney,
Member of the BPCC Group, Aylesbury, Buckinghamshire.
Bound by Haddon Craftsmen, USA.

Printed in Great Britain

Ναῦται βαθνκυματσδρόμσι
ἁλίων Τρίτωνες ὑδάτων
καὶ Νειλῶται γλυκυδρόμσι
τα γελῶντα πλέσντες ὑδάτῃ,
τὴν συγκρισιν ε'ίπατε, φιλσι,
πελάγσυς Νείλσυ τε γσνίμσυ.

P.Oxy.III.1903,no.425,p 72

(For translation see page 207)

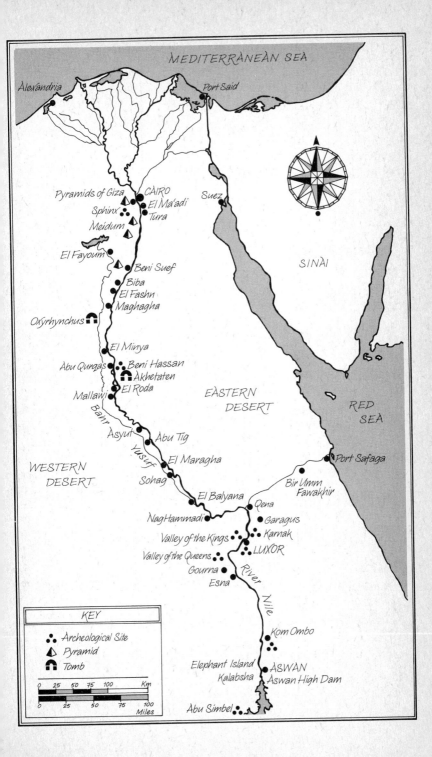

The genesis of this book has been peculiar and its aim in doubt. For the last sixty years I must have read every popular book that anyone ever wrote about Egypt. In common with my generation I found a deep and so to say natural attachment to things not so much just Egyptian as Ancient Egyptian. Perhaps for us all, the supposed immobility of ancient Egypt stood over against the change which is the experience of daily life. This was not quite a yearning for a lost paradise but it was certainly a yearning for something or other. Perhaps we could divide the children of that generation into those who read Conan Doyle for choice and those who read Rider Haggard. The concept is attractive. You can, by falsifying the nature of both men somewhat, put them at opposite ends of a spectrum. On the one hand, we have the creator of that egotistical male, Sherlock Holmes, and on the other hand we have the creator of She Who Must Be Obeyed. Here we have set up as an ultimate the logic of deduction, there we have Mystics Who Know and do not Need To Reason. And so on. It would not do, of course, for Conan Doyle was the one who ended up looking at photographs of little girls in Art Nouveau costumes and believing they were fairies. We may be simplistic but life isn't. Nevertheless there was in the two men a tendency towards one rather than the other of two worlds.

Haggard, of course, was hooked on the mystery of Darkest Africa. Of this mystery Egyptian history was no more than an extension. His novels *The Moon of Israel*, *The World's Desire* and *Cleopatra* either imported or recognized what was implied in our view of ancient Egypt – the mystery of magic, the presence of gods, the power of a priesthood, the attraction of anciently, the glamour of kingship. Then into this partly realized connection between us and them was stirred a catalyst, the excitement, the hullabaloo, the world interest of Tutankhamun's tomb.

Now though I read Conan Doyle when he came my way, I did not buy him and I did not borrow him even from the library. But on Haggard I would spend my all, walk miles for one of his books, read and reread without end. I still think he has scenes of an overwhelming power. C. G. Jung, in the days when not just a diminishing group

9

of addicts but everyone took him seriously seemed to give Haggard a validation. He cited She Who Must Be Obeyed as the archetype of the Anima.

But to us as children and adolescents what was Egypt to be? The young Farouk was to be seen on a stamp, unlikely looking heir of the pharaohs. There was the administration of Egypt by Great Britain, such a benefit to the place. There were the papyri. There were the biblical connections. There were in every museum some of the anthropomorphic, the mummiform coffins that stared at us with all the awesomeness of death, magic, terror, mystery. Yet the official source of all our views of ancient Egypt came by way of archeologists who were just beginning to use science and adopt a wholly rational approach to it – science and rationalism in the service of magic and mystery! It was a great confusion.

My childhood's stance, then, was romantic though terrified, even a bit religious though pagan. Mummies, the mere thought of mummies, put ice on my skin, but at the same time I could more readily believe in Ra, Isis and Osiris than in the Trinity. To me the contradictions of Egyptian beliefs were not implausible; or rather, since they were religious beliefs, contradictions were just what I had come to expect.

Yet all the time, as far as the adult world was concerned my preoccupations were with the rationally explored and logically treated discoveries of scientific archeology! This was a tension of which I was only partly aware and which died a natural death as I grew older and was more caught up in life and love around me than in an imaginative dialogue with death and magic.

And yet – !

It would be going too far to say that I felt myself to be an ancient Egyptian. But I felt a connection, an unusual sympathy. It became, absurdly enough, a feeling of responsibility as if I owed the country something though I had never been there. There is even the possibility that this book is an unsuccessful attempt to pay that debt.

So there remained a link with ancient Egypt in me until past my middle years. It was only then – and about ten years before the publication of this book – that my wife and I made our first visit to Egypt. Why so late? At any time in the previous twenty years we could have gone. But there had turned out to be so many interesting things to do, so many other countries to visit, such boats to sail, such money, such reputation to be chased. . . .

Nevertheless, at last go we did and I found that the Egypt of the mind simply did not exist. I had to rearrange everything. Egypt was more – much more! Even the archeologists were not what I had supposed. For instead of being the rational creatures I had anticipated they were as crazily imaginative and as well disposed to the Mystery as any child could have wished sixty years earlier. When, for example, the question arose of a dear lady who believed herself to have been a priestess of a particular temple, they did not dismiss her as a crackpot but agreed that *she had something*.

Then – well, a year ago – I was approached and asked to write a book on Egypt. The prospect of another visit to Egypt but this time with a Minder who spoke the language (what our Victorian forebears would have called a 'courier') was attractive. But I had no particular view, had no axe to grind, had read widely but not deeply. I pointed out to the publishers that the book could not be authoritative. To my surprise they were aware of this. It was to be, I found, a book about me as much as about Egypt. It would contain photographs, mostly photographs of the country but some of me.

This seemed to be the perfect assignment. We discussed methods. I had an idea which seemed plausible. The last time my wife and I had been in Egypt the greatest difficulty and danger we had faced was to get rooms in hotels. I was, or had been, a sailor. I sailed in my youth, spent the war years in the navy, some of them in command, spent more years after the war teaching sea cadets to sail. After that I sailed my own boat on the north coast of Europe and topped the lot off as unpaid hand in my son's canal boat. Then why not hire a boat, a yacht on which we could live, proceeding up and down the Nile, stopping off at such places of interest as Oxyrhynchus and Abydos; and mingling light-heartedly with live Egyptians instead of dead ones. For during our previous visit I had come to a simple truth; that Egypt is a complex country of more-or-less Arab culture and it is outrageous for the uninformed visitor to confine himself to dead Egyptians while the strange life of the valley and the desert goes on all round him. The tourist (and I was not quite that) who has limited time and money may well confine himself to the monuments of Pharaonic Egypt. For us, handsomely supported as we were and able to take what time we chose, it would have been an insult.

I flew out to Egypt for forty-eight hours to find a boat. In this I was not so much helped as *carried* by the young Egyptian gentleman, Mr Alaa Swafe, who was to be our Minder. There were very few boats available. The concept of private persons travelling on the Nile in a hired boat and not as one of a tour was, if not new, at least unusual. We searched the waterfront at Cairo with growing despair. I quote from my journal.

The boats were awful. There weren't many of them. Perhaps Alex would have been a better place but I had some delusion that Cairo would have river boats. I suppose some vague picture of possible luxury was floating about at the back of my mind. 'The barge she sat in' and all that. But the boats were either plastic skimming dishes or rotting old houseboats where the decaying curtains were pulled apart by their own weight and carpets under foot squelched with water from the bilge. The hire price averages £250 (E) a day.

I had a gloomy lunch with our bilingual Minder. 'There's one boat left,' he said at last. 'It's up river a mile or two at Ma'adi. I don't even know if she's for hire.'

Of course that was the one we hired finally. She belonged to Dr Hamdi and we came to an arrangement. The boat (named *Hani* after Dr Hamdi's son) looked a bit more solid than the skimming dishes. She wasn't over-engined as they tended to be. There was a central space containing the galley and a console of controls. There were two cabins with four berths in each. There was a fo'c'sle for two. There were also two toilets, or 'heads' in naval parlance. If my account were to be relentlessly factual those heads would loom as large and important as any Egyptian ruin that ever was. But at first sight they seemed all right. After all, I thought, if anything nasty happens – it always does in boats – we could get out and walk or take a train.

I flew back to England a few hours after I had left it. I was immediately caught up in a whirlwind of controversies, interviews, parties and publications which I need not go into here. But Egypt and the boat and the book became more and more uneasily part of a twingeing background. As the days slid away and the *fact* that we were actually going came nearer and nearer I was overcome with a feeling of sheer folly. I was seventy two. I did not need the money. I had awful memories of dirt and helplessness. Yet here I was engaged to fill an as yet empty book. Determinedly then I set to and planned what I would do. I should expand the experience of Egypt beyond the valley – visit the Red Sea coast – try to get there through the desert, the Desert, the DESERT! It was a breath-stopping concept.

12

I rummaged among my books.

... Where the soldier of a hundred years ago was buttoned up tightly in thick uniform, the modern resident of Egypt seeking comfort wears thin white cotton or silk clothing, consisting of shirt, trousers and jacket, white canvas boots with thick soles and a light but inch-thick pith sun-helmet, possibly with a further protection against the sun in the form of a spine-pad inside the jacket. The only vulnerable spot is then the eye....

Well, I knew better than that, at least. Also we had thoughtfully decided to go in February when on the one hand we should benefit from the mild Egyptian winter and on the other miss at least some of the fierce English one. We should come back when the flowers were in bud and the cuckoo cucking.

Then I fell sick and the date of departure moved on me through a maze of more interviews, sittings, doctors, parties meant to honour but sources of desperate strain. During increasingly wakeful nights I began to plan ahead, feverishly. Preface? I would have no preface, thus saving time, money and exertion. I would have no index because – well, because it wasn't going to be that kind of book so out with the index! After that, the bibliography might as well go too and for what I consider a plausible reason. This was literally journalism and journalists protect their sources. Farewell then Gilson, Major Charles, and Balls, Mr W. Lawrence, adieu Maspero, Professor Gaston Camille, and Gautier, M. Theophile – I wrote a list of subjects and I decided precisely how I would treat each. Really, I was planning to write the book without needing to go to Egypt at all. Confused, more and more convinced that I should find too little to write about, I saw myself creating most moving soliloquies in the desert, particularly in the more neglected sites. Bending down, I would detect, sticking out of sand the corner of a roll of papyrus – or pretend I had detected.

The day of departure came inexorably. We took far too much clothing in three large suitcases. We took too few books. I was obsessed with the horrors of Cairo Airport. I could not find Plutarch's account of the story of Isis and Osiris and this seemed a disaster. For I felt I should not be able to verify certain quotations. When fit and well I don't verify quotations. However good and beautiful a phrase or sentence may be in its original place, the unverified version has an additional beauty which it derives through tumbling about for a generation or two in the mind. Moreover an unverified quotation is always apter to the new context than the original stuff would be by reason of a nice derangement of epitaphs which is the operation of the unconscious, holy be its name! Yet now I feared to make a mistake and must therefore have been really sick. Then again, there were the sixty photographs with which the book was to be littered and thickened. I had never been in the position of writing a book which would be illustrated with photographs and did not know what I was supposed to do about it. Would someone photograph what I had written? Should I write about what had been photographed? Should we ever meet? Ought we not do the thing together? Would it not be better – a seductive thought, this one – to leave all the writing until the photographer had finished? Would it not be better if I confessed to the frivolity attendant on the advance of old age?

We landed and passed through the 'horrors' of Cairo Airport in five minutes flat. We were wafted. Our Minder met us and drove us straight to the Sheraton in Giza.

All the same, when he left us, the complex of minor irritants that Egypt provides you with even in the most luxurious surroundings presented itself again. The traffic was thicker than before and even more hysterical. Even with the double-glazing of our room we suffered once more that whining, parping, screeching, howling disharmony which is the background to life in Cairo. Neither of us could come by sleep. Perhaps we tried too hard. The traffic, oh the traffic! It was like a fever. There is a period, and only one, lasting about an hour in the early morning when the noises cease as if something has been turned off. With common and unspoken consent we got out of our beds, opened the French windows on to our balcony and stood looking down at the Nile where it glimmered among the high-rise buildings. The corniche that lay beside it and beneath us was empty. Then a solitary little red car came along the corniche and it was parping fretfully.

'He's lonely,' said Ann. 'He can't stand the silence.' The car passed below us still parping in the direction of the pyramids. Faintly from over on the island of Zamalik a voice began to cry. It was a muezzin. Soon his voice was joined by others.

'Remember?' Once we stayed in a hotel on Zamalik. The concourse or rather convocation of muezzins had not annoyed me

14

but brought on a fit of piety. I had got out of bed and tried to write down my impressions. Now I carefully closed the French windows on them.

'We shan't be bothered with muezzins where we're going. I've decided we'll tie up by the bank in deep country. We'll see towns during the day and press on during the evenings. Of course, when we have tied up alongside we may very well be able to stroll about in waterfront villages before we turn in. . . .'

'Bed.'

I suppose we got a bit of sleep before next day. We spent most of the morning turning three suitcases into two. After that, we went to have a quick preliminary look at the boat which Ann had not yet seen. She lay alongside a pontoon that was reached by a catwalk. We did not stay long since there were a number of apparently shy persons who stood up when we came near and then sat down again. Nor did we go on board but stood on the pontoon and looked at *Hani* as wisely as we could. She had been cared for. She looked clean. All the same a young man in a blue tracksuit picked out with white stars and wearing a close, blue turban was cleaning her with the frenetic energy of someone working under the immediate eyes of the boss. I felt for him and smiled but he did not notice. He simply went on polishing the mahogany trim – a redundant activity for it already shone under the chilly February sun.

Somehow it seemed improper to go on board, as if we were not yet entitled. More than that, I found myself becoming more and more incredulous of the fact that we were actually going to put ourselves, at *our* age, into a boat again and allow some strange people whose language we did not speak to convoy us. We came away and the strangeness of the circumstances seemed emphasized by a most extraordinary tree. It was average size for a tree but the flowers were enormous. It was only after close examination and a few double takes that we realized we were looking at our first banana tree in bloom. The farce of the situation seemed emblematic. I dare say if you look you can find a banana tree in bloom at Kew. Then we went back to the hotel and prepared for our evening party by spending the afternoon in bed.

At Dr Hamdi's sumptuous flat we were shown photographs of reclamation work and we were video'd. We met various police who were active in various Middle Eastern countries. We met some teachers, school and university. It was at this party that our Minder and Dr Hamdi discovered that they were not too remotely related. Dr Hamdi made it clear (in order I suppose to relieve me of any feeling of responsibility) that our Minder Alaa Swafe, was in charge of the boat. This put me in the position of being a passenger, a position in a small boat to which I was not accustomed. Still, there was no denying that without Arabic I should not have been able to take charge of the boat in a proper manner. In any case I had to accept the position whether I wanted to or no.

Next morning we were taken with our suitcases to the boat again. Our Minder had hired us a cook and he turned up, carrying a lute. I asked our Minder if, since he was responsible for *Hani*, he knew anything about boats. No, he said, with what I hoped was modesty, nothing at all. It all seemed a bit surreal. The crew consisted, then, of one engineer, one cleaner, one cook with lute and the *reis*. Our Minder, Alaa, told us that Shasli was a *reis* – *Reis* Shasli – and to be addressed as such. *Reis* was a dignity he stood on. It didn't mean 'captain'. It meant 'Foreman of these circumstances'. But a crew of four to handle a boat not as big as one I had once owned and sailed! I looked at them and they seemed to avoid my eye – or did I avoid theirs? I strolled away, leaving Ann to talk to Alaa and pretended to examine the banana tree. But really I was remembering a painful quotation from one of the books I had not brought with me.

> ... English go their way ... with their habit of looking "through" persons who do not interest them, and of waiting for friendship rather than going to seek it ... the British are the most foreign of all the foreigners in Egypt ... prevented ... by their temperament from assimilating themselves to the life of the country....

It was true. I could feel a lifelong experience of being a particular sort of Englishman building up in me like a wall. It was more impervious than a wall of language. It was assumption and custom. And I was the one who had hoped that my book would not be about temples but about people!

I turned back to the boat. The crew had gone aboard. Alaa and Ann were talking animatedly. Near them was a frail old Nubian, black and crumpled, in jeans, grey jersey and close turban, messing tremulously with ropes. He had a dazzling white moustache but looked strangely sullen behind it. Dr Hamdi, his son and charming wife turned up together with the females of Alaa's apparently extended family. It was a scene of much animation and reminded me of such pictures as *The Departure of Christopher Columbus for the New World*. We said our farewells and went bravely aboard. *Reis* Shasli, a slight figure in grey galabia and large, grey turban ascended to the glass box which housed our wheel and slave controls. His face was black as the Nubian's. It was well enough featured but mud-coloured from heredity and exposure. Our engineer, a sophisticated man in western dress and with a Ronald Colman moustache was busy over the engine in the centre compartment. The cook had stowed his lute and was in the galley. Shasli started the engine. The Nubian cast off ropes, the audience waved and took photographs.

The Nubian clambered aboard as we moved away from the pontoon.

Crew of five.

The main thing was to get away. We stayed on deck, waving and shouting absurdities and not understanding the replies. Presently a gaggle of yachts at anchor hid the pontoon and we could be said to have started. Ma'adi is a nondescript suburb of Cairo. We left it and the high rise area of the city behind us at 11 o'clock. Industry clusters by the water and the suburbs stretch south for miles. It was cold and the river Nile, most famous, most exotic of rivers, was about the same size as the Thames by Tower Bridge and the same colour. The adverse current meant that we made little headway – surprisingly little since the boat was allegedly capable of eleven knots. We were using no more than five of them from which the adverse current subtracted one. There was nothing about the scene to distinguish it from any river scene in any city. The pyramids, of course, were hidden by buildings. The grey, poppling water and the occasional barges were too matter-of-fact for description. *Reis* Shasli didn't steer straight up the river and I thought at first that he might be following a winding channel, but no. He went from boatyard to boatyard, zigzagging from one bank to the other, each time hollering to a chum on shore. I thought at first he was showing off his splendid command, but in fact he was wanting to borrow a bit of rope and a thingummybob, a *machin*, a what d'you call it. He was – is – steersman of one of the Nile tourist boats and only allowed to hire himself out to us because his own boat was being refitted. We went below to look at our cabin. Ann discovered at once that there was no hanging space for clothes, something I had not noticed when I hired the boat. I tended after that to avoid catching her eye. We put up the upper bunks and used them for stowage of clothes (of which we clearly had too many). I pretended to find this just as convenient as drawers and cupboards but deceived neither of us. I didn't like the look of our lavatory, toilet, loo, heads, admiral, either. The bore looked small to me.

Reis Shasli brought us alongside a floating restaurant and went aboard it. Presently, staring through our windows (they were too large to be called ports), I saw him coming back with the old Nubian, who was carrying a grapnel. So we had had no anchor either! I saw no more of them for the young man, Faroz, in his blue tracksuit, started to clean the outside of the window six inches from my face. Shasli took us back into midstream.

We wrapped up even more warmly and went on deck and stood, chillily in the cold north wind. On the left, a mountain of white stone lay perhaps half a mile from the eastern bank of the river. There was much machinery, smoke and clouds of dust. This was Tura with its quarry for fine limestone. Chephren faced his pyramid with it, all blinding white. Five thousand years of quarrying had put half a mile between the mountain and the river. It was something to have seen after all and consolation for not being able to see the pyramids from the river. After Tura the banks became a bit more countrified and even Egyptian. There were plantations of date palms and lines of delicate green trees – tamarisks, I think. We passed a huge dovecote built in the distinctively Egyptian manner, massive mud walls then domes and minarets with niches for nesting. There were donkeys, untethered and grazing on the bank where it was clear of reeds. It seemed odd to see a donkey doing what it liked and not laden to death. But this was February, the Egyptian winter, and a relatively lazy time for man and beast, unless your business happened to be with the water traffic or you were a woman. The Nile was very low and women were washing clothes on the mud beaches. A solitary man moulded mud brick and women processed up the bank with huge water jugs on their heads. The palms, I thought, looked like bottle brushes – but then did I know what bottle brushes looked like? Here and there brickyards or brickfields obtruded most rawly into the Nile with great screes of red fragments. There were sailing boats moored alongside the screes taking in loads of red brick. Rarely the interruption to the mud bank was not red brick but stone foundations of some vanished building which might have been any age.

Then, in broad daylight – with hours of daylight left – we tied up to an open sailing boat that was moored next to a whole mountain of straw pecked over by pigeons and rat-rustled. The straw, being in a brickyard, was, I supposed, the stuff which Pharaoh wouldn't give the Hebrews. As far as I was concerned (and the rats poked out their noses or rustled invisibly) anyone could have had it.

The first bad news of the journey filtered through to us. The boat carried neither sheets nor blankets. Alaa and the cook, Rushdie, scrambled ashore over the sailing boat and rustling straw and went to find a place where they could buy what was necessary. The crew evaporated. Fish jumped round the boat. The wind blew. A pulley block tapped the mast of the sailing boat, tap, tap, tap for ever. Dusk approached quickly. The sky was covered with high cloud and it was cold.

Alaa came back with sheets and blankets. The crew materialized and music, Arab music, resounded from a loudspeaker. It was nearly 6 o'clock and sunset. We have, I said to Alaa, a few more hours of the evening in which we can make more distance. This remark was translated to the *Reis*. It stopped the music, stopped conversation, even seemed to stop the block tapping, or perhaps it only stopped the wind. The answer to my remark filtered back to me. Nobody uses the Nile after dark.

Then why, I asked, have we those little green and red navigation lights up forrard? This piece of expert knowledge created a pause. But once more an answer came filtering back. Nobody uses the Nile after dark. You have to have permits, which can only be got back in Cairo. There are regulations. The river is low. There will be trouble.

Everyone was smiling in a friendly manner. It was an Egyptian smile. I had seen it many times on statues but now for the first time I understood it. We should only move between the hours of six in the morning and six in the evening. There was no question of working watch and watch.

In that case, I said, we would start sharp at 6 o'clock in the morning. The answer filtered back again. We would start as soon as possible but there might be fog.

Fog.

Fog, the seaman's bane was the captain's friend. I envisaged him lying in while the early sun dried up a trace of mist, which had lain, but penetrably, about the banks.

Well, there was nothing to be done. Once, I remembered, an old

19

lady told me about her young brother, a midshipman. He boarded a slaver in the gulf while his gunboat rushed off to chase another dhow. He was unarmed. He drew a chalk line across the deck and forbade the slavers to cross it. (Provenance of chalk not stated.) Hour after hour he paced the chalk line until his gunboat came back and arrested everybody. Aye me!

No, there was nothing to be done. The generator and the lights started up and the music. I was informed by a smiling *Reis* that we had come seventy-five kilometres.

After some time the generator stopped and the lights dimmed as the music faded. Presently light and sound faded right away. The block tapped.

I lay on my bunk, fully dressed, wrapped in a sheet and blanket, my head, since we had no pillows, on a rolled-up raincoat. Across the cabin Ann shivered a little under a whole heap of clothes.

It seemed that I would never get to sleep. I began to reflect glumly on the inadequacy and incompetence of my approach to this business of finding out about Egypt.

My childish approach had been replaced gradually by an adult one which had become more and more complicated. It was not just an inability to meet people, it was a question of the inward eye. My whole imaginative concept of the country had changed because of the explosion of knowledge, not just about ancient Egypt or even modern Egypt but about what might be called geological Egypt. All the way up the Nile valley there had been made, I knew, boreholes for water; and, of course, there had been much exploration not just for ores or water but for oil as well. In addition, the massive evidence for plate tectonics and continental drift had put the northeast corner of the African land mass firmly into a more general picture. My imagined Egypt (the one which would have to go into the book) now included this majestic history, which by its very nature was difficult to assimilate into the more limited human story, even when that was stretched to take in the successive changes in the nature of *Homo sapiens* himself. It was a question not of thousands but of millions of years which conditioned the imagination. I knew now, as I had never known when I was a child, that there had not been just one Nile in this valley but five Niles successively. By the standards of some of them our present Nile was no more than a trickle. But to exercise that geological imagination it was necessary to see through the surface, to

20

turn back, as it were, successive blankets on a bed of rock and to realize vividly – *poetically* – that this was a place like any other, welded into the total nature of the planet and an expression of it.

Stars shivered at me through a gap between the curtains which covered the window behind my head. They were piercing stars and emphasized the major history over the minor one. The fifth Nile clucked occasionally under our bilge.

This was my ludicrous problem. In imagination I had filled something like the Grand Canyon, only larger, with evaporites, boulders, crags, fossils, gravel, sand, clay and mud so that its cliffy sides projected from the rest no more than a few hundred feet – and that was now my Egypt, impossible to gather into a simple picture. The canyon was no plausible guess. Echo-soundings and drillings have mapped it all. The time scale which used to stretch over ten thousand years must now be stretched to cover ten million. The story of Man himself, it seems, has occupied at most no more than half of that. We must adjust ourselves to time scales that differ by a factor of a thousand.

I thought of the famous statues that now illustrated both scales so that a man needed an impossible depth of imaginative focus to appreciate both aspects at the same time. There were, I seemed to remember, worked stones from temples which included a fossil by accident. Even without the fossil the type of stone was significant and evocative. The archaic figure of Zoser in the Cairo Museum takes us into the inconceivably distant (on one scale) past of nearly 3000 BC. We feel that, and are perhaps awed by it. But our other eye, other focal length, must recognize that it was made with stone from Tura, that mountain of fine, white limestone we had passed earlier in the day, and multiply the time if not the awe by a thousand.

I was warm enough now, but my bald head was cold. I felt round in the dark and found my floppy sun-hat, crushed it over my head and waited for the heat of imagination to be useful for once.

I remembered an incident that happened to me years before across the river, at Aswan. I was up by the tombs on the fringe of the Western Desert. I saw, lying in a ditch near them, an ancient maul. This was a lump of stone, rounded so that it could be held with reasonable comfort in one hand. It was the earliest of all stone-working implements. All you did was to pound persistently at a slightly softer rock until it crumbled away. The day before I had seen

21

the results brilliantly illustrated in the *unfinished obelisk* on the other side of the river. There I had inspected the wavy surface of stone which had been worn away by this method and marvelled at the length of time the workers must have spent, prone or supine, pounding unhandily at the bottom of the object to undercut it. They had failed to complete the obelisk because it had split from a flaw not at first detected. But they had succeeded in leaving behind them an object lesson in the powers of persistence and elementary sculptural technique. Now here on the other side of the river and at my feet was an example of the primitive tool. Facing me was an outcrop of the same stone as they had pounded into the near shape of an obelisk. The rock was red Aswan granite. There must be few major museums which do not preserve a specimen or two. In the British Museum, for example, the huge head and forearm of Sesostris are fashioned from it. Experimentally, then, I lifted the maul and examined it closely. There were no visible marks on the surface. But then, why should there be? You can scratch a steel knife with a diamond, which remains unaffected. This stone was dolerite from the shores of the Red Sea and twice as hard as granite. I began to pound solemnly at the red Aswan granite of the outcrop. To my surprise it cut easily. Before I tired I cut a groove a foot long and half an inch deep. Of course, near the surface even granite will have undergone a delicate chemical change on the road which will (after a few million years) rot it down to kaolin. Nevertheless, even after I had penetrated this skin I went far enough down to find that virgin rock was workable. How was one to cope with such an experience? To me, it was delightful and significant – but of what? There was the knowledge that the granite was a geological event in one time scale, that the dolerite maul was in the same time scale but a different event. There was (coming down to the other time scale) an attempt at imaginative identification or empathy with the workmen, fellaheen, slaves who had fashioned this primitive implement some five thousand years before.

What I am trying to convey is the confusion of a lifelong relationship. I needed to find a centre to knowledge so wide yet superficial and a treatment which could contrive to be comprehensive without falling into the jejune. I could only see that the cohesive element would have to be my own individual experience and the impact of disparate and dissimilar phenomena on my particular sensibility.

My head was warm, not to say hot. Huddled under my heap of clothing, with one star glittering past the curtain, I lay, feeling that if anything, my head was now steaming. I had an illogical feeling that something had been accomplished. I must have slept.

I surfaced – probably from sleep though I couldn't be sure at the time – at about a quarter to six. It was still dark outside and cold. I looked out. Strange! There were robed people about, some in boats, some on the bank but no one was moving. The water was so flat that the current was not visible. The stillness of the scene was such that the figures of robed men seemed to brood as if contemplating some inevitable and awful tragedy before which movement and noise were useless and irrelevant. Had they, I asked myself, sat, crouched, leaned or stood thus all night? Were they – were *we* since the night had left me diminished – like lizards, which require the sun's warmth before their muscles can operate? I watched them as the dawn lightened swiftly and the faintest trace of mist drew away from the water. A fisherman was crouched in his rowing boat, his ridiculous oars (two unshaped baulks of timber) lying idle along the thwarts, his head closely wrapped against the chill of dawn. He was moored only ten yards from us. He never moved, wrapped elaborately in a thick galabia. It was as if the night was a time for grief from which men had to recover daily.

The east lightened all at once. A woman crept out of a house with a tin water vessel on her head. She came slowly down the mud bank and the tin flashed as the first grain of the sun struck it. The fisherman lifted his head. Figures began to move on the bank. It was theatrical in that it led from the first tableau of grief to the common preoccupations of day in two minutes flat. A woman led a donkey. The fisherman shipped his ridiculous oars and rowed slow strokes. Two men spread their robes and squatted by the water. The rising sun grabbed the hill of straw and at once turned it to the gold woven for the girl in the fairy story. The pigeons started to peck, the rats to rustle. A big sailing boat, her torn sails wrinkled like ancient skin, came with a just perceptible movement as the current brought her towards us. She was empty, going north. A smaller boat stood south towards us but did little more than stem the current. She was loaded deep with raw, red brick and seemed to have no more than six inches of freeboard.

Alaa appeared, blinking. I asked him what the sailing boats were

24

called. He did not know but put the question to *Reis* Shasli, who was climbing aboard at that moment.

'He says they are called "Sandals".'

Reis Shasli was bowing sinuously and smiling.

'Please tell him I hope we get further today than we did yesterday.'

Alaa translated. Shasli continued to writhe, answered, then swung himself up into the glass box which housed our wheel. Alaa translated. I could not believe what I heard.

'*What?*'

'"He who rides the sea of the Nile must have sails woven of patience."'

I was speechless. The philosopher of the Nile started our engine and we moved off. Alaa went below again. The ancient Nubian, who I had thought to be an employee of the yacht club at Ma'adi, appeared and began slowly to coil ropes. '. . . English go their way . . . with their habit of looking "through" persons. . . .' I went and stood next to him feeling that even if I had no control over events at least I could do a violence to my own reserve and get to know this crew. The Nubian turned his back and went below.

We were not moving very fast. Nor could the scenery be said to be exotic or even interesting. It consisted of two river banks, each of mud. To our left the heights of the Eastern Desert were just visible.

I began to realize yet another miscalculation. In a big tourist boat you may see over the banks. But from near water level, where we were, and with the Nile at its lowest in February there was nothing to be seen but the two faces of the banks themselves. You could not in these circumstances move up the Nile examining the width of the valley but see only the severely restricted life of the water and the waterfront. More than that; the Nile in common with all rivers which flood has for countless years deposited silt on either bank, more silt near the channel than anywhere else so that the banks are raised, which of course is why they are called 'levees'. Not only was our view restricted by the mud banks, the land beyond them was lower than we were so that our normal view was of the tops of palm and nothing else. For a while it put me in a panic, the thought of sliding all the way up the Nile, hundreds of miles, in a confined and muddy ditch.

The cook, Rushdie, appeared and said that supper was ready. I explained that he meant breakfast, and went below. Ann had used our heads and was looking sick. I did what I could to remedy matters. Let that story remain untold except to say that during our trip the crew got the heads working adequately but no more.

After breakfast we wrapped up, for the northerly wind pursuing us was faster than our speed and cold, and went to sit it out on the upper deck. The Nubian was standing by the rail, holding it for support. This was not seasickness but age. I asked him his name. He muttered that he was called 'Saïd' but seemed to resent giving the information. We were approaching an island, it appeared, for the river here divided. There were whole plantations of palms and enclosures of heavy wire netting as though the place was a prison. I asked the old man what the island was called.

'Fisher.'

'Fisher? Fisherman? Fisherman's Island?'

'Fisher. Englishman.'

'English fisherman?'

His Arabic became voluble and, I thought, resentful. When he had said his say he went below.

If we were confined to the river the least I could do was find out what I could, make what deductions I could. There were sizable palms and tamarisks growing in the levee and what looked like a few acacias. Well – for sure the acacia is an Egyptian tree! It turns up in the ancient literature time and again. Some of these trees were no more than four or five feet above the present water level. Yet before the building of the high dam at Aswan the flood had sometimes risen many feet higher than that. Even down here within fifty miles of Cairo it would have drowned these trees. They had rooted during the last fifteen years, then, and here the permitted rise of the river could be no more than four or five feet.

Alaa appeared.

'How high does the river rise in these parts nowadays?'

'Oh,' said he, 'not more than four or five feet. In February – now that is – they only let enough water through the high dam to keep the hydroelectrics working. Nobody gets any irrigation water in February. That's why the Nile is so low. It's why Shasli is going zigzag. He has to keep in the deep channel and even then there's only just enough water.'

'At least there'll be little current against us.'

'On the contrary. Shasli says that when the Nile is low all the water is in the deep channel so it runs faster.'

'When will they raise the level?'

'In a few days' time, February the sixteenth or thereabouts, Shasli says. What happens is this. They shut the first barrage down by the sea and wait until that bit of the river has risen behind it. Then they shut the barrages one after the other, all the way up the river, waiting for each section to rise. After that they begin to let water out of the main channel for irrigation.'

'Then there won't be any current at all.'

'Hardly any, he says.'

So much for planning, I thought. My idea of going up the Nile against a slight current and coming down with a fast one was exactly wrong. We should go up against a fast current in the deep channel and come down a broad river with no current to help us.

I watched the banks, apparently inching past.

'Alaa, what about those eleven knots we're supposed to be capable of? We're only using five of them.'

'There has', said Alaa gently, 'been a little bit of trouble.'

'Oh God.'

'It's the water pump. Akhmet the engineer thinks there's something wrong with it.'

I opened my mouth and shut it again. There was, I thought, probably some flowery Egyptian proverb on the tip of Alaa's tongue and I did not want to hear it. The old Nubian, Saïd, crept out of the main cabin, crept forward and disappeared behind the bulk of the wheelhouse.

'Why is Saïd so sulky?'

'It's a delicate matter.'

'Come on, come on!'

'Well. He was down in the Suez area, oh forty years ago. He worked for the English. He hates them.'

I thought back then, more than forty years. A world clawing itself to death: the Atlantic; storm; a helmsman, his neck broken by a single wave; D-Day.

'So that's why he knows a few words of English.'

'That's why.'

I remembered.

'He said something about this island we're passing being "Fisher-man", or "English".'

'Oh, yes.'

'Tell me, then.'

'You really want to know?'

'Of course.'

'It was years ago. There was an Egyptian owned half the island. Some high-class tourists came up the river in their own boat like you – like us. One was called Fisher. He wanted to buy the island. The Egyptian invited him to a meal but the Englishman wouldn't come.'

'Why not?'

Alaa was betrayed into a high, very Egyptian laugh.

'I suppose he thought the native was dirty.'

There was no possible reply to that. Presently Alaa went on.

'However. The Egyptian gave Fisher half of the island as a guest gift.'

'But what on earth . . .'

'He persuaded the owners of the other half to sell it to the Englishman cheaply.'

'I don't see . . .'

'Egyptians are very hospitable. They offer the guest what they have.'

'Like the Arab and his horse.'

'That's why it's called Fisher's Island. Of course, after the revolution Nasser nationalized it.'

I reminded myself never in any circumstances to admire anything. I also came at once to certain defined but private opinions over the matter of Fisher and the Egyptian. The Egyptian was a dislikable fool. Fisher was just dislikable.

It was a pity about Saïd, though.

'I don't suppose the Fisher story has lost anything in the telling.'

'Saïd heard it from Fisher's daughter.'

The wind seemed colder, the boat slower, the banks even less interesting. Those ancient Egyptians, what would *they* have made of the stranger in their midst? But they were fading from my mind, had been obscured on our first visit by the lively crowds of brown men so unlike the hieratic, sideways-standing figures of my childhood. And now the truth of it, the likes and dislikes, hatreds and hysterias, the ingrained, sullen memories, the old man, lifted from his easy job at the yacht club and made to set out with us for whatever reason, a reminder perhaps. . . .

'Alaa.'

'Huh?'

'What do they think of us? Two old people setting off in not much comfort to do whatever it is?'

Alaa thought.

28

'I'll find out.'

I went below to record all this river-sorrow in my journal, but stood for a long time looking grimly out of a window, at brickstacks and the chimneys of brick kilns. A sailing boat lay waiting at each brickyard. I thought to myself that these graceful 'sandals' with their simple, elegant lines and single huge sail were going to be one of the consolations of the trip. One standing north inched past us. She was, so to speak, *rigged for straw*. She looked, as she receded, like a mule with paniers on either side. She was built out amidships an additional hull's breadth and the load of straw was delicate gold against the dirty white sail. The steersman, standing aft of the load of high-piled straw could see nothing ahead of him. But after all, steam gives way to sail or does so in most waters. We passed a mud bank palpably dried out in the middle of the river and lined with the seagulls that the Egyptians call 'Iraqi Geese', I don't know why.

I shook off my slight depression and set myself to look for interest. At the time, apart from the occasional river boat my interest was forced to concern itself with bricks. Well, after all, bricks are not without interest. In this part of the river I could see a preposterous collection of kiln chimneys. I counted thirty in sight at the same time. It is symptomatic of the state of Egypt that this absurd over-production is frowned on by the government, which tries to stop it but can't. It's not that bricks in themselves are a bad thing but that there are two sorts. There is mud brick, which any peasant can make on any bit of river bank; and there is burnt red brick made from the heavy, eternally fertile red clay of the valley. There can be few things in a civilization uglier than a red brickyard. Mud brickyards are minimally less repellant. But there was only one yard of mud brick among the thirty red brickyards – long brown walls of the stuff with a single workman turning the bricks to let the wind and sun get at the other side. Here and there among the fields and date-palms were mud brick buildings. The walls of a properly built mud brick building are 'battered', that is they lean in towards each other for support, an immemorial angle. Yes, that was it! The whole of Egyptian history seems subsumed in that angle. I remembered, not successively but in a whole expansive moment, one of those decisions I had come to at home, one of those chapters in this book I had not yet written, a planned essay ready in my head and lacking only the confirmation of coming and looking at the place itself – it was a process, I had said to myself. The angle, the one I had called 'immemorial', increased from this mild slope of batter, increased to the steeper angle of a temple pylon, back through the steeper slope of stone temple walls here and there, then closed in still further to the ultimate steepness of a pyramid, where the walls collided and shut out any possibility of a roof altogether. There it all was in my head. I saw the increase in angle as an increase in weight, in domination of the country by privilege. In my head I saw the temples as heavy, brutal. They said, 'You peasants have your mud-angle, a timid thing. We gods have ours. Fall on your faces. Sacrifice!' Now here, glimpsed beyond the levees and among palms were mud bricks and mud brick houses not plainly seen yet but promising to be (when I got them in full view) confirmation of the chapter lying in my head.

However, houses nearer the levees and easily seen were red brick, staring red brick, uglier, if that were possible than the brickyards. When a brickyard reached down to the river it turned the bank into a scree of broken brick. Sandals lay alongside and were sometimes being loaded. Only in one place as far as I could see were bricks being loaded unfairly into big trucks while sandals waited, empty.

In Egypt you don't shift or load bricks with a crane. If you want to fill a sandal you do it with muscle and a sloping plank. Hodmen have a plank not sloping but strapped upright against their backs from above head level down to the waist. The plank has a projecting shelf at waist level. Bricks are loaded on this step, right up to above head height, two or even three columns side by side. So the hodman carries a section of red brick wall behind him. Loaded with these dozens of bricks, hands clasped tightly at their chests as if to prevent the rib-cage from bursting the hodmen shuffle down a bouncing plank from the scree of red into a sandal then down again into the hold. A fellah heaves the bricks off the step in a few heavy lifts. The hodman rushes back for more torture so there is a constant ant procession. They take their red, empty planks back up the plank and appear again in seconds it seems, loaded down and hands clasped, all too soon. The bank, the whole yard, the sandals, the men, all is dusty red. But where there's brick there's brass. One of the sandals had a new white mainsail. I had an eerie feeling of certainty that it was someone's dowry.

All this, appropriately enough, was a stretch of river parallel to the line of pyramids that reaches down from the level of Cairo – though because of the levee or the trees we could not see and had not seen a single pyramid. In fact, to the west of us as far as we were concerned

30

there might have been no desert at all. The palms and occasional buildings, the raw bricks and tall chimneys might have stretched between us and some ocean or other. There was nothing beyond that bank and its greenery and brickyards but sky. To the east things had been a little different. The Eastern Desert was there and now and then with some sand hump beyond the levee you were reminded of it. The high escarpment of desert rock which had withdrawn from the river after Tura and its quarry now showed signs of approaching us again. For that is the odd thing about the desert confines of the Nile Valley. It seems rather as if you yourself do not move but that the desert sneaks nearer, furtively, and looks over trees or houses then goes away again. You begin to give it character, that cloudless, brown, yellow-ochreish escarpment with sand shuffled up round its feet. You cannot define that phenomenon, only describe it crudely. But once seen, you remain aware of it and you watch out.

Then after we had dragged for hours upstream we came to open country with strangely less levee. We could see for a mile or two on either side of the river – on the left looking out to that Eastern Desert, which came sweeping in closer as if to ride over and blot out everything. There was a rim of life along the edge of the river but perilously thin. Women squatted in clusters by the water's edge with the desert hanging over them and only held back it seemed by a palm or two and here and there an ancient village wall. The women wore red or blue or black. They were not using the old *balaas* the waterpot of heavy clay – so soon does everything change I never guessed that we had seen, ten years before, the end of six thousand years of the *balaas*! Now the women cleaned and carried pots made of metal – aluminium or tin. The pots were lighter but bigger. Clearly it didn't do to spoil women and what you save in weight of pot you can make up in weight of water. Some women – blessed champions among their sex – paced along slowly under bins large enough for trash or rainwater. Those bins were more properly to be called water butts and the sight was painful, though perhaps the women were proud of them and of carrying them. Those pots, bins, tubs and pans flashed in the sun. A procession of women, red and blue and black, all stepping with that most graceful and majestic pace are a sight lovelier than the caryatids of the Erechtheum – and as cruel. For were not the daughters of Caryas enslaved by the Athenians and set to carry burdens as a punishment? We think of all that, when we think at all of all that, as art which excuses everything.

Here and there were floating patches of what we call water hyacinth on the river. This is the plant which is busy blocking some of the great rivers of the world. It is native to equatorial Africa and to South America. Now it is to be found everywhere there is water warm enough for it. I tried a bit myself in my own water garden in the south of England, but of course the winter killed it. I saw it, I remember, spread in great fields in the river by Brisbane, Australia. In China, cannily as one might expect, they feed pigs on it. In the New World they just try unavailingly to get rid of it. Just possibly it may remain and collect metals! And now here it was, floating past, held up by its bladders but brown with the chill of winter Egypt and its winter water. The flower is pretty, of course, but the plants on the way to the sea, or at least the seaward barrage, were past that. The Egyptians, I found, call the plant *Ward el Nil* or Rose of the Nile. Somewhere or other I had heard the story that the plant got into the Nile from central Africa by someone using it as an ornamental plant in a water garden at Khartoum, but I don't know if that's true or not.

On this afternoon, I remember, Ann braced herself and started to sketch. She tried for a village on the east bank but it got away. However, in what for this boat was rapid succession, we passed two others just like it so she was able to complete the sketch after all. It was a sketch which, being not exactly like any village, was instantly recognizable as what a Nile riverfront village is like, thus illustrating mysteries of art, geography, observation and all kinds of things. I think she tore it up.

It is symptomatic of the sameness of the Nile that I found myself struggling to find variety to put into my journal and without much success. I decided to list any stuff there was floating in the water, but there was nothing but the odd clump of the *Ward el Nil*. It's a fact that there's no litter in the Nile. The water at this low period of the year was soupy, grey-green with an underlying tinge of brown. I was reduced to staring into the water and reflecting on the many diseases said to lurk there. I was cautious. Out in the middle where we were – the deep-water channel – there might not be the obvious parasites of bilharzia or guinea worm or any other of the ghastly parasitic infestations, but that still left bacterial and viral diseases. That fairly innocent-looking soup might still give you polio or hepatitis if you treated it too casually. It was all very odd, I thought. Down at Cairo they hold international long-distance swimming races round the islands. Alaa had been an oarsman and said how he used to drink

32

vater out of the Nile when hot and thirsty. He was hefty and healthy. However, disease or no, the Nile is free of litter and refuse. Perhaps here's nothing to throw away.

The river broke up around more islands. I wondered frivolously to whom they had been given as tokens of Egyptian hospitality. Napoleon, now there was a man who brought a library to Egypt with him and might well know this curious virtue or alleged virtue that obtained in Arab countries. Why had he not ridden forward at the Battle of the Pyramids and pointed out to the Mamelukes that he was a stranger in their country, that he wanted the pyramids, and that *herefore....*

We passed moorhens swimming in line ahead. The Eastern Desert, which had been stalking us all along, now pounced in to within yards of the eastern bank. I watched a woman take advantage of western technology and fill blue plastic bags with water. She hefted them on to either flank of an ass so that they became water panniers. Like the women with their lighter metal pots, the ass got no benefit from his blue plastic panniers. They were bigger, that was all. When the woman had the bags in position she topped them up with water and directly they were topped up and slopping over, the ass turned away without an order and plodded up into the desert. I couldn't see how far he had to go but clearly enough from the map there wasn't any green stuff between him and the Red Sea. The sun was very bright and there was a cold wind.

At about 3 o'clock in the afternoon while we were still waiting for lunch the boat swerved violently. I rushed up on deck. It was clear what had happened. The linkage between the wheel and the rudder had parted. The crew, with the exception of old Saïd, was running in circles. There was much argument. The boat, engine out of gear, was now drifting rapidly back in the direction of Cairo. What had seemed an irritating impediment to our progress upstream but no more than that, I now saw to be a considerable current. The banks – in a way familiar to all wretched rivermen – seemed to be fairly streaking past. A young man whom I had noticed vaguely before – he wore a blue tracksuit trimmed with white stars – threw the foolish grapnel overboard but it did not hold. Shasli manoeuvred with short bursts of power as the boat swung until the bows struck the mud beach of a little island. The blue tracksuit dived for the beach, took a line, made it fast and there we were with the Nile clucking gently under our bilges.

The crew gathered in the central area of the boat and discussed what to do. Alaa and Rushdie, the cook/lutanist, jumped ashore. A fellah appeared with two women, one donkey and a water buffalo. He laughed a lot, particularly at me. Now there was a crowd on the beach all talking and laughing. A smaller crowd in the central cabin was examining a length of wire rope which had parted in the middle. They were trying to tie the wire rope. I suggested that they should try splicing it but I don't think anyone understood. Indeed, they thought plainly enough what is this passenger doing poking his nose into something which only we seamen can understand? We retired to our cabin and discussed the speed with which our little expedition was getting nowhere. After a while Ann looked out of the door and returned with a fit of the giggles. She said the committee was trying to tie the steel wire rope together with blue nylon cord. It was a situation too comical for despair. It was like all those years of hapless messing about in boats, the years of making do, the animosity of inanimate objects especially when waterborne.

I went up on deck again. The village clown once more thought I was very funny. I suggested to Alaa that there was a degree of simple-mindedness to go with the clowning and he agreed, saying that the laughter wasn't all our fault! I took a snap of the crowd and Alaa took a snap of the crowd and me. It was reasonably matey but no more.

Below decks I found that the crew had cannibalized some wire rope from another bit of machinery. God only knew, I thought, what other bit of gear would prove to be inoperative for want of wire just when we needed it. But at last we got under way again. We came to more brickyards. Upper Egypt, it appears, is constructed of red clay and brickyards. One group of chimneys stood on ornamental bases, which seemed very odd. An ornament in a brickyard seems a contradiction in terms, since brickyards are of all places the rawest and most irremediably ugly. Adornment may well wait for bricks; but in their place of making they are a kind of architectural plasma undifferentiated into grace or beauty. The attempt at amelioration was wrongheaded.

A huge crane and a water tower appeared on the southern horizon. I was beginning to grasp the character of the land. You can tell a town from a village because the town has a water tower for which the water is either drawn from the river and purified or drawn straight out of the new, deep boreholes which will make such a difference to Egyptian health. So we came to Beni Suef.

34

Apparently this was where we were to stop. We tied up alongside a station for the river police. This sounds more impressive than it was. The place was on the slope of the levee with two shacks, some ramshackle boats and a dozen young men who were dressed in seamen's uniforms which were ragged and dirty. They were heavily armed, however. A sentry cradled a submachine gun of some sort or other and it was nastily clean. Here, Alaa produced our trump card – a letter he had obtained from the Chief of Police in Cairo directing all river police to give us every assistance, et cetera. So we were fixed up with water and fuel, the second everywhere in short supply. It was dark now, a darkness which began at about 6 o'clock in the evening and lasted a full twelve hours. We moored at some ornamental steps, which were convenient for shopping. We went ashore with Alaa and were 'hello'd' by men and boys. Indeed, I was even asked my name by a gaggle of schoolgirls in western dress who then fled with shrieks of laughter, 'appalled at their own temerity'. Near the river there was a small public park, very neat and clean. All the roads were tree-lined. There was a social centre further on, with a theatre and a cinema. But dust was king and made a drabness in what might have been elegant. The sparse street lighting competed unsuccessfully with the darkness of early evening. There was a street of small shops and stalls. Here and there these stalls were operating by the light of acetylene flares which took me back more than half a century. It was indeed curiously like revisiting the past. For the tendency of our street lighting is to spread round. It is hoisted up by wire, or what John Betjeman called 'seasick serpents'. This gives a height to the lighted area which enhances a sort of public bleakness as if something is being revealed which had better not be shown. But these lights were low down, at head or even waist height and shuddering. They were not so much bright as flaring; and they hollowed out a comfortable warm space like a cave in which human activities could go on in the full importance of bargaining and gossiping and quarrelling without being staringly lighted into insignificance. They were a proper light for the oranges and mangoes and bananas and for the ubiquitous carriages, the *calèches* of the Nile Valley which clopped and creaked here and there. There were patient donkeys being ridden by large men who sat well astern and by small boys who sat amidships as it were and pretended they were riding horses. There were trucks, bicycles and a few young men on unsilenced motor bikes. The costume was, on the whole, drab western. But the place was quite uncivilized. You could walk down the road, not on the pavement, and the traffic would divide round you as if pedestrians had a right to live. So we shopped, buying towels and tangerines and bananas. The bananas weren't very big but that was because they were straight off the tree.

We found our way back to the boat in nearly complete darkness. There was music on the corniche above the boat, music on the ship's radio – or was it a tape? – Arab utility music sounded strangely familiar. And once Rushdie had got settled in, his lute began to compete. The crew chattered busily. We seemed, I thought, to have been in the boat for a month though it was no more than two days. We were sixty odd miles from Cairo. I reminded myself that we still had a meal to come before we tried to sleep – but the meal didn't come. Instead, the chattering died away, the generator stopped and slowly the lights in our cabin faded until all that was left was a faint glimmer through the starboard 'window' from the street lighting of Beni Suef.

3

It was another cold and restless night. Since we were moored alongside quite a large town we could hear the muezzins competing from their minarets at that point of the night, 'When a white thread may be distinguished from a black one'. I personally did not sleep after the competition. We were under way by about half past six. There is a bridge at Beni Suef but it is only half built. In Cairo I had been told that the bridge had already been ten years in the building and certainly the unfinished end where it hung out over the water had a rusty and depressed look about it. Just beyond the furthest point to which the bridge reached, an iron stake stuck out of the river at what was clearly the wrong angle. It was not buoyed. I should like to have found out the history of that stake but never did. In any case, there are so many quaint stories about bridges over the Nile one more would make no difference. There is the story, for example, which I told Alaa that very morning as we were passing the dangerous-looking stake on our way out of Beni Suef. I wanted him to tell me if it was true. There was an architect who designed a swing bridge for Cairo and it was completed and the king of Egypt turned up with much pomp and circumstance and pressed the button but nothing happened. Nothing ever did happen according to the story and the swing bridge stayed where it was without swinging and the pomp and circumstance left for other places as if for a previous engagement. Well, was it true?

'No,' said Alaa, 'it wasn't.'

'But my dear boy! I was told in the minutest detail – the architect went straight home to his apartment on Zamalik and shot himself. Architects always shoot themselves when things go wrong. It's a tradition. I bet the ancient Egyptian who made a mistake over the "Unfinished Obelisk" shot himself.'

'Where is this bridge?'

'You tell me.'

'I've never seen it,' said Alaa brusquely. 'I know the story. It's about Aboul-ela bridge. And in any case he didn't shoot himself. He went off and built something else. Maybe he built the Eiffel Tower.'

The wind of morning was keen.

'I expect the truth is he shot himself and *then* built the Eiffel Tower.'

All the same, there are some strange and authenticated stories about building bridges over the Nile. They are based in the huge, mild power of river water, with its unceasing pressure day and night, year in, year out. There was a bridge built with the best of intentions and the most elaborate of calculations, only somehow the river had not read the calculations and did something which was not in the figures. It just ignored the bridge altogether and went somewhere else so the bridge was left high and dry without any river to give it a reason for existing. Once a large river boat full of stone sank in midstream. The hulk broke the current at that point so that silt fell out of the water where it was slowed. The silt became a mud bank and then an island which is still there, all because of one boatload of stone. I wondered what the water would do with that stake at Beni Suef and its obviously wrong angle.

The river seemed a little wider above the bridge of Beni Suef than it had been in Cairo. As the dawn mists cleared away we could see that there was some evidence of prosperity over on the eastern bank – houses and villas and estates stretched out among palms under the brown and yellow desert. The levees were lower now and we could see over them. On the west bank by contrast and only a mile or so beyond Beni Suef there were real hovels and the abjectly poor fellaheen so often written about. There were small enclosures made of nothing but dried sugar cane or perhaps maize stalks, mud huts with a few canes laid across one corner to serve as a roof. Then we came to an unconcealed mud brick village and my facile ideas about the 'immemorial angle' were at once complicated out of existence. There *was* no immemorial angle; or rather there were all kinds of angles and curves; and all plainly the 'incompetent angle', for if the fellaheen had ever known how to build in mud brick they had forgotten now. Some of the angles actually went the wrong way so that the building leaned out instead of in. That this was a mistake was plain to see because some of the buildings had actually fallen and blocked alleys. One ridiculous hut had the left-hand wall leaning out and the right-hand wall leaning in so that the whole building leaned to the left and looked as if it would slump sideways at any moment. Reeds were employed in this complex of misuse, but scantily. It was all hopeless. Once again we were in time to see that curious moment when the trance of the night turned into the slow movements of lawn. The first movements came from small children who ran about to keep warm. Women wrapped in black slowly crept out of holes in houses. Goats and donkeys moved but only just. Then we had left them behind and never saw the brisker movements of their day. That's the traveller's trouble when he's carried in a vehicle that he doesn't control. I've never forgotten travelling by express train on the old Great Western Railway and seeing a cricket match going on. The batsman had hit enormously towards mid-on, who was running frantically to catch the ball. He stretched out his hand and a house hid him. That's fifty years ago and I've often wondered whether he caught the ball or not. Silly. Anyway, we left the village coming back to life such as it was.

Alaa got out his battery of cameras. They were more costly than the boat, I should think. As the day broadened under a low sun we began to meet the Nile barges, powered craft called trams (the 'a' is long) which can take up to a couple of hundred tons of bulk cargo. Some craft are combined as you may see on the Rhine or Seine, one pushing the other. The bows and stern are so shaped as to interlock. The first one is called the 'pusher', and the one ahead of it the 'sandal', though it has no sail. Both together make up a 'fleat'. A tug is called a 'kicker' and usually pulls a line of sail sandals. The first pusher we saw had a large cabin right aft, rather like a landing craft, with painted kerosene cans containing hopeful shrubs. This was rare. Egyptians don't often go in for private gardens.

Now we entered a stretch of river with palms to the left and a low island on the right which seemed to consist of nothing but reeds, phragmites, set in shallow water and so close together you could not force a canoe through them. Once upon a time the island would have been nothing but papyrus, but not any more. Somehow, phragmites, the same tall flowering reed you can find by the Thames or any canal in England or indeed Europe, has ousted the famous paper plant. Now, except for some specimens cultivated in the Delta you have to go all the way down to the Sudan to find papyrus growing wild. These reeds were very tall, ten or twelve feet, I should think. Here and there fishermen were holed up among them in heavy rowing boats and looking rather like they do in Chinese paintings. Their oars once more were plain baulks of timber, the looms square, the blades non-existent. I asked Alaa what was the point of these seemingly ridiculous implements which are common on water from one end of Egypt to the other. He said you could consider the timber to have a long thin blade rather than a short broad one because of the huge weight of the heavy rowing boat. So there is another example of the apparently ludicrous having a logical explanation.

There was a faint breeze blowing the wrong way. I mean it was blowing from the southwest, which is where the hot *Khamsin* is supposed to come from, unseasonable at that time of the year. In any case, it was not only blowing the wrong way, but it was also cold. A notable phenomenon was the behaviour of the small sailing boats, which the Egyptians call feluccas, pronouncing the word 'fe*look*ah'. Well, the feluccas, not much bigger than rowing boats, can startle the curious onlooker because they appear to be contradicting the laws of hydrodynamics and aerodynamics all at the same time. They stand within less than one point of the wind. This is impossible. I was delighted for a while. But if you should see a felucca behaving so, look closely ahead of it among the reeds, and presently, fifty yards ahead of the boat you will detect a small boy plodding through the shallow water and attached to the felucca by a long, thin line. He is usually dressed in dirty brown and thus camouflaged by the reeds.

As the sun rose, the two levees which hid Egypt from us disappeared. It seemed a contradiction in the behaviour of water but I was glad of it, because now we could see countryside. Between us and the Eastern Desert, that brown cloud on the horizon, there were miles of scattered scrub and palms. By 8 o'clock in the morning the laden trek to the water was beginning. The women came from more than a mile away, but with huge baskets on their heads. The baskets were full of a clover of vivid green for the donkeys that had been left overnight by the river. Perhaps with the dense rural population and inchmeal farming the narrow strip by the river was the only grazing.

The Eastern Desert changed from a cloud to solid fists of rock and swept in towards the very bank of the river. It became a cliff dominated by a cemetery which dogs liked. On the western shore there were no brickyards eating up the rich soil but maize, sugar cane and date palms, with not a smoking chimney in sight. As for the eastern shore, it was edged by the speeding water. There were obvious shallows and rips. The current was faster in the tortuous channel that Shasli was following. The whole scene, river and shore, was wholly unlike the Nile of further north where we had seen the kilns and brickyards. Here all was rock and water. There were lines of foam, then patches of flat water where it welled up again from the bottom after falling over a hidden ledge. There were more fleats and rams. We were following a whole line of them, all doing their best to wriggle through a complicated channel. But then there wasn't so much a procession as a crowd, some of them tied up two or three deep along the western shore with others dotted here and there, fast aground. There was much shouting and manoeuvring. I stayed in our cabin watching the whole affair through our ample windows, well out of it as our crew ran round the deck, poled with a boat hook, swore, invoked Allah and a whole litany of what I supposed were saints and shouted and gesticulated. We hit, of course, hit hard in a river which I had always fancied had a deep mud bottom, but my goodness no! It was a nasty crash and grind. You could feel every bit of stone gouging at her hull and worse still at her propeller as the current drew her off. She touched on what must have been compacted gravel. Shasli went slow ahead when we were free, feeling his way along a ledge, bump, bump, bump-*here*! So we were able then to thread among the stranded pushers, fleats and trams for we drew less water than they. There was a crowd waiting for the sixteenth of February and the ponding of the water behind each barrage in turn. It looked like a long wait.

We came through at last into calmer water between Biba and El Fashn. Looking back I could see how the Eastern Desert had projected into the river in a white headland. Once, Tura must have looked like that before the pharaohs began the gnawing at it that has been continual for five thousand years. They could start all over again on this white headland. Presumably all the shallow water and the complicated channel were caused by an extension of the white cliff but under water, making a kind of mini-cataract. This is not the same as the real Cataracts, the maxi-cataracts as it were, which are pink, black-spotted granite, but something like, done in hard limestone. Certainly the eastern side of the river was becoming increasingly dramatic. It was not just the white headland with its spectacularly layered rocks, but further on, vast limestone cliffs, sheer at the top with the bottom two-thirds hidden by screes of white stone. There was busier than usual river traffic here, cross-river traffic, for the western bank (a levee once more) was being revetted with blocks from the screes and cliffs of the eastern shore. The traffic was conducted in the sailing sandals. It is one of the few places left in the world, I suppose, where the use of sail is economic and it was very pleasant to see. Now we were in calm water I went on deck and asked Shasli if there were different names for small sandals and big sandals.

41

Yes, there were. They were called small sandals and big sandals. Was there a special name for a big sandal with two masts? Yes. It was called a big sandal with two masts. I decided there and then to put together what I found out about Nile traffic as an essay. To tell the truth I was finding it more interesting than the temples. Jacob Boehme said that by the Hebrews' spoiling the Egyptians of their golden ornaments was meant the taking away of their wisdom and mystical power. Certainly the temples seem empty like brown cardboard boxes. Hieroglyphics? It's not that I don't know about them, I've forgotten them!

Hereabouts the sandals were loading busily. Because the white blocks of limestone were irregularly shaped and big, they were carried down individually by labourers who – how madly subjective – seemed to treat them with a kind of affection as though they were more important and had more individuality than bricks. A sail full of wind has the richness of a pregnant belly. We all know that, the words are there. A sandal loaded *down* with no more than six inches of freeboard but with a neat cargo of white limestone stacked under the boom, the crew sitting about on it as the huge sail moves the whole slowly across the water is wholesome, is wealth, is good. It is the epitome of industry with a human face; for the crew that loaded the sandal on one bank takes it across and unloads it on the other: and four or five men share the labour. Now it is easy to sentimentalize all this and I do not wish to. But if appearances are anything to go by, it is a happier fate to work white with the powder of limestone than red with the dust of bricks. However, my hands were clean and I was a temporary spectator. Nor do I know the relationship between the crews of the sandals and the men who were working in the cliffs of the quarries. For that job as far as I could see would have been better left to goats. There were pathways netting down the screes and men scrambling about on them. Their purpose was plain. They would start a block tumbling down the scree, working with others poised above them. The object was to clear the scree of its blocks, working upward from the bottom. Once a scree was clear it became a quarry, not of blocks but of rubble, which could be carted away and burned into quicklime. But in the quarries we passed – they seemed to impend over us – half of a scree would be dug away, leaving a vertical cliff. Since the angle of a scree is by definition the angle of rest of the material in it, this vertical cliff must be a deadly menace. It seems plain that this method of getting rubble out of a quarry is hideously dangerous. Here and there men were working at the very top of the screes close under the sheer cliffs. They must have known what they were doing; but by the tracks left in the scree from blocks that had fallen out of the cliff itself you could see their work was no more nor less than a kind of Russian roulette.

So they work. It is a stone area, no doubt about that. The white rocks tumble down the eastern cliff and on the western shore the lime kilns billow out smoke into thick pats that drift up and along and obscure the sky. Even so, smoke or no smoke, the blinding white cliffs on one side and blinding white revetments on the other will dazzle you into a headache in no time. It was quite a relief when that beast – I came to think of the desert in such terms – retired from the water and we chugged past miles of reedy marsh again. Here there were mud huts, built crazily as usual. But in the western shore were openings, the entries of canals which would parallel the main stream all the way down as far as Cairo possibly, or swing off into the Fayoum. There was only one use for brick in this area. Each time the great gates of an irrigation channel appeared in the west bank there would be a *house* – not a hut – built next to it for the gate keeper. He is clearly a man of power and prestige so only brick is good enough for him. But here is one aspect of present-day Egypt made plain. The brick is used as crazily as the fellaheen use mud, with not a vertical line anywhere. Has no modern Egyptian heard of a right angle? To think their ancestors were the first people to investigate the nature of a right-angled triangle! Today there doesn't seem to be a T-square or a plumbline in the country.

I had thought that we had done with the Eastern Desert for a bit; but just as I was getting accustomed to the marshes that tawny beast crept close then sprang at the water again and we were back in rock-country. But there was a difference. Back by the white headland and the quarries rock had dominated by sheer size and weight. Now it was rock's turn to suffer. Now we could see just what the earth was indifferently capable of in the way of twist and upthrust. Here, the top thousand feet of that mud-sand-boulder-filled canyon which is the Nile Valley exhibited contortions beyond belief. The whole place north of Maghagha is frozen in the act of a most titanic violence. Those strata which had lain level in the quarries, impending brutally by sheer dead weight, here were flicked and crumpled like so many sheets of paper. They, in their countless millions of tons, were flipped upright as if the demiurge's secretary had freed them for

43

restacking then flung them down or sat on them or screwed the lo
up. There was fire, too, extinguished now or tamped down, fo
darker leaves of igneous matter had been injected between the white
limestone layers, had been forced up, squirted up, held so till they
cooled and solidified. Those rocks have resisted erosion so that they
jut at the sky like blades of knives. Here and there huge portions o
the whole broke off and slumped forward in days before the canyon
filled. Now their unburied tops remain as separate hills, castles,
forts, contortions that seem too strange to be natural and ask fo
topographical names of genii, wizards, devils and the spirits of the
desert, the Afrits. One of those dark leaves of igneous rock lies in the
river next to the eastern bank. When we passed, the water being low,
it was high and dry, a row of nasty teeth with a broken felucca chewed
to pieces among them.

So. There are dangers, then, even in this apparently mild river.
But here the shallows began again and the river seemed strewn with
the typical Nile barges. Then just when it seemed we had entered the
desert for good, this stretch, more dramatic than any other between
Alexandria and Aswan, came to an end and we were chugging once
more slowly between low banks, or call them little cliffs of brown
mud. There was a large blue sky, unsullied by the smoke of lime kilns
or brick kilns and coming down everywhere to a close horizon. These
mud cliffs were so vulnerable that piles of dirty white limestone were
placed in the water as jetties or groins to keep the current in the
middle of the river. The mud cliffs are scored with parallel lines and I
supposed these to be the marks of flooding, silt laid down year after
year then revealed as the river ate its way, sidling from west to east.
But the marks were so wide apart. I could not believe so much silt
came down each season, but silt it was, for mile after mile there was
not a stone or pebble. Every few hundred yards now there were
tractors standing at the top of the little cliffs, each linked by a
widebore pipe to the water. Despite that mechanization, women still
processed down the cliffs and carried water away in metal or clay pots
as if the ancestral rite was not to be abandoned for mere convenience.
Indeed, I saw one little girl who could not have been more than six
following a string of caryatids with a pretend pot on her head. This
was my fabled region of Oxyrhynchus – more of that later – but the
site was ten miles away across the fields and out of reach. The west
bank was beautifully fertile with beans, drying maize and clover.
The mud cliffs were fledged or hidden by fig trees. Wild ducks flew

round in 'V's and fans.

Alaa and Rushdie descended into the stern sheets and played music. In Arab music if you have a good thing you don't let go of it. The first three notes of *Three Blind Mice* but in the minor mode lasted them for rather more than half an hour. Of course after each repetition Rushdie did a tiny embroidered 'arabesque' but the sound was hypnotic. It was also quiet.

Just when I had decided that the striations in the mud banks could be nothing but markings of the seasonal flood before the building of the high dam we came to a section where they lay aslant in such a way that they could not have fallen out of water. A syncline? Cross-bedding? Terms vaguely remembered and perhaps never clearly understood floated through my mind. All that mattered really was that the river bank was not going to yield to quick amateur investigation. It seemed clear, too, that the apparent mud was harder than mud would be. I called it 'mudstone' and abandoned my inquiry.

Then I found that by the *force majeur* of Shasli and the rest of the crew, all speaking the Arabic I could not understand, we were now to tie up again well before darkness. I expostulated with Alaa, who explained there was nowhere between us and El Minya where we could tie up without finding ourselves too isolated in the deep countryside. Isolated? What were the dangers of lying to by ourselves? We tied up on the west bank but nowhere in particular as far as I could see, or find out from the map, among a gaggle of fleats and trams. We were alongside a lighter. I salaamed the *Reis*, or watchman, and got a magnificent navy salute in return. Why navy? The mudstone cliff now we were near enough and still enough to examine it, I saw to be pockmarked and stippled with holes. Swarms of birds were wheeling about outside them in the tangerine light of the sunset. If they weren't swifts, they were swallows. For a moment or two, caught in this slow boat and frustrated I wished I could migrate with them back to Europe. The Western Desert was still out of sight but the eastern one lay crouched again far inland and contorted against a darkling sky. One contortion – but I couldn't be exact – was called Dilel Afrit which must mean the 'Demon's Tail', 'Devil's Tail'? Perhaps this was a haunted stretch of river, then, and all this traffic was huddled together for the night in fear of the supernatural.

I went below. We were caught between the ship's system doing its

45

economy music and sounds from other craft. I stayed below to fill in
my journal while Ann went up on deck well wrapped against the cold
and anything else that might be going – bogles and beasties and
rivermen. I tried to work out from the map where we would get when
and decided that at our present rate of progress we could do no more
than half of what we had intended.

Presently Ann came down again.

'Two men are smoking a hubble-bubble on the next tram,' she
said. 'You ought to go and look.'

'Why?'

'They're stoned out of their minds.'

This was exotic – practically King's Road standard. I went on deck
but the men had taken some hint and had vanished, leaving behind
them nothing but a faint and rather sickly smell. There was light,
though, for some of the craft had rigged up naked bulbs on deck.
Alaa appeared and inquired how much money I had with me. When I
told him he gave it as his opinion that we should last out. Then he
wandered off across several decks between us and the bank, climbed
it and vanished into the darkness of the countryside.

I stayed where I was, then struck by a sudden thought went to the
bows and looked down at the Nile. Here the water was still. Either
the grounded craft or the moored craft or perhaps the conformation
of the bank ensured that there was no current at all. But in the light
from the few naked bulbs hung here and there among the gaggle I
could see the surface of the water. It did not boil or seethe. But it was
thickly patterned with interlacing circles, ripples, blips and pips. It
looked as if small fish were gorging themselves on insects at the
surface or on larvae hanging from it or swimming free. It was my first
intimate glimpse of what one might call the private life of the Nile,
the nature of that water when stagnant. I cannot say I cared for it.
But how much of my distaste was reputation? Tourists are strictly
cautioned against drinking Nile water or bathing in it. Yet where the
water moves it seems no more than a trifle muddy. But near the bank,
where the water does not move? Or in small, stagnant side canals? No
indeed! I had now seen – ticking the events off on my fingers – people
spitting in the Nile, pissing in it and shitting in it. On the same mud
beaches where these events were taking place I had seen people
standing in it, washing in it, bathing in it and drinking it. I had even
seen a mother scoop a tinful of the stuff and give it to her small child
to drink. Well, I thought to myself, see what happens to them, poor,

benighted people! And yet it did not appear that anything happened to them. Whatever a medical man might have said, to the layman's eye there was nothing to distinguish these men and women and these cheerful, active children from their European equivalents brought up on company's water. Perhaps the lame and the halt and the blind were lying up, tucked away in those crazy mud huts or shivering under roofs of maize stalk. To be able to reach the water's edge and so be subjected to the stare of the passing westerner was in itself a sign of some health. For the rest it would be generations, I thought, before these people living at the waterfront would learn only to drink from the deep boreholes or the purified water of the towers. Meantime there was nothing to be done but remember with relief that we ourselves were drinking mineral water and never touched that sinister soup with its pips and blips.

I looked round and up. The sky was brilliantly loaded down with stars and all the hazier companies of heaven, but the air was cold.

I went below again. Ann had already climbed into her bunk and was reading. There was nowhere to go and nothing to do. I lay in my bunk and thought about geology and astronomy and anthropology and theology and zoology and parasitology and the intestinal flora and fauna of Egypt with its claws and teeth. The book I had promised to write, where was its centre, what was it all about?

Home seemed a long, long way away.

That night we were too far from a mosque to be wakened by the muezzins and their chorus at dawn; but I woke all the same as if expecting it. The air was still colder than the night before and the time somewhere near 5 o'clock. I dressed in darkness, wrapped up and went on deck. A cold breeze as distinct from the rest of the air as a river was wandering here and there among the mass of moored craft. There was a trace of mist on the water. There was nothing, but nothing to show that we were not on some wintry stretch of the Thames. Idly I looked round for a sign that we were indeed in Egypt but could not find one. Only an expert could tell the difference between these working craft and what you might find in Europe. Then at last, as a trace of light began to define the high line of the Eastern Desert I saw the only sure sign that we were indeed on the south side of the Mediterranean. A fellah was sitting on the high mud bank above the swallow holes – had been sitting there, presumably all night. He was cross-legged; but this had to be deduced. So accustomed was he to sit thus that he seemed cut off at the waist. It was a position no European could imitate.

Suddenly the light widened into day and the mist drew back. Here we were, three days out of Cairo and we had seen nothing, done nothing! All I had to take away with me was this close look at a river no wider than the Thames no matter how long it was! Who was going to be interested in quarries and brickyards? Even the long line of pyramids that marches south from Giza all the way to the Pyramid of Meidum at the exit from the Fayoum had been hidden by the high bank, the ugly Cairene suburbs as we crept south against the current in our ill-equipped boat. We must get on. Angrily I stumped round the deck, making as much noise as possible. Even so, for a while nothing happened. Then *Reis* Shasli emerged, not from our boat but from the tram alongside where doubtless he had found one of his many Nile acquaintances. I began to make furious gestures to hurry him up and get him into the wheelhouse. He in his turn made deprecatory then soothing gestures and went in the dignity of all his robes to ease himself over the stern of the tram. When you got to go you got to go. A lifetime's conditioning made me turn my back.

48

The engine was started at a quarter to seven. At a quarter past, Rushdie brought us tea in our cabin, and Alaa made an appearance. I began to expostulate at the wasted time but he waved my objections away.

'You are making plans,' he said. 'It is useless to make plans. What will happen will happen.'

'Not if I can help it!'

It was a collision, not so much of east and west as of north and south. The south won. Alaa made soothing gestures. Then, 'You see, it is Friday.'

Of course. Friday for Muslims, Sunday for Christians – did we have a Jew on board? If so, Saturday would be out too – a four day week. Through one of our windows I could see the old Nubian Saïd doing his religious duty, with his rump in the air and forehead to the deck. I hoped he knew which was the direction of Mecca. I certainly did not.

'And then too,' Alaa went on, 'we cannot go beyond El Minya. They need time to dismantle the water pump and get spare parts. There is no point in hurrying the pump.'

'It is the rhythm of the Nile.'

'Yes,' said Alaa with surprised pleasure. 'You said that exactly right.'

We were now, I saw, in banana country – that, and sugar cane. It seemed that Friday meant that people were at leisure – even more leisure than usual for the river banks were more thickly crowded. Here we began to see the coloured dresses more specifically associated, in my mind at least, with middle and upper Egypt, all gaudy nylons, electric green, orange, staring red. The average skin colour was darker, too, moving towards the jet black of Nubia. This darkening of the skin tones down the glaring colours, I don't know why. They certainly seem to be appropriate.

So we came to El Minya, Minya for short. I had seen the city from the road years before and we had actually spent a night there, but the water front was dusty and confused and not at all like the comparatively well-ordered city I remembered from before. Here the river swarmed with craft, a good many of them doing the local ferry work, for Minya also has the stump of an unfinished bridge that has been years in the making. Minya is a major ferry-point. There are two mosques and a Christian church lined up above the corniche down which much rubble has cascaded. We tied up once more at what was officially the station of the river police though only the uniforms, the dirty 'square rig' of the other ranks, distinguished it from the rest of the river front. As usual there was a guard on duty and he carried a gleaming submachine gun. We had not been tied up for more than five minutes when all the crew, including Alaa but excepting Saïd, processed ashore. The Nubian with slothlike speed arranged some kind of portable pump and proceeded to empty our bilge. We sat around. Then, bored, we walked on the river front. The ferry boats crossed and recrossed, always full and loaded to within an inch or two of the gunwale.

We sat around some more.

The sun set dustily crimson beyond the minarets, then as the dusk welled out of every corner and quickly swamped the river our crew came back. There were no spare parts for the pump in Minya. Someone must take the train back to Cairo.

Listlessly I saw the Nubian Saïd chivvied off the boat to take the train. The crew had the floorboards up in the central cabin and were dismantling the pump in readiness for the spare parts when they came – if they came.

'We need a full day's travelling from Minya,' said Alaa. 'Shasli won't set out for our next stop – Asyut – if there is any danger of having to stop halfway.'

'Why not? We spent last night nowhere in particular. Why can't we do it again?'

'Shasli says there is a stretch of river he doesn't want to spend the night in because of pirates.'

'Are you serious?'

'He is.'

In the end, since we were stuck anyway, I decided we would spend two days in Minya so that I could see what I could, find out what I could. Ann was feeling altogether off colour. I should have to leave her in the boat. Alaa explained that he had contacted the assistant to the Director of Culture for the Governate of Minya but the director himself could not be contacted because he was at home and his assistant was afraid to telephone him.

The crew went ashore one by one and we were left alone. I busied myself with my journal once more, adding up the poverty-stricken list of things I had seen while we lay here, clueless, languageless, engineless. The river had been more various – marshes and the desert, villages, cliffs and quarries. Now there was the ample ferry traffic of Minya and beyond it miles of desert cliff at the top of which, every few hundred yards were caps of harder stone. Between these successive caps the rock was worn away in a gentle curve from cap to cap. Was that after all Dilel Afrit? I remembered seeing those cliffs the first time we had come to Minya. We had left Cairo at dawn and got to Minya so early in the day that it was not worth stopping the night. But on the way back down the valley we had stopped there, spending the night in the Lotus Hotel. We had sat drinking tea in the top floor restaurant and looked at these same cliffs and agreed what fun it would be to examine the overhangs for flints and bones and pots! Surely, we said, prehistoric man must have used those overhangs; but now we were nearer by a mile and knew the overhangs were hundreds of feet up in the air and quite inaccessible. That time, too, we had sat listening to Sadat orating for hours on the tiny black and white television set, talking on and on; and at last our few words of Arabic seemed to be deceiving us – for surely he was throwing the Russians out of the country? We must be wrong – but we were not. It was a triumph for Sadat and for our half a dozen words of Arabic plus a few dozen inspired guesses.

Now, what we had for entertainment was the ferry. There were two-storey launches chuffing either way. There was a larger ferry to take cars and trucks but it was 'temporarily' out of order. There were also a dozen sandals going back and forth and loaded so deeply with people it was a wonder the ripples from passing trams did not sink them. There was, too, constant illustration of the Great Egyptian Mystery. Where do the crowds come from? In Egypt a crowd simply materializes, there is no other word for it. One moment you have empty air. The next moment one car bumps another or some vegetables fall off a truck or a child cuts its knee – you lose sight of the event because there is now a crowd round it ten deep. Opposite us on the other side of the river was a landing jetty which was empty most of the time. But did a sandal with its load touch there and before one crowd was properly off, the jetty would be thick with another one waiting to do the journey back. There was never an empty sandal or two-storey launch moving either way yet the jetty was always empty until the frantic two minutes of loading and unloading. I had a look at the water alongside and decided it was particularly soupy and wondered if this was an effect of the city. The *calèche* drivers had brought their wretched horses down to the water, driven them in and gone in after them to clean them. It was impossible not to wonder whether the horses were acquiring new diseases or merely exchanging old ones.

As dusk fell nothing moved on the water except a huge tourist boat which attempted to come alongside the corniche but found insufficient water and stuck about fifty yards offshore. With night the stump of the unfinished bridge a hundred yards south of us stuck out into the sky with an odd air of pain about it as if sheer suffering kept it in this gesture. I did some more sitting. Ann lay, trying to doze and shivering now and then. The crew came back. They started the generator and the boat lit up from stem to stern. Rushdie was getting us a meal and brewing the bitter Egyptian coffee. We had grasped the nature of Egyptian meals. They are not feasts but they are movable. You could say we ate now and then. But Alaa's letter from the Chief of Police had done its work. A cable was run on board and we were hooked up to shore lighting. A hose came next and filled our tanks with pellucid water from the water tower. Another hose filled us up with fuel. An officer of the river police, a very young man but in a beautiful khaki uniform came aboard bowing and saluting in every direction. Alaa came too, and explained that he had been unable to contact the Director of Culture. He would try again early next morning. The meal and the coffee were very good. I managed to get some extra things for our bunks – coverlets which helped to keep our heaped-up clothes securely on top of our single blankets. I simply do not know why I had not the sense to buy other blankets – it did seem impossible with the crew sleeping rough.

With free power from the shoreline we ran the generator all night and the boat became almost warmer than we wanted. I stayed awake most of the night so comfortable in the warmth I didn't mind a bit. Even the dawn chorus from the minarets seemed in better voice and so soothing that I slept after it. Ann was definitely better.

Alaa came back after breakfast. He had contacted the Director of Culture who had blasted his assistant from Minya to Khartoum when he found how Alaa had been kept waiting. El Minya was ours, we had only to ask. The Director himself, Mr Ahmed El-Sherif, arrived at midday. Tomorrow he would take us for an audience with the Secretary General to the Governor of the Governate of El Minya. Unfortunately the Governor himself was in Cairo otherwise he could imagine nothing that would give him greater happiness than to lay the place at our feet. Meantime, here was an assistant, Madame X, interpreter and guide, and a sergeant of the Tourist Police. Madame

52

X spoke French. What did I want to see? Ann pleaded indisposition but the rest of us went off together.

The most important sites are tombs to the south of Beni Hassan on the other side of the river. We drove through the city then on to the main road and stopped to examine a Mameluke Palace, which by now had been turned into tenements. It was an elaborate structure, with lots of marble courtyards and patios and galleries. Minute shops huddled close to it. Then we drove south for about twenty kilometres along the side of a canal in sugar cane country. I looked at this canal until it became ordinary to me. It was a canal, that was all. Idly, I asked Alaa which canal it was and he said it was the Bahr Yusuf. I was moodily and quite illogically vexed. For this Joseph's Canal is alleged by all persons like myself who prefer a good story to literal historical accuracy (whatever *that* may happen to be) is, I say, alleged to be the very canal that Joseph – he of the coat of many colours – built for Pharaoh. They say – *that lot* say – that it isn't Joseph's canal but a canal built by a much later Joseph. Did you ever hear anything so silly? Before I had seen it I had already made up my mind that even if it wasn't biblical Joseph's actual ditch, his must have lain along the same line so what's the odds? You put a canal in the best place for it so the later one was no more than a restoration of the original. I had promised myself such a thrill at seeing it; but now I had been looking at it for twenty kilometres and made it so ordinary to myself that my promised *frisson* was entirely lacking.

But still, it was Joseph's Canal. It was, I think, a greater, a more impressive, a wilder leap of the imagination than the pyramids. There was and is a great depression in the desert on the western side of the Nile opposite Cairo. This is the Fayoum, between twenty and thirty miles square. Right back in the earliest pharaonic days someone conceived the idea of deflecting surplus flood water from the river into that depression and then – here is the leap – of letting it out again into the Nile when a flood was inconveniently low. But this join between the main stream and the Fayoum could not be made down by Cairo. The main stream for obvious hydrostatic reasons had to be tapped hundreds of miles to the south so that the gradient of the canal would be so gradual the water would be controllable. So there the canal is, huge in length, vast in scope and breathtaking in the sheer imaginative size of the conception. Now here it was, a canal like any other and I found I had to screw my wits up to remember what it was I was looking at. This was Joseph's artificial river (to match his

53

granaries) which turned the Fayoum into the first man-made lake.

At last we turned left across the canal and towards the river through much fertility. There aren't many crops they don't grow in Minya. The handout lists sugar, cotton, soya beans, garlic, onions, vegetables of all sorts, tomatoes, potatoes and grapes. I add to these the clover and wheat that I saw with my own eyes. The crops are so much better than the houses! So many houses, imposing or would-be imposing brick buildings are unfinished and left so. Here and there even the land was left overgrown and gone to waste. That in the supreme and historical treasure of Egypt is preposterous. I asked about this and got one of my few Minyan insights. Apparently the fellaheen are deserting the land in droves. They can make more money in the cotton factories or sugar factories and there aren't enough of them left to till the land. Those who are left demand such high wages that 'the landowners cannot afford to pay them'. Worse than this from the government point of view, fellaheen sneak off if they can, somehow get abroad to other richer Arab countries where they do the dirty work in oilfields and the like. Then they come back home with a bit of money which enables them to escape the old back-breaking toil with a hoe and open a small shop or some other minute sort of business.

All this means, said Alaa that the price of food increases. Now in Egypt, only the relatively well-to-do can afford it. This leads, he said, to *trouble*.

'What trouble?'

'Riots.'

'Not recently, I hope.'

'A month or two ago.'

The village towards which we were driving, Abu Qurgas, was Coptic Christian. In what I supposed was a graveyard, crosses remained in position if they were made of metal but if they were wooden the cross members were all torn away.

We went down to the ferry and climbed aboard. I saw that the engine had been designed some forty or fifty years ago by my brother-in-law, which completed my feeling of fantasy. The ferry chugged downstream for a quarter of a mile then turned in behind an island and butted the further bank. This was steep sand and we had to jump. A huge, streamlined tourist boat was moored a few hundred yards further along the bank and seemed empty. We walked through scrub and sand to a causeway that led into a more fertile area, perhaps

54

the most fertile bit I had seen to date. There was a water pump further on which served this area and gave it water and enough to spare. So the half a dozen green fields of beans and vegetables were running with water all channelled in the old manner, a miniature demonstration of the system which the pharaohs or their viziers invented. The area was heavily screened off by date-palms and felt cool. One small field was under water entirely with some crop only just showing above the surface. There were a few large, white birds picking about in the water and on the banks. They were the *Amis des Paysans*, or mock ibis, the Farmer's Friends. I asked about them, 'investigatively' and found that they are decreasing in numbers because of the build-up of insecticides. Here too, in this little paradise!

The causeway led on to a resthouse, then across desert and an increasing slope. We came to the foot of the desert cliff, that same escarpment which had stalked us, brown beast that it was, all the way from Cairo and would stay with us in this river valley as far as we chose to go. The causeway bent upward sharply, smooth portions interspersed with groups of 'donkey steps', deeper than steps for men but the rises no higher. The tombs I had come to see – or rather the tombs thought suitable for me to see – were visible as square black doorways high up in the cliff. We toiled up, rested on seats provided thoughtfully at the halfway mark then braced ourselves and reached the level path along which are set the tombs. The tour from the tourist boat was already there but just finishing and turning to go down back to the sunlit boat, a perfect model of itself in that clear air. The tombs are of much importance to Egyptologists for the light they throw on conditions during a troubled period of history, though to the ignorant eye they are less impressive than the ones at Luxor in the Valley of the Kings. They date from the Middle Kingdom and are painted with all kinds of secular events. The paint is not as vivid as it appears in illustrations. But the subjects *are* interesting and the Department of Antiquities in association with the Governate of Minya province has cared for them elaborately, and for the visitors as well, since they have filled the grave shafts with sand and gravel and made them safe.

Here Madame X began to speak. Dear lady, years of guiding, do what she would, had given her set speeches a degree of flatness that combined with the slight echo to make them as soporific as informative. She spoke the French of Egypt and when she had finished she did it all over again in Arabic for the benefit of the rest of the group. I nodded my way busily through the French. Outside the brightly lit doorway the tourists were now visible making their way back down the path. Beyond them the tourist boat lay, waiting for some child to give it a shove or see if blowing would make it move like a real steamboat. It was *so* streamlined. The glass and metal of the hull was sheer and there was simply nothing to break the monotony of glass, metal, glass, even her upper works. I saw, suddenly that she was all *wrong*. This was fashion and nothing but. It was like the absurd streamlining of cars that are never going to benefit more than about one per cent from it. She was a river boat confined to a narrow river. She had no storms to face, no waves bigger than ripples. Her greatest inconvenience would be the wash from some sister ship. Well then, why was she not fantasticated? She should be a barge fit for Cleopatra or a whole group of international Cleopatras and burn on the waters with gold and purple and red. As for all that glass: every window should be graced by a window box and her upper works green with scented shrubs.

I came to with a jerk to find that I had been nodding busily through the Arabic version intended for everybody but me. At the end I carefully asked an intelligent question to show I was with the party; but an awful possibility presented itself to me. Was I in fact a *philistine*? Would Schumann have dismissed me? Or would he have dismissed the tombs? They had some degree of interest about them after all. The particular one we were in was illustrated copiously, as they used to say of books, by various martial arts; from which it had been deduced that the local magnate had got as close as he could to having his private army. And so on. The trouble with so much Egyptology is that of necessity the story is often conjectural because hard evidence is difficult to come by. The links are almost always so tenuous and since the strength of a chain is that of the weakest link. . . .

Madame X returned to French and I to my legitimate nodding. The tomb, compared with the bright afternoon outside, was chilly. I nodded on as a desolating truth became clear to me. I had suspected it ten years before but here was clear confirmation. Unless you are a professional archeologist there is more interest to be found in an illustrated book of a tomb than in the comfortless, rock-hewn thing itself. There is a primary degree of experience which lies in a touch of the hand on rock, as with the pyramids for example and the realization that *I am here*! After that, what is most of interest is the unexpected and all the unforeseen surroundings of an unexpected event. Still, the martial arts *were* a bit interesting as was the uncompromising secularity of the tomb.

We came out into the sun and commenced our return. The tourists were already piling aboard their streamlined supership, *Canopus* perhaps, or *Ramesses*. We crossed again by the ferry, and drove back to Minya along the line of Bahr Yusuf, my old friend. In the boat I found Ann was somewhat recovered and had passed some of the time doing a river sketch to be worked up later. We were bidden that evening to the Palace of Culture, where we were given tea and shown round. Perhaps the most impressive aspect of the visit was the fluency of the English which was spoken, not only by the staff but by such of the students as we met. We came away, identified the Lotus Hotel where we had stayed before, then went back to the boat. Alaa sat with us for a while. He explained what had not been made clear before. The fellaheen do not emigrate. They scarper. They are, as near as nothing, tied to the land though there is nothing legal about it. Minya is a centre for scarpering, for fading away, for disappearing into the blue yonder. It is a centre from which roads lead out to the west through the desert. These roads lead out to the oases. If you want badly enough to get away and you are able to pay a certain amount of money, there are secret roads leading from the oases west into Libya. You go by land-rover or camel and it is inadvisable to be caught by the police of either country. In fact from Minya there is run what amounts to an 'underground railway' into Libya, the proper Homeric epithet for which is 'oil-rich'. The Egyptian/Libyan frontier has been closed officially for years so this traffic is not advertised widely.

Saïd, our Nubian, was back from his trip to Cairo and he had succeeded in getting the spare parts for the water pump. However, he was not feeling well. I asked that my commiserations for his sickness and my thanks for his double journey should be conveyed all the thirty or so feet from our cabin to the fo'c'sle. I was anxious not to be associated in Saïd's mind with Fisher of Fisher's Island or with the English he had hated. I was a bit servile, I think. Alaa declared he would say what was appropriate. I never knew what that was.

But it had been a better day. I at least, and Ann to some extent, had been out and about. We had climbed out of the ditch of the Nile and been interested. That evening the generator ran late again so the boat was warmed through. The stars that sparkled through the chinks between the curtains of our stern window were dazzling just as in all the right travellers' books of the country. I tried to keep my eyes open for the sheer pleasure of seeing them but was not successful.

The next day was very mixed. The events were not so much incompatible as events designed for several people each with different interests. That I found them all interesting meant that any book I wrote eventually was going to be incoherent. The Director of Culture called for us early in the morning and we walked along the corniche where I expected our first stop to be at Government House, but not a bit of it. There was fronting and hanging over the corniche a large kiosk, or, if you prefer, a small shop. This was full of tourist objects. It was crammed with tourist objects. There we might have bought ourselves galabias and turbans – not such bad purchases, either, since they are the best wear for the climate and only poverty of imagination combined with a reverence for national costume keeps the westerner fouling his crutch with pants and underpants. Or we could have bought imitations of the more famous Egyptian *objets*. These, of course, are not so much Egyptian as ancient Egyptian; and their best description is contained in the new Arabic adjective for everything Pharaonic; 'Pharoni'. That is what they are, they are 'Pharoni', whether it be a plastic copy of Narmer's slate palette or El Sheik done in wood but only six inches high. Far and away the most popular of the 'Pharoni' *objets* is the head of Nefertiti. If she weren't so elegant, what a bore the woman would be! Was she anything but beautiful – but then I ask myself, did she need to be?

But here in the kiosk she was not beautiful only repetitive *ad nauseam*, *ad infinitum* in bronze, brass, copper, iron, tin, lead, alabaster, plastic, sandstone, granite, pottery and embroidery. Perhaps the one most reduced, the ugliest, most along the lines of 'a present from Margate' was a section of bamboo hollowed out as a vase with a few hieroglyphics and the invariable head of Nefertiti done on it in pokerwork!

There were also some modern imitations of 'Pharoni' pictures but done on genuine papyrus. 'Genuine' must be the word; for the Ministry of Culture has – laudably I think – caused papyrus plants to be reintroduced into gardens near Cairo so that the stems may be made into papyrus, following exactly the ancient method. The paper

59

is good, then, and a sight of it highly educative to children though the coloured pictures tend to be less authentic than eclectic. But what seemed strange was that we were obviously expected to buy something! Well, after all, we had had fuel and electricity – why not? I had my eye on a very reasonable pastiche of ducks in the Akhetaten manner, partly because it was a pretty picture and partly to buy papyrus for grandchildren and partly – since we were supposed to buy – because in these days of air travel one must assess purchases for weight as well as value. But as I reached for it, Alaa muttered that the Secretary General would unquestionably present us with some papyrus on behalf of the Governate so we had better leave it alone. Finally we chose some small pottery heads of Akhnaton and Nefertiti which were inoffensive, not too heavy and in the last resort readily disposable. We concealed these about us and walked on to Government House which was guarded by soldiers as ragged as the river police. They made tentative gestures towards shouldering and presenting arms but then decided not or that they didn't know how and gave up. We went in. The ground floor was notable for some brilliantly coloured maps of new Minya, wherever that was. We were shown in to the Secretary General, a very imposing gentleman whose appearance, I think, made Alaa's our minder's Egyptian limbs quake with an apprehension old as the pharaohs. In fact the situation was just that little bit 'Pharoni'. Here was authority and power without any doubt whatsoever. The Secretary General seated us, called for tea, got rid deftly of some previous suppliants and asked what he could do for us. To this the answer was, of course, that his underlings in their serried ranks had already done all that could be possibly done and that we were overwhelmed with the kindness and generosity of the Governate of Minya and so on. Well, so we were. But I tended to overdo it. There has descended on me since I have found myself brought willynilly into the presence of the great ones of the earth an orotundity which I have come to define in my own mind as *Nobelitis*. This is a pomposity born of the fact that one is treated as representing more than oneself by someone conscious of representing more than himself. The Secretary General and I now began to use *Nobelspeak*, suffering as we both did from *Nobelitis* or inflammation of the membranes of the ego. The Governate of Minya was peculiarly honoured and I was peculiarly honoured. The Governate could not express its sense of what I could not express adequately my sense of – and so on.

Finally we got down a bit nearer to ground level. Was there by any chance any question that I desired him to answer?

Yes, there was. I wanted to know Minya's plans for the future. This was the right question. Had I noticed the bridge? When that was completed – and all it needed was the root on the other bank and the centre section – it would give immediate and easy access to the other side of the river. On that side, they would build New Minya, which in time would be as big and prosperous as Old Minya, where we were now. They would also make use of the desert. I had noticed the desert on the other side of the river? They were experimenting and there was no doubt that after the teething troubles were over, they would have a method of making bricks out of sand. This would mean that they would no longer have to use the fertile soil of the valley but be able to keep it for growing things. Had they produced any bricks from sand? Not yet but shortly he had no doubt whatsoever – he expatiated. Finally he asked me for my criticisms. What had I found *wrong*? They were only too anxious for constructive criticism. At that I replied in fluent *Nobelspeak* that we were guests in the land and would not offer criticism, only thanks for hospitality. He implored me to find fault. At last I suggested hesitantly that I had noticed a certain – how should I call it? – a certain dilatoriness in the execution of a project. I had seen so many houses that had been left uncompleted and land, precious land, not put to its best use.

How true that was, said the Secretary General, so true! It was a great problem. Perhaps I knew that the fellaheen, good enough people in the main but not, no, not intelligent, were demanding wages so exorbitant that landowners could no longer pay them so that it had become uneconomic to work the land. He himself knew of many people who were simply unable to keep up their family homes and had been forced to build themselves smaller ones. It was a tragedy. Some, as I had so acutely noticed, were unable even to complete the smaller houses. What would become of such people?

We would not take up more of his valuable time. We rose. He rose. We were, he said, guests of the government. Meanwhile, as a token of their respect and admiration they begged we would accept these trifling gifts as mementoes of a happy occasion. He clapped his hands. An acolyte came forward. The Secretary General took from him a papyrus picture for Ann, who was delighted and for me, also delighted, a bamboo vase with the head of Nefertiti inscribed on it in pokerwork. We bowed over our presents and withdrew.

The minibus took us back to the boat, where Ann descended t hole up with her paints for the day. The rest of us set out for th domain of the Great Heretic Pharaoh Akhnaton. The minibus nov contained me, the director, Madame X, a sergeant of the touris police and two young men who looked literary and carried notebook and pencils. We drove again by the Bahr Yusuf but much furthe south this time – to the very borders of Minya Province. As we wen the two young men questioned me. I was disconcerted for this was ; reversal with a vengeance! I had proposed to ask questions but here was, answering them! However I replied as elaborately as I could te the questions I have answered a thousand times, and at last we came to Deir Mawas on the Nile. Here, while we waited for the ferry boat I found that one of my own wishes had been anticipated. I was tc inspect the house of a 'poor fellah'. I had indeed asked to meet people, in a grand, rather pious, sociological gesture. But now, faced with the actual eye-to-eye contact I felt bogus and embarrassed. Why?

The man and his wife were handsome and dignified. They welcomed me in a way that increased my unease.

'They are very poor,' said Alaa. 'This is the father and this the mother, this is the peasant son, I mean the one who stays here to work the land. The elder son is at the university.'

The living space was an irregularly shaped and unroofed court-yard. Sugar cane was heaped by the wall. In a niche was the only visible sign of their abject poverty; a television set, but black and white. A face – I think it was President Mubarak's – was opening and shutting its mouth soundlessly. The family beckoned me into their bedroom. It contained three enormous beds and nothing else. Well, in a bedroom what more do you want? Inspired, I asked about grandchildren. This was popular. The family tree down three generations was unravelled for me. There was in the courtyard a huge columnar structure, not free-standing but bonded to the wall among the heaps of sugar cane. It was about the same size though not shape as the huge storage jars in the palace at Knossos. The father, or rather, as I now knew, grandfather, seeing my interest bent down and fished some grain out of a hole at the base. I examined it wisely and nodded. I shook hands all round and the exquisite old lady – she must have been within a few years of my own age – finished me off by kissing my hand. Then to my intense relief we were outside again. I

62

walked away, realizing at last how difficult, even impossible, it was going to be, to be more than a tourist with a bit of extra privilege. All those journalists who appear on television with intimate views of huts and families and explanations of absolutely everything – what foreheads of brass they must have! I walked away, the two young men with me, pencils at the ready.

Another fellah was arguing fiercely with Alaa, who turned to me, amused. 'Do you wish to see a small, private sugar factory?'

Yes, I said defiantly and to Alaa's astonishment, yes I did! So off we marched again between the mud-built, lime-washed huts with their crazy angles – oh that elaborate immemorial angle! – through dust and dried dung and straw and sticks of sugar cane, among droves of small children, goats and water-buffaloes. In an open courtyard was a machine, all clanking wheels and travelling, flapping belts with what I think an engineer would call a 'hopper' at the top. Two men were filling the hopper with sugar cane which the machine instantly chewed. I was presented with a bit of sugar cane and did not know what to do with it. Alaa began to eat his bit the way the machine was busily chewing a far larger mouthful. Sugar cane is about an inch thick and I remembered the children's book (was it *The Swiss Family Robinson*?) in which the characters are delighted with the thick juice running so I took a bite and nearly mashed my teeth out. Cane is cane is cane and you could use sugar cane for a walking stick. We went on and into another more-or-less open courtyard. Here the heat was fierce. There were half a dozen steaming vats, their mouths only inches above the floor level and men were scooping off the scum with long ladles. There was fire below us and the floor was hot to the feet. There were sacks of quicklime for purifying the juice. I was given a saucerful of juice from each vat in turn and of course all were sickly sweet. But there was a noticeable transition from coarse to pure. I did much nodding. The last offer was a saucer of glue which I was encouraged to taste and of course it was molasses. Alaa translated that molasses was the end product as far as this little factory was concerned. It was stored in earthenware pots and sent off to a larger factory for refining. But molasses was a panacea, like 'royal jelly'. I applauded the sweating company with clapped hands as if I were a soviet delegation, hoping the gesture would convey an amiable interest and admiration. Then we came away with my attendant group and an attachment of children who had come along for the show.

We went down to the ferry which to my great pleasure proved to be a felucca. There is an inexpressible delight in sail. I think it must consist in the sense that you are using directly one of the huge, simple forces of nature and for that time are a conscious part of her however differently you may phrase it. In calm water and slight air the quiet movement is ineffable and I settled to enjoy a holiday. But now the two young men sat either side of me and began to ask literary questions. It was difficult to switch back from the Nile to a seminar but I did what I could. Even what I could do at such short notice was not really adequate; for I was bemused by this example of the biter bit. The various fellaheen we had left there on the western bank were as like as not still exclaiming at my interruption of their work. Now here I was in the guise of Visiting Writer half way across the quiet Nile and having to give opinions on my contemporaries. It was just, tiresome, and funny.

Across the river was Akhetaten, that space on the east bank to which Akhnaton, the heretic pharaoh, retired when he shook the dust of Thebes off his feet. The place is a plain, bounded by an arc of the tawny desert escarpment to which the Nile lies as a string to a bow. From the river as you approach you can see nothing but the greenery, palms, acacias and crops of the river bank. I thought how the day had got out of hand. It would be hard to get the experiences of the sugar refinery, the travelling seminar and of Akhetaten under, so to speak, the same hat. We landed and climbed the bank of what looked like a dry canal leading inland. By the few houses a wagon was drawn up, a springless char-à-banc which I saw was to be pulled by a tractor. Our party climbed aboard and the tractor set off at about six miles an hour. We passed through an area of strangely empty houses and then the plain burst upon us in all its spectacular aridity. Really, it is as if some god had blasted the place! In all those square miles there is not one eye of green and the only variations are between the whitish yellow of sand and the yellowish brown of rock. Ahead of us, a few miles across this most deserted of deserts was the escarpment with a track leading halfway up it to another row of square black holes. But the track itself was almost too rough even for the tractor. No car could have gone a yard on it. As for the wagon it seemed to be most of the time in the air, a few inches between bump and bump. The noise was explosive and hideous. Our bodies were bounced six inches off the wooden seats at each explosion and through it all the questioning went on. Airborne, I heard the shouted

64

uestion, 'What is your opinion of Virginia Woolf?' It was too much.
burst into rude but unstoppable giggles, tried to explain but gave
p as we continued on our Brownian way. How awful to be a
iolecule! It was not, I believe a successful interview; but that was
ot entirely my fault. The char-à-banc stopped after about two miles
the foot of the escarpment. It was easy to confuse this place with
esterday's Beni Hassan. There was the same carefully constructed
scent with its donkey steps and seats for the weary or defeated and
ie same rows of holes at the top, the same tour coming away from
iem as we arrived. Once more Madame X talked and we listened
nd nodded.

Nevertheless here was something to see. The story of Akhnaton is,
f course, that of the conflict between two gods – Amun and Aten.
'he heretic Akhnaton tried to popularize if not enforce worship of
he sun disc', but after his death the forces of Amun triumphed
gain so that, for example, Tutankaton became our familiar
'utankhamun. All that is popularly known from a hundred novels
ince Akhnaton was described as the first individual in history – I
on't know by whom. As Egyptian material for the novelist he has
eplaced Moses and the pharaoh of the Exodus almost entirely. But
ere you could see with your own eyes the evidence of what riotous
assions were loosed in that remote conflict. It made them vivid and
ontemporary. For the priests of Amun had cut any reference to
xkhnaton out of the rock, and to his queen, poor, over-reproduced
Vefertiti, too. You could feel the hammer and chisel in your own
ands. They had carefully emptied the shape of those strange bodies,
ollowing the outline so passionately that the chisel had gone through
he gypsum and chipped the solid limestone beneath it. By this
neans they had rendered permanent what might have faded in time.
Here and there, high up or low down, they had missed a hand,
erhaps, or a few sunrays from the painted solar symbol with its life-
ffering hands.

There had been, I knew, in the last few years, a swing against
Akhnaton – or at least a reassessment. First regarded as a towering
nonotheist, a mystic, a religious genius, he was now argued to be a
lictator with a purely material idea of his god the Aten, the physical
lisc of the sun. He was thought also to have made a god of himself –
vhich is not surprising in view of the accepted status of a pharaoh –
ind to have declared that no one could approach the Aten except
hrough Him. But then, I knew also that during the last year a text

had been discovered the alleged translation of which made a point(
reference to a spiritual reality behind the physical object. That wou
put Akhnaton back on line once more as an original religious think
– a mystic rather than politician. However, archeology always do
things by halves and it seemed unlikely that a single text should tu(
up to settle a vexed question. I wanted to talk to the discoverer a(
translator of that text in Luxor.

Madame X was continuing to talk and our really rather large grot
stood round. I was thinking of Amun and Aten and deciding that I
least knew little to choose between them when I chanced to lift n
eyes away from what was in front of us and look up into the shadov
nearer the roof.

The generous, life-giving hands still reached down, in th
wonderful symbol of divine and natural abundance. Even th
individual rays led upwards and inwards from the hands toward
their source; but someone had take his chisel and carefull(
methodically obliterated the sun.

The sun was blinded.

You can say, of course, if you want to slice things small that the su
is not always beneficent in Egypt, is to be avoided in some season
and is a breeder of plagues. But despite that the Egyptians alway
knew that the sun was the giver of light and life. If he sometim(
killed or blinded, well, what would you expect from a god now an
then? Are there not the afflicted of Allah? Was there not a fig tr(
blasted once and a man struck dead for trying to support the Ark (
the Lord? But here, for all that, a chisel had been driven deep into th
very heart of life. Somehow that obliterated, that gouged-out disc (
the sun settled the whole argument for me as between Amun an
Aten. It spoke of a bigotry and blasphemy, a dark and cruel intentio
as if the priests of Amun had been worshippers of a black sun.

We came away, back down the path over the donkey steps, back i
procession to the char-à-banc and jolted once more across utterl
desert Akhetaten to the village and the river. I had always intended t
walk along the south part of the bank along what had bee(
Akhnaton's royal way where the strange family of king and queen an
small daughters had ridden in their chariots by the water in th
sweetness of living. But now I saw how naturally everyone wa
assuming we were homeward bound, having seen what was suitable
I knew I could not ask our assembly either to walk with me or wait
So we moved back across the river and I was questioned some mor(

nd answered where I could. A conference of writers in Minya was
roposed to which I regretted I could not commit myself as it was so
ar ahead.

We stopped far short of Minya. This was a sugar refinery and a
ery big one. The director used all his status to get us in and had to
ign many papers. We went first to the recreation centre, which was
mpty except for a huge television set showing a man orating to
obody in particular. Presently a youngish man came in, seated us,
eated himself and began to give us statistics. Egypt manufactured a
aillion tons of sugar annually. There was such and such a number of
mployees in the place, which was owned by the government.
Behind the speaker's head the programme changed on the television
et. It was a lecture by a doctor on diseases of the eye. I tried to look
way but found it impossible. The facts and figures continued. The
oung man, feeling himself in competition with the television turned
he sound down and went on with his stream of information. A
aideous series of eyes in one state or another of decay, eruption,
nalformation, obliteration stared at me over his shoulder. Presently
ve all stood up. The young man led us away and left the eyes still
lemonstrating themselves.

The factory was huge, covered acres. This time, instead of the
aopper I had seen earlier in the day in the little machine at Abu
Qurqas there was a gigantic trough. A truckload at a time the cane
ascended a gantry then was thrust into a trough to be crunched with a
ound as of dinosaurs at dinner. It entered a complex of machinery
which jetted heat and steam and noise and clank and squelch. We
ascended like the cane to move among machinery on walkways of
teel net. We followed our leader between boilers and vats and
varicose piping. The temperature was well over a humid hundred.
Here our introduction was shouted to a young man who proved to be
he engineer in charge. His face was extraordinary and stripped by
his enthusiasm or passion or obsession to skin and bone from which
unblemished eyes stared as if they saw a single truth which must be
proclaimed no matter what. The thought flicked through my mind
that there was a little of Akhnaton left about the place. The young
man never blinked. He grasped me by the arm and led me into the
system, inventing English as he went in the passion of his
explanation. Here the juice boiled while *this* was added, the effect of
which was to remove *this* here. Now the juice was affected not by
steam – he was insistent it was not by *steam* – but by *vapour*. I was to

inspect this gauge, at such and such a temperature. Here the lime w‹
added, whereas here. . . .

It was extraordinary and moving. The explanation, if such it wa‹
of his actions came to me late because it was at first sight
implausible. He comprised in himself the machinery and tʰ
process. He had swallowed the factory, become it, in his singl‹
minded passion. He was not so much an engineer as a refinery. So ɪ
drew me on between the jets of steam, the blasts of heat from one va‹
blip, blip to another, blop, blop, then onward to where things we‹
cooling and cooler; and so at last to the great, revolving drums fro‹
which, lo, a powder of white crystals fell – he thrust his hands into
sack and held out these elements which had achieved such a glitteriⁿ
transmutation through his own body.

'See. Take. Eat.'

After that and our thanks we walked away through stocks of suga‹
machinery, old boilers abandoned, and metal shapes of unknow‹
name and function, through lessening noise and heat until we we‹
out from the artificial light of the factory to the light of the real sun.
by now, was exhausted and glad to see our minibus; but the day ha‹
not quite done. In the first place I saw a man on the other side of tʰ
canal using a shadouf, that primitive, counter-balanced machine f‹
lifting water which is now disappearing from all over Egypt to ᵇ
replaced by diesel engines. A shadouf in the Bahr Yusuf! Then aga‹
on the other side of the road was a narrow gauge railway; an‹
presently we overtook a train on it. The railway was the sugar can‹
railway and here was the sugar cane, truckload after truckload, pile‹
so high, heaped so thick that small boys were running beside it an‹
tugging lengths of cane from the trucks. The minibus stopped and a‹
the passengers except me piled out and took part in the plundering.
merely took a photograph – or thought I did, but the film was n‹
advancing. The person most amused by all this carry-on was tʰ
driver of the train.

So then we arrived back at the boat. I thanked everybody in sigʰ
profusely, thanked and apologized to the young men whos‹
notebooks I hoped were full. I went down to the boat where Ann ha‹
sketched and not been satisfied with her work. I had so much for m‹
journal. I did my best; but beside the phenomena – the Secretar‹
General, the 'poor' fellah, Akhnaton, the engineer – anything I coul‹
do seemed hardly worth the trouble.

I did not hear the dawn chorus of the muezzins and woke only when the engine came to life at half past six. By the time I was dressed we had left Minya, and fast too. It seemed that we had acquired a couple of extra knots, courtesy of the mended water pump. Rushdie, in his capacity as cook, had by now discovered that we liked meals at set times where possible. So we actually had a bit of genuine breakfast, bread and cheese and mineral water, round about half past seven. I asked for coffee in my rudimentary Arabic and got it between eight and nine. Hardly had I finished drinking this when through our stern window I saw that the Nile was black with smoke. My first thought was that we were overhauling some craft very much in need of de-coking. My second was that this is *always* one's first thought on sea or river or canal and one is *always* wrong. The trouble is *always* with one's own boat. But this, as had been made abundantly clear, was not my boat. All the same there are some things . . . I went on deck. Sure enough, a quarter of a mile of thick, black smoke was trailing from us astern and blotting out a view of the suburbs of Minya. I gesticulated at Shasli in his glass box but he only nodded and smiled. We were certainly moving along fast enough – doing a good three-quarters of those alleged eleven knots we were supposed to have at our disposal. I did some more gesticulating at Akhmet, our engineer, but he shrugged resignedly and pointed upwards, either at Shasli or Allah or both. I turned back to watch our smoke, and as I did so, a police launch moved out of it and began to overhaul us. I cursed Shasli for a fool, thinking that we must be breaking some river law by our filthy pat of pollution but while I was still finding unusual words to describe him my irritation changed to incredulity. The old Nubian Saïd was kneeling up in the launch and waving a handful of dusters.

Shasli slowed down and the smoke diminished as the launch came alongside. Rushdie and Akhmet hauled Saïd shivering out of the launch. The two policemen, first making the launch fast to one of our cleats, followed him into the centre cabin. Alaa appeared and at last I got an explanation. Saïd had been sent ashore for dusters in Minya and had been mislaid. When he got back to the police station we had

gone; so with a simple faith in the importance of people who went f[o]
an interview with an Egyptian Secretary General and came back i[n]
one piece he had commandeered the launch on our behalf and set o[ut]
in pursuit. The launch was open, the morning chilly and they had a[ll]
three, Saïd and the two policemen frozen solid. They would war[m]
up soon, said Alaa. In fact everything had ended happily except f[or]
Faroz. My heart sank. Well, what had happened to Faroz? He had s[et]
off to look for Saïd in Minya and must have missed him but anywa[y]
he would be able to rejoin us further on. But, said Alaa, we must n[ot]
worry. With that he went below, where the policemen and Saïd wer[e]
being revived with some refreshment or other. I stayed on deck an[d]
tried to convince myself that this sort of accident could hav[e]
happened to anyone. I examined our wake, under a trace of smok[e]
which had appeared again. Shasli was speeding up – not very much[,]
of course, for the police launch was still made fast alongside. [I]
decided I had found a reason for his hysterical burst of speed whic[h]
had made so much smoke. He had seen the police launch following u[s]
and had thought of his sins, or ours, or the crew's and he had decide[d]
to try and make a bolt for it. The thought was curiously pleasant.

We passed a peculiar thing lying in the water which was made t[o]
waggle a bit by our decorously small bow wave. 'Nonsense,' [I]
thought to myself. 'It's only a dead fish.' Odd, rotting stuff gave it th[e]
appearance of having four legs – illusory, of course, for what fish eve[r]
had four legs? I went below, and found the frozen three restored[.]
Two of them got into the launch and swung away from us. [I]
congratulated Saïd on his initiative, then went into our cabin, feelin[g]
a bit chilly myself and watched the world for a while through ou[r]
ample windows. I was rewarded with two splendid sights: first jus[t]
above El Roda I was delighted to see a very small felucca with a loose[-]
footed mainsail towing a larger rowing boat heaped high with brigh[t]
green clover. In sail and towing! It was a vision to restore a man'[s]
faith in the use of nature; second El Roda itself (fronted by a high
revetment of white limestone of which huge semicircles ha[d]
collapsed) was all beset with trees, big trees; and for a mile or tw[o]
thenceforward the trees were so full of *Amis des Paysans* roosting
among the branches that they looked like sulphur cockatoos i[n]
Australia. Come to think of it the trees may well have bee[n]
eucalyptuses, which are notably established in Upper Egypt, unles[s]
my eyes have deceived me. But more poetically than cockatoos [I]
decided the mock ibises, the Farmers' Friends – I cannot be officia[l]

out them, getting either the language or the apostrophes muddled I decided they looked like white magnolia blossoms.

The two sights put us both in a cheerful mood for the day. I was le to point out to Ann the tombs I had examined in the previous vo days, those square black holes halfway up the eastern cliffs. But ter Akhetaten – Tell el Amarna I suppose – the escarpment came ose to the river and spread out in whole libraries of geology, fawn, ff-white, yellowish and light brown. Cultivation still clung to the ist bank under the cliffs, but only just. In fact we saw (and hotographed on actual rather than conceptual film) the Last Palm f Akhetaten. Every now and then there were more holes in the cliff, me square like those at Beni Hassan and Tell el Amarna, some napeless mouths, caves it might be for anchorites or corpses or both, dits for any sort of mine you care to think of, refuges for – who can iy? They are all 'published' somewhere if you care to chase through library after them, all dealt with if you have the patience. leanwhile they were enigmas, square holes, round holes, lopsided oles, here and there a speckle like a group of swallow holes and here nd there a black hole with a white scratch of path leading up to it. he sky was bright blue over the cliffs, and opposite them the other ank of the river was flat and fertile. The Western Desert was still out f sight. In fact, since leaving Cairo, had we not previous experience, ve might have thought the fertile western part of the valley stretched nd stretched away for ever, or to the Atlantic at any rate. The Nile self was still greenery-yallery with a bit of reflected blue mixed in. Vile Roses were drifting past in green patches. There was some parkle.

To the east, cultivation began to come back. Every few hundred ards there were feluccas drawn up on the bank. They were a new reed, very small and very lightly built. They looked as if they might e made of hides stretched over keel and timbers. There were crazily ngled mud huts again and a single, crazy wooden one. A woman quatted before a tripod of sticks from which hung an inflated goat's kin. She was pushing and pulling this vigorously, churning milk nto butter. There were, here and there, a few prosperous houses, ach with a hand pump well away from the river.

The note of the engine rose. I glanced aft. Sure enough, our trace f smoke thickened, became the usual pat, thick, black. I rushed out f our seclusion and found Alaa.

'You are planning again. Relax! It is not your boat.'

71

'It isn't Shasli's either!'

The argument went no further. Short of physical violence there was no way of stopping Shasli handling the boat any way he liked. invented sayings. Behind the apparent amiability of the Egyptian is steely determination not to be moved out of his habitual indolence And so on.

Near Mallawi we saw a young man standing up to his knees in water on the west bank and signalling with his shirt. It was Faroz. We picked him up and found he had been waiting for us for hours having taken a taxi from Minya. The time was 5 o'clock and after moving on a mile or two we approached the west bank again and made fast to a tram among some others. We were now in the allegedly piratical stretch of the Nile. Shasli thought there was safety in numbers. The crew drifted away to the other trams or to the shore We discovered the water was off. In any case we could not have had a bath but only a minimal shower. Presently it was explained to us that the crew was fetching water so that they could drink. We frail creatures, of course, stuck to mineral water from plastic bottles Night fell, almost, one felt, with a crash. Rushdie made us coffee After we had both drunk it he explained it was made with 'good water brought from ashore'. He added as an afterthought, that boiling the water had 'killed everything'.

Almost certainly it had been a dead fish and not a crocodile.

Alaa brought his coffee along to drink with us. He mentioned that Saïd was proposing to spend a night with his people at Aswan in Upper Egypt when we got there.

'We shan't get there, Alaa. You know that. We shall be lucky to get to Luxor in this boat.'

'That will suit Faroz.'

'Why?'

'He comes from a small settlement on the west bank just beyond Luxor.'

'What about Shasli?'

'He comes from Qena. . . .'

'In Upper Egypt on the way to Luxor. What about Akhmet?'

'He was born in a small village some way ahead of us on the east bank.'

It is not that Egyptians are particularly devious. It is that they all from Hamdi down, believe in killing as many birds as possible with one stone.

72

The engine started in twilight.

'What's happening?'

'I don't know.'

But Shasli was only manoeuvring from alongside the tram to lie alongside a big sandal with a cargo of sugar cane piled in its hold to the height of our bridge. Some of the sticks overhung our deck. I remembered how everybody had run along beside the sugar cane train and grabbed bits of cane for themselves. Now it was sticking out and to be had for nothing, nobody bothered. I sat and filled in my journal by the dying, or at any rate fading, light of a small strip. Never mind I thought – if that were the only problem! What great works have been written by the light of a penny dip.

It was a non-place. Perhaps the half a dozen trams and two or three sandals had indeed huddled together to avoid pirates or thieves as they may have been. After all in Chinese waters they used to say the rivermen would sell you an anchor chain at the stern while paying it out over your bows. It was all a very honourable profession and perhaps 'piracy' on the Nile was the same. I slept the worse not for thoughts of 'piracy' but from the cold. We both got to sleep at last under piles of assorted clothing. I dressed at dawn and stared through the port window. We moved away from the gaggle of craft and all set off in procession. There were much bigger rafts of Nile Roses coming down the stream. The cliffs were *in* on the east side and there was an orangey glow of sunrise behind them. It looked as if dust or smoke was hanging in the sky. I could not believe there was water up there – but why the dust? And now, as the sun pushed up, character entered into the cliffs, as the play of light and shade, all sharp in contrast, created an infinite variety of forms in the rock. There were faces of men and beasts that changed into cities and fallen trees. A sleeper lay, his head pillowed on a coign of vantage. As we moved past, the face fell in, the sleeper became a clenched fist then vanished altogether. The sun, blazing now, was parodying or analogizing in rock its own acts of universal creation. Oh, yes – to cut out the disc of the sun was a dreadful thing.

We moved over closer to the west bank, which was burstingly fertile now but swept by a considerable current. There were groins and little promontories of limestone in the curved shelters of which the water and the masses of Nile Roses gyrated. *Reis* Shasli sent down a message that we were passing by a notorious pirate village. There seemed to be no inhabitants and only one small rowing boat was drawn up on the mud beach.

We went on deck and waited for the barrage at Asyut to come in sight. It was impressive. It is essentially a road stretching across the river with one hundred sluice gates ranged side by side below it. At one end there is a kind of travelling crane made of what looks like gigantic meccano. This machine is the size of a four-storey house, the bottom storey of which straddles the road, while leaving a hole in itself big enough for any truck to pass. The whole huge contraption travels on railway lines set on either side of the road and running from one end of the barrage to the other. So the crane can move from sluice to sluice and adjust each of the hundred massive gates as required. As we approached it was plain that the river had not yet been ponded for the replenishment of the irrigation system for all the gates were letting plenty of water foam through. On the righthand side of the barrage as we faced it, were lock gates with trams and sandals waiting for them to open. Getting through into that lock, and getting out of it afterwards was a slow business. The in-between business was terribly slow. That whole operation took us about three hours. 'He who rides the Nile must have sails woven of patience.' The word that proverb uses for 'Nile' means 'Sea' so perhaps the whole thing is mock-heroic. How can you tell, in a language you don't know?

Once clear of the lock we went roaring up the river at our top and smoky speed and were chased at once by a police launch. I had just the same nervous reaction you feel, however virtuous your conduct, if the police stop your car. But Alaa's letter from the Chief of Police was now working its magic more potently the further we got away from Cairo. The police launch merely wanted to know if we required anything. Shasli, never missing an opportunity, got water and fuel with a quick tie-up at the police station.

The Nile is notably broader above Asyut. Most rivers get a bit wider as they approach the sea, since tributaries increase their flow. But the Nile has no tributary to join it anywhere north of Khartoum. So the flow, what with more than a thousand miles of evaporation and irrigation, decreases all the way to the Delta. To say thus is to simplify a process that is vastly complex and, be it said, not yet fully understood by the people who study the water or administer its distribution. There is, for example, seepage of unknown quantity – unknown because for some ineluctable reason the seeped water sometimes elects to flow on underground and rejoin the Nile at a

74

point further north, thus making a nonsense of exact calculations. To complicate the complications there is what geologists call 'juvenile water' – the stuff that bubbles up from the endless crack between the two Atlantic Ridges – which may have been trapped somehow in the exhaustingly ancient African landmass before there was life on earth or even a decent stretch of sea. That water runs under the Sahara – possibly. Perhaps it's as well that there are still mysteries left for our grandchildren to solve, even in something as apparently simple as a river.

Here, then, and for whatever reasons, the Nile was majestic; and as if wealth were to be gauged exactly by the size of its flow, mile after mile, south of Asyut the banks were dotted with villas splendid by Egyptian standards. The weather, as if it had been ponded behind the foaming barrage of Asyut, became significantly warmer. I began to rejoice, feeling that we were getting on. But just as I began to rejoice we tied up at a place called Abu Tig. Nobody had told me anything; but to my surprise Alaa and Rushdie asked me to come and see the town. So ashore we went. An aspect of any Egyptian town that is bound to surprise a westerner – northerner – is how the children swarm everywhere. They seemed healthy enough to me as did the population generally. There were no ghastly cripples begging beside the road, no children too listless to move. Even so, the children stopped their playing as we approached and waited. They did not bother us, however, but only examined us curiously and from a distance. This is a change that has happened in the last ten years. It was not because we were 'convoyed' by Alaa and Rushdie, who look as Egyptian as anyone can. It is the result of a push by the authorities to get the bakshish boys off the backs of foreigners. Ten years before we had been plagued by them and they have been notorious for generations. But as far as my experience goes, from one end of Egypt to the other the bakshish boys are gone. So in Abu Tig we were able to walk free and unhindered. The streets were a little untidy but not dirty. There were small shops which seemed to stock only a few goods, except the tobacco kiosk which was loaded down with every kind of tobacco product. The Egyptians make 'hubble-bubbles' out of a can and a length of bamboo. Those who could afford the earlier, ornate versions of the hubble-bubble now smoke western style. But the average Egyptian if he is not dragging at his bamboo pipestem is smoking a cigarette. Everybody smokes hash now and then. Officially the police are supposed to stop it, but wink.

Beyond the kiosk we came to Nasser Park. For a small town it was a remarkable place. There were winding walks under trees, all concrete and all swept clean. The trees were festooned with fairy lights. There was also a zoo with animals in rather cramped cages. The captive birds seemed depressed. What I found remarkable was the fact that the place had many statues; and these were mostly reproductions of 'Pharoni' works. They were made in the appropriate stone, granite, basalt, limestone, quartzite, but reproductions nevertheless. The effect was curious in a way not easy to define. For outside Cairo and Alexandria the craft of statuary is not much practised. Off hand, I could only think of one attempt at a modern 'work of art' and that was the war memorial in Asyut, which seemed to be made of aluminium and to my untutored eye was dramatically inartistic. But then, what war memorial isn't? Perhaps the strange effect of these reproduced 'Pharoni' statues was because in most western countries we have the genuine article and connect fake Egyptian with those super cinemas of the Twenties and Thirties. I still can't quite account for my bewilderment at meeting a Ramesses or an Amenhotep quarter size in a bed of Strelitzias. The statues drew me on until we discovered that we were back at the corniche and only fifty yards from the boat; so we climbed a fence illegally and went back on board. It was early. Ann stayed in the middle cabin to be taught her numbers but even this palled. The time was just after six and it was growing dark. There was nothing left to do but read our minimal supply of books and write my journal. Bedtime could not be before 9 o'clock and that was a long haul. I still do not know why we stopped at Abu Tig and forgot to ask Alaa, having by now become a little fatalistic in an Egyptian way about the reasons for things. It was a defeat.

In the morning the engine began to tick over at a quarter to seven but we did not get up until a quarter past. The Nile was copious as if we had passed the principal points where irrigation drew it off from the main stream. The air still felt a bit warmer. There was some temptation to relax into that warmth and forget the duty of being interested. Shasli was pushing the engine, I thought, and we were still trailing our thick black tail. We made the day noisome for any craft that followed us too closely. Fishermen, sitting in their rowing boats and rocking in our wake did not like us. To tell the truth, both Ann and I were prepared to admire nothing so much as a comfortable hotel with large, clean bathrooms and large, clean beds with large, clean sheets. They awaited us at Luxor, still a long way ahead. Meanwhile, I fulfilled my duty by noting the river craft – still more interesting than temples – or rock tombs at any rate. This stretch of the river above Asyut appeared to breed a standard small felucca, lightly built – skin on ribs? – and setting one of those loose-footed lateen sails which can be so adjusted as to seem to be *lifting* the craft along with something the aspect of a hang-glider. They all carried the standard Nile variety of sculls – that is a pair of lightly shaped baulks of timber. These boats draw next to nothing. Under oar they are ideal for fishing. The fisherman lowers a stone buoyed by a tin then rows towards the bank, spreading a net behind him as he goes. It seems infallible. Fish never learn.

By now our crew, including Alaa, had adopted the habit of having all their meals in the centre cabin without benefit of tables, chairs, or stools. They set out as much as a dozen plates of various foods on the carpeted floor then squatted round cross-legged and ate. I felt it looked exotic and grubby; but on analysing this reaction discovered that *I* was the exotic one with my needs for and assumption of a rich paraphernalia for the daily business of eating. The crew had been amiable enough, but since we could only communicate minimally unless we used Alaa as an interpreter, they remained *other*. There is no doubt that with sufficient enterprise along the Moorehead or Stark lines I might have found out more about them. The fact was – and I here put it down in black and white – I was *shy*. Invite a Frenchman to translate the word into his own language and he is likely to come up with '*réservé*', or '*timide*', neither of which will do. A Greek will give you '*deilos*', German '*scheu*' none of which is appropriate since it misses out the 'I would if I could but I am not able' which is inherent in 'shy'. It is no good asking an Italian for a translation for the concept of shyness is unknown to him. But here I was, a week in the boat, living cheek-by-jowl with a crew and unable to catch their eye in a matey way and with not even the courage to try to learn a word from anyone except Alaa! I had to stand round, humming and nodding on the edge of things, even when Ann was learning numbers from them and having Egyptian bread explained to her. Significantly enough, I felt I knew Saïd the Nubian better than the others because he had a genuine, simple reaction to us. We were English and therefore to be disliked. The others might think that but would be too complicated or, if you like, too sophisticated to say so.

My small stock of Arabic now contained, however, the words for 'north' and 'south'. They were interesting. 'South' is '*qibli*' which is of unknown derivation, as if the south anyway was a mystery; but 'north' is '*bahari*', which simply means 'towards the sea'. The interest in that is partly because we were approaching the 'big bend' which is so notable in maps of the Nile, where the river kinks violently in a right angle then gets back on course again. So for a time the river does not run north and south but east and west. Nevertheless, what was really east would still be '*qibli*' and west would be '*bahari*' or in the direction of the sea, though the nearest water in that direction would be more than three thousand miles away in the Atlantic.

At about midday, while Rushdie was giving us an elementary but I am afraid misleading lesson in hieroglyphics – children are taught a list of the 'alphabetic' signs at school – while, I say, we were having our names written out with no benefit of syllabic signs or determinatives, the rudder lines parted again. Shasli repeated his former manoeuvres and we half-motored, half-drifted to the western shore. It was the more comfortable one. On the east bank, while Rushdie scribbled, the cliffs had become high and spectacular again. Directly opposite there was a quarry and while we watched, it blew the day's charges, making much dust and rubble but having little effect on the cliff. We cast off from the shore and with a jury-rigged rudder went looking for a bit of wire from a passing tram. It had no wire but agreed to give us a pluck. The energetic young man Faroz, officially our cleaner – but on *Hani* there was no demarcation – Faroz in his blue tracksuit with its white stars and his rakish blue turban, seized what I think must have been our only bit of rope and leaped across about six feet of Nile on to the tram. He made the end fast. That was fine and gallant except that no one was holding our end of the line and it was not made fast to us either so we lost Faroz once more and our rope. Since our rudder was jury-rigged we could not manoeuvre and the tram had to do the job. I watched with a mixture of keen enjoyment and irritation. We got alongside at last, made fast, and retrieved our rope and a crestfallen Faroz, though it was no more his fault than anyone else's. He is a likeable lad and we thought he would be excellently cast as Aladdin.

We were provided with a full police escort into the city of Sohag – or to its corniche and police station. I felt that had we come by road,

Alaa's letter from the Police Chief would have ensured us motorcycle outriders – what fun! The police were helpful. Sohag is a big city with housing estates and many mosques. More than that, Sohag has a bridge going all the way across the river so that the city lies on both sides of the river as Minya will do when they contrive to get the root built on the east bank and a bit in the middle. I noted yet another example of our confined inability to make contact with people. Rushdie spent most of the afternoon with Alaa's head in his lap, reading aloud in Arabic what Alaa called 'A tale by some Lebanese idiot'. They were hysterical with laughter every now and then but I saw that it was useless to try to find out what it was all about. Nothing is so impenetrable as laughter in a language you don't understand.

We had tied up by a quarter to five and I was by that time resigned to wasted hours that might have been spent making headway. The reason this time in any case was sensible – an effort to find the correct flexible steel wire for the connection between wheel and rudder. Five minutes after we tied up, Ann and I were alone in the boat. There was nothing to do but wait and watch. One of the consolations was a beautiful sailing sight. As we waited for the quick dusk to well up round us two huge sandals came up the river before a following wind. Each had her lateen spread out to port and a 'balancer' to starboard. They were laden deep with white limestone. Their sails caught what light was left and the water was so smooth now that as they inched along they were mirrored faintly in it. I took more shots with my camera – wishing all the time for Alaa's battery, but felt I was preserving this magnificent sight for posterity. I had an uneasy feeling that we were among the last people who would ever see sail used as an economic proposition – used, as it were, *healthily* and not preserved for occasional pleasure or to dress a tourist scene. For, of course, the huge trams, able to transport hundreds of tons of stone or brick, must end by pushing the exquisite sandals off the river and they will finish by being preserved only to take tourists on sentimental journeys. However, the thought struck me that they would be an even more magnificent sight if the *Khamsin* started to blow and they had to beat up the river at top speed!

The crew drifted back having failed to find the bit of wire they wanted and the police this time were unable to give us fuel, having none for themselves or saying they had none. We were, therefore, in a mild kind of fix. Shasli said he thought he would be able to get fuel from one of the trams, once we were out of sight of the police and the city. How odd. However, we had taken water aboard and could wash if nothing else.

7

In the morning the engine started at a quarter past six but I did not get up. I lay, instead, trying to deduce what was happening from what I could hear. It was complex. Just when I thought we were all set to roar smokily off up the river, Shasli put the screw out of gear for a couple of seconds. Then he moved our boat by a series of delicate little engine-nudges, each time only using the screw minimally. He was going alongside something again. We bumped. I got out of my bunk, drew a curtain and stared out. I got a shock because there was a limestone cliff only a yard from my face and for a breathless moment I feared the worst. But in the next moment I saw that this cliff of limestone was supported by a tram and we were now tied up to it. The tram was moving too and soon we were off up river, our engine just turning over while the tram hauled us along faster than we could have gone under our own power. I dressed after that and went on deck to see what was happening. The cliff of limestone reached up about six feet above the gunwale of the tram and must have been at least twenty yards long. The steering position – but this is customary and a definition of 'tram' – was right up in the bows. The engine, engine-room and engineer were right aft in the stern. The engine-room 'telegraph' consisted of a piece of string laid sloppily along the top of the stone cargo. Presumably if it was pulled it rang a bell in the stern and presumably the engineer knew what the signals meant. But in any case, when I came on deck there was no engineer in the engine-room at all. He was forrard in the steering position together with the tram's crew of six and most of our own crew. It was a matey and animated scene. Shasli was bargaining for fuel; or rather both crews were bargaining for it. As far as I could see there were at least ten people in command. I understood that the only male in either craft with no contribution to make was myself. I felt not so much a passenger as a bit of lumber. Alaa emerged from the after part of the tram.

'Nice simple loo,' he said. 'A wide bore pipe and straight through into the river. No problem.'

Akhmet, our engineer, walked aft along the tram carrying a towel.

'He is going to have a bath,' said Alaa. 'Not very hot, though.'

81

Maybe we should have hired a tram.

The bargain was struck. Both crews busied themselves with the job of manoeuvring the craft so that a fuel pipe could be joined between them.

'Why are they taking so long about it?'

'It is difficult,' said Alaa. 'Very difficult.'

I remember coming back from Gibraltar with Force 'H' at twenty-eight knots. I was in the destroyer *Orion*. There was a moderate sea. We manoeuvred alongside the battleship, *King George V* was it, or *Anson*? – I could not remember – or *Prince of Wales* – no she had been sunk by then. But whatever ship it was, we lay, our captain conning his ship by fractions of a degree ten yards from that brutal citadel of armour plate and steel while mail was passed and a fuel line linked. The contrast was entertaining.

I remembered what I had come for. Those deep insights and profound thoughts did seem a little thin on the ground – or water. It had become obvious that I was an observer of the trivial and would have to record it or come home with nothing. It seemed an appropriate moment for learning about trams. After all, they are the powered workhorses of the river. I began to make inquiries, no doubt getting in everybody's way – but then everybody got in everybody's way! These craft were not being run by captains or committees or even majority vote. It was all happenstance and worked, which was what mattered. This tram belonged to the biggest sugar company which was government owned. Egypt produces a million tons of sugar every year, refining it from the raw cane in the extraordinary bowels of the engineer who haunted me with his passion. This tram would distribute its hundreds of tons of limestone for purifying juice to half a dozen refineries in Upper Egypt.

'Bigger than the one we saw?'

'Much bigger. Newer.'

The tram, when it had shot its cargo, would bring back molasses in special tanks. The company – the government, in effect – had two hundred trams. Who, then, in the long run would pay for our fuel? The taxpayer, I thought, most likely.

However, I was now a little enlightened. Why, this was *almost* 'investigative journalism'! I saw now the difference between the government trams, grey painted but rusting and the privately owned trams which went up and down the Nile touting for custom, ready to carry anything from bricks to grain or sugar or straw or crowds of fellaheen on a religious outing. The private trams needed to be seen and had not an assured market. For this reason they were brightly painted and decorated and beflagged. They were covered with advertisements and pious exhortations, the two sometimes mingled for in Egypt you can see 'God is greatest' written in the most unlikely and perhaps inappropriate places. Most trams are to be defined by the position of the wheel right up in the bows and by the size of the wheel. Since it is right up forrard, no matter how your cargo of, say, sugar cane towers astern of you, you can still see what is in front. However, a corollary of this is that there is a distance of about fifty yards between the wheel and the rudder it controls. Sizeable chains link the one to the other and consequently the effort needed to shift the wheel and the chain and the rudder is enormous. For this reason the wheel is as large as that of a ship of the line – six or seven feet in diameter. For the slightest change of course you see the helmsman spin the wheel, bearing down with his weight on one side of it. He needs all the mechanical advantage he can get and the big wheel provides it. Power-operated steering would be uneconomical because as usual in Egypt – except when raising large quantities of water – it is cheaper to use human muscles. I had seen one example of a new mark of tram. This was a larger vessel altogether and had the wheelhouse right aft. But it was moored by the root of a bridge which was being built and had been imported specially by the foreign company which was building the bridge. It was, I say, the shape of things to come, and I regretted it, sentimentally. There were in this stretch of the river, a few of the big tourist boats going up and down. They were the modern sort, four-deckers and streamlined. Only once, when we were moored in a creek, I happened to turn round and saw a different tourist boat slide past the opening of it – a large, wooden, fantasticated job which was probably used for the film *Death on the Nile*. On the other hand, the sight was so brief I wondered if I had dreamed it. Then again, there are launches with awnings overall for day trips and these seem very popular with middleclass Egyptians rather than tourists who prefer to take their whole world with them and, indeed, as we saw, can do very little else. It seems that different governates – what were once called 'Nomes' – favour slightly different craft as though natural selection was for once performing its textbook operation.

Yet it is difficult to see any real dividing line between these governates. The division noticeable from the river – and it is only notional as a division – is where the Eastern Desert swerves in and brushes the water then swerves off again. That must interrupt or at least diminish communication along one bank; but then most communication in Egypt from prehistoric times onward has been on water.

I had now become all eyes in my search for interest, however trivial. The stretch we were in was once notorious for its dullness. That decisive-minded traveller, T. G. Bowles, took the 'Post Boat' up this stretch and did not think much of it.

> As for the voyage, it is dismal beyond expression. The melancholy succession of flat mud banks rarely broken by as much as a single tree, still more rarely by a village, and never by single houses is quite depressing, and offers no inducement to linger, while the crowd of half or wholly naked urchins who at each stopping place howl for bakshish makes one wonder what kind of people it can be that succeeded those who built the Pyramids, and what kind of system it can have been that has thus degraded the inhabitants of the richest soil on earth.

Today, I thought, things had changed beyond measure. The abundant fertility of that soil was now evident to the very edge of the water and the urchins might be seen passionately playing football wherever there was a space for them.

The tram to which we were hitched was loaded with the soft limestone of the mountains over to the east. I knew it was soft because I broke a piece off the cargo and crumbled it easily between two fingers and a thumb. No wonder it was destined to purify sugar. It seemed less a stone than a spice or even an *eatable*.

We came to Balyana and cast off from the tram for it was stopping there. Shasli pushed ahead. Plainly he scented his home comforts at Qena. Immediately the scene was obscured by our long tail of dense, black smoke. I stopped peering at Balyana which did not seem worth more than a glance, and went below, where I was told that Saïd now had tonsillitis. Poor old man, the devoted journey after dusters and subsequent wild pursuit in the police launch had done for him. He was looking very miserable. I exerted all my will on this momentarily malleable crew member and got him to go and lie down on his bunk. It was not that he went off duty, for the distinction in *Hani* was without a difference. No one was ever on duty except the man at the wheel; but then no one was ever off duty either. They just did, more or less, what was to be done and at varying speeds. The lad Faroz – Aladdin – was officially cleaner, but handed, reefed and steered, if by reefing may be understood rearranging the long cushions which had been placed in more leisurely days on the upper deck for lounging passengers. He also cooked, as did Akhmet the engineer. Poor Saïd on the other hand, aged and ill, did nothing but stand about and go the occasional useless errand if we chanced to be tied up at a town. It was wholly bad luck that he got left behind and exposed to the elements in the police launch. Shasli, of course, did nothing but steer and give orders which was fair enough since he was the *Reis*. Rushdie steered, cooked, studied business management, taught elementary hieroglyphics, played the lute and occasionally sang. He had other talents which had not yet emerged. But what proper systematic naval arrangements could be made with such a job lot? It was no good saying they were efficient. The boat did not allow efficiency. On the whole they had kept her running but only just and with intermissions. As for Shasli, I swear he was now overrunning the boat and our tail of smoke was a quarter of a mile long and almost as wide.

Alaa emerged from the fo'c'sle and said that he thought the old man was bad. I asked what help we could get in those parts. Apparently there was a hospital at Nag Hammadi and one at Qena. What we must do, I thought, if he got no better, was to put him into one of those hospitals and collect him on the way back. I even considered leaving someone to look after him and wondered who could most easily be spared but came to the conclusion that that someone was myself. That day, for some reason, Rushdie cooked us a colossal lunch.

After the lunch I was watching the now fertile east bank – the tawny desert had slunk away again – when I saw a 'Return of the Native'. It was remarkable. There was a mud cliff about six feet high, some trees and among them a long straggling village. A procession was moving under the trees. Everyone was dressed in the standard costume native to Egypt, with much brilliant nylon. But *leading* this procession with children dancing round him was an elegant young man in a western business suit of light grey and very, very sharp with flared bottoms to the trouser legs. His hair was set carefully. He carried a small suitcase while a little boy struggled after him with another. It was without doubt one of those moments when the son of the village comes home from foreign parts having, let us hope, made

85

his modest fortune perhaps as a construction worker among the rigs and who was now all set to become the great, rich man in his village. It was as clear as an illustration in a book, this glimpse of a process, the man returning with city shoes already dusty as the bus which had brought him home went trundling back along the bank. Well, I thought to myself, you have seen it, you have seen the historical process which is remaking not just Egypt but the whole Arab world in one way or another, possibly for the better. It could not surely be for the worse. But could I, in my unwritten book, give that scene the importance it deserved? Probably not. After all there had been that other Arab in the foyer of the Sheraton. He was just in from the desert, you could see that clearly enough, but the modern desert with its land-rovers, roads, airfields and imported water. He had come in to shop and now was carrying back his purchases. Some of them were in the suitcase he carried. The suitcase was of shiny gold.

There was another barrage at Nag Hammadi. It was identical to the one at Asyut, one hundred sluices with a lock-gate on the western side. We approached it at speed as Shasli wished to get in before the lock-gate shut for the night; and as we entered the lock there came a thunderous knocking sound from under our stern. We stayed in the lock for hours, it seemed, but no one bothered to go below and examine the stern gland. When we came out of the lock it was to the same thunderous accompaniment from our wretched screw. I felt a mixture of fury at the sheer incompetence of this ship-handling, which would inevitably mean a shorter trip altogether, and a gloomy satisfaction at seeing my prognostications fulfilled. We had a malaise, it sounded to me, somewhere between the screw and the engine and the possibilities were multiple. Knocking and rattling as we were, Shasli manoeuvred us to a berth. The crew set to work excavating round the engine and Alaa came presently with the news that, 'The bearings have gone'. That settled it, I thought. We should simply have to hire a car – but not a bit of it. Shasli wanted to press on regardless, knocking and all. The whole crew were now within reach of their homes and were not going to be thwarted by anything as trivial as an engine dancing in its bed. This was the nearest my minder and I ever came to an outright quarrel. I pointed out that this breakdown was not like the others. To carry on might well finish the boat off completely. To this, the answer that filtered through to me from Shasli was as before: why should I worry? It wasn't my boat. After a row, we reached a compromise. Alaa would ring the owner in

Cairo and suggest that a new set of white metal bearings should be flown or trained up the Nile to Nag Hammadi. So Alaa went off to find a phone and Ann and I sat speechless.

Alaa came back. The owner had said, *Push on and see if it gets any worse.* So that was that. There was nothing for it but bed, where at least we were both beginning to sleep warmer. In the morning the pre-dawn chorus seemed more prolonged than usual, aimed, I thought, at the very large Christian church alongside which we were moored. The *Reis*, eager now for his home at Qena, was up before anyone else and got away in the semi-dark as he might well have done on other days if his sails had not been woven of Egyptian patience. Now, apparently, that patience was threadbare. The propeller shaft bounced and banged deafeningly under our cabin. I stared out of our stern window and could see nothing but the usual black smoke. We were doing our best speed, something like ten knots, and it was a toss-up whether the propeller shaft or the engine would smash first. I thought moodily of the ship which broke her propeller shaft in mid-Atlantic, stabbed herself with the broken end and foundered slowly. At least we weren't at sea for all their silly names for the Nile! The propeller shaft would chatter for a while like teeth as if it were cold rather than hot. Then, as if trying to jump about to get warm, it would imitate one of Liszt's *Hungarian Rhapsodies*, the final *prestissimo*. I got up. Ann was endeavouring or pretending to sleep through it all and thus be somewhere else – home, perhaps – but I don't think she was really succeeding. Then, just when I was thinking that the only thing left to do was to abandon ship, the *Reis* knocked a knot or two off our speed, the *prestissimo* became a gallop and the black smoke astern became a cloud of white steam. I say the *Reis* knocked off our speed but this may have been done by the engine itself in a desperate attempt at self-preservation. Then it, or the *Reis*, slowed down still more. He was trying to find the speed which would do the least damage and so enable the boat to get him home. He achieved a node among our vibrations in which the engine did not clatter or chatter its teeth but kept them too tightly clenched as if in permanent anguish. It was better for us, I suppose, but you could still feel the boat suffer.

I turned away from our boat with much determination. There was, as far as I could see, nothing to be done. At Qena or Luxor if we were still afloat, I thought, there might be a boatyard capable of doing something. Meanwhile, the only way to make use of our progress was to ignore as much as possible this horrid vibration through the soles of the feet and continue to watch the river and the countryside. There was, for example, that fisherman. He had his blessedly vibrationless rowing boat holed up among tall, flowering reeds. As we passed he hauled up his fishtrap, which was like an openwork dustbin of thin wire, and lo, he emptied a small fish out of it. Then we came to fishermen and boys, two by two, one of each in successive rowing boats and they all had long, thin rods out over the water; and like rodmen everywhere, not catching anything. I thought then and still think that I've never seen anyone with a rod catch a fish. The rodman is *stasis*, permanent gesture, meditation. Take the hook off the line and you would suppose yourself passing a series of Buddhas. In this stretch of water, oddly, there was no net fishing at all. There must be a reason for the change but it was not in my competence to discover one. Rushdie appeared with breakfast. It was bread, cheese, slices of cold sausage all washed down with mineral water. Before we had finished, he brought us cups of tea, the surfaces covered with a close interference pattern.

We wrapped up and went on deck. There was sun and wind sparkle. We were, I thought, turning to the *qibli* – *gibli* in the local dialect. In other words, we were turning to the south which was really the east. *Bahari*, or north, was increasingly to the west of us, for we were beginning to enter the huge turn, the kink the Nile makes which is such a plain feature on the map. I ought to add that this was the morning on which our loo came clean and we were able to pump river water through it. All the vibration of our careless speed – beggars on horseback – had achieved what neither we nor the crew had been able to manage. Every cloud has a silver lining and so on. So we sat on deck, and turned more and more to the *qibli* with the morning sun straight ahead of us. The wind breathed wooingly for a change so that at length both of us unwrapped cautiously. There was no doubt about it. The weather was changing with the bend. Had we reached the point where the warm south really began? There was much life about on the nearer, eastern, I mean northern bank. It was often intimate. At that time of the year, Egyptians wear a vest and long johns under the galabia. The long johns have no fly. An Egyptian about his early morning business pushes the long johns to his knees as he squats and lets the galabia spread round him. Away it all goes and as he is in a tent he is happy enough performing in broad daylight and within a few yards of other people. Sometimes a second galabia is worn under the top one. Ann said that our *Reis*, sophisticated man that he is, and living as he does on tourist boats, had his galabia made of modern material with rayon in it. She added that the shoulders and sleeves were of a modern cut. Women's costume was changing in these parts. They sometimes wore trousers tight to the ankle but under a calf-length skirt. The colours were ever more garish, the faces ever darker. Here, too, there were scarecrows, not metaphorical but real; and either I only just noticed the custom or they were the first to be used between Alexandria and Qena. It seems odd; for an agricultural country must surely be up to every dodge in the battle of the fields. Perhaps the population lower down the river and in the Delta is so dense the birds don't get a chance. The whole area of the Big Bend seemed prosperous with here and there a quite large villa. Some villas actually had steps going down to the water and a moored boat.

Now, for the first time since leaving Cairo – from the terrace of the yacht club at Ma'adi you could just see the very tip of the Great Pyramid and so know that the desert was there – now we had a hint that there had been a western desert tucked away beyond the cultivation of the western bank. For now, to the south (which was west) the huge browny-yellow Theban hills billowed into sight above the horizon. Presently the great bridge of Qena stretched across the water before us.

Akhmet the engineer came rushing up on deck. He was, I thought, about to announce some catastrophe. But he reached into the wheelhouse and sounded our siren. I did not grasp the significance of this and wondered what signal it was. Perhaps those who ride the sea of the Nile have the equivalent of 'get out of my way because I can't get out of yours'? But why the engineer?

Alaa explained in due course. Akhmet had been passing 'his' village and was letting them know he would be home soon. Then, with the suburbs of Qena stretching along the bank on our left Shasli did the same thing only more prolonged, a blast. The two others, Saïd and Faroz, were up on the fo'c'sle staring ahead at the Theban Hills which sheltered Faroz' village and suggested the long way up to Saïd's. Saïd came back to the centre cabin. Before he went below I asked him if he was feeling better. Oh yes, he said, he was nearer home. Shasli slowed then manoeuvred us against some broad steps above which there were trees with fairy lights and loudspeakers and people looking down curiously at our little boat; for this was a place where four-decker tourist boats were accustomed to tie up. It was a park and religious music was being broadcast from all the loud-speakers in the trees. Shasli was ashore, up the steps and out of sight before I could ask him anything.

The engine, which had been idling, now stopped. Faroz and Akhmet appeared in bathing trunks. Before my startled eyes they waded from the steps into the soup, then swam round our stern. I looked to see them collapse, die at once, or bloat or shrivel, or scream then sink, bubbling. But nothing happened. Faroz seized the propeller and shook it. You could hear the shaft knocking about in the stern gland. I went below. Saïd had a floorboard up and there was water in the bilges. I asked Alaa where the best boatyard was and how soon we could get new white metal bearings or at least have the defects assessed by an expert.

He laughed. 'You are planning again.'

We had not been moored more than a few minutes when a procession came down the steps. It consisted of the Director of Cultural Affairs, the Director of the Palace of Culture, a police inspector, a policeman, one actress and one theatre director. The police did their paper duties, whatever those were, and went away. We were invited ashore. Presently the cultural directors said their welcomes and farewells and went away. The actress and the theatre director remained. They proved, conveniently, to be friends of Alaa.

I knew what I wanted to do. One's image of Egypt is of a long thin valley stretching south from the Delta, and wholly isolated from the outside world. It was a matter that could be vivified by consideration of two pictures. On the one hand, you have consumptive Victorian ladies going into a decline, carefully carried up the Nile to Luxor, where the poor souls hoped, in that milder climate, to be cured of a disease we now know to be a bacillus. The other seems a different planet. It is the picture of other ladies going out to India, their ship touching at Egypt, sliding through the Suez canal and then making the long passage down the Red Sea. It had seemed necessary to me to understand the physical barrier between these worlds, the awful stretch of desert that lay between the River Nile and the Red Sea, the two different worlds separated by the desert, the tawny creature that had looked in on our river, slunk off again and sidled back, always barren and terrible.

There were tracks through the desert for I had traced them on the map. In terms of miles, less than a hundred separated Qena from the Red Sea. Well then. To join as an experience the fresh water of the river, however soupy, to the hot, salt water of the Red Sea would be, I thought, a startling association of places, as unlike any other hundred miles as it could well be. It would be space travel. It would shortcircuit distance. Now I inquired if it would be possible to undertake that journey, east through the desert from Qena. Alaa's friends nodded. Yes, it would be possible, if that was what we wanted to do. I elaborated, daringly. I had seen on the map that there was a track along the shore of the Red Sea and a second track which came back through the desert to join the road along the Nile, perhaps

91

twenty miles above Qena. Would it be possible to do the round trip? Yes. It would be possible. By car? Most certainly. Well, then.

So it was arranged. We would set out at crack of dawn in the morning.

We returned to the boat. Rushdie, I learned, was in his bunk, sick. Saïd, having taken up the floorboards, was sick too. Ann admitted that she was feeling off colour. I was surviving. Alaa was surviving. So were Faroz and Akhmet, both of whom had immersed themselves cheerfully in the Nile water. I sat on deck in the sun. Alaa was below, tending our two sick men. Ann sat with me, wondering how long it would be before she had to take to her bunk.

We were treated to a splendid sight. Akhmet appeared on deck, said his goodbyes and strolled away up the steps. He carried a small suitcase. He was dressed as usual in western style but this was such a sharp suit he was wearing! It was a wonder he didn't cut himself on it or at least nick any passerby so rash as to brush against him. It was an exact repeat of that village scene we had watched a little further downstream – the return of the native in all his sophisticated splendour to dazzle the stay-at-homes. In my mind's eye I could see the procession and the little boys who would compete to carry his suitcase the last quarter of a mile from the bus to the mud hut on the crumbling bank.

Akhmet was hardly out of sight when he was *obliterated* from consideration by the appearance of Faroz, now no longer in a tracksuit and playing the part of Aladdin but positively *en prince*. He wore a light blue galabia as a foundation. Over this was a darker blue outer garment open down the front. He had topped everything off with a turban of positively brilliant blue. He displayed himself before us with the unconscious self-satisfaction of a peacock then wafted up the steps and disappeared. He had no home locally so we could only suppose that he planned to make some section of Qena's population happy.

I think Ann saw it first, or perhaps we saw it together, a wonderful black-and-white bird working the waters along by the bank; and now, in our and its time of tranquillity, it was willing to work the waters even before the steps of the park and the kiosk. There was no doubting for an instant the nature of this bird. It was a Nile Kingfisher. The black-and-white markings were so distinct and methodically distributed that the bird seemed to be chequered. As far as body, wing and head were concerned it was all kingfisher, undoubted in shape, quite, quite unmistakeable, even to the straight, powerful beak. What was different was the tail, long as the body, spreading in a fan for flight and again, black and white. We sat perfectly motionless and it hunted the river past us. Its method was to fly along about five yards from the bank in a series of loops, swooping down to the water and up again. At the point where these loops joined, points as it were, of suspension of the chain of flight, the bird would hover, peering down. Here it would perform its characteristic manoeuvre, impossible to our native kingfisher with its stubby tail, and still hovering, with flirts of its spread fan of tail feathers it would spin on its axis, still peering down and round on every side. Then it would swoop away again in another loop, or perhaps drop on a convenient branch, or, as often, drop on its prey. When the Nile Kingfisher drops he hits the water with a heavy, almost clumsy action and a sound like the fall of a small axe. There he was then, in that brilliant sunlight, looping along the side of our craft and the steps and the bank, hovering, spinning, diving, sparkling it seemed, in his clean black and white. For the time we were able to watch him he was worth our journey.

Alaa appeared and reported on his patients. Rushdie was not so good but Saïd was determined to avoid hospital and reach his family in Aswan in one way or another. I said that with the engine in the state it was we could not possibly get the boat beyond Luxor. In that case, said Alaa, Saïd could leave us for the time being, take a communal taxi and go home.

We found *Reis* Shasli who insisted on buying us tea. *Reis* Shasli was a rich man. He had a house not a hundred yards from where we were sitting. His wife lived there. Well, one of his wives. He had two. Generally, one wife lived there in Qena and one down in Cairo. He had two children by one wife and three by the other. They were both Qena girls and had shared a house for some years without difficulties. Of course, he himself was away from home a lot of the time. When he had been on the Alexandria to Cairo run, and then the Cairo to Aswan run, having one wife in Cairo and one in Qena had been very convenient. We agreed it must have been. While Alaa translated all this, the *Reis* kept bowing round the circle as if he were conferring favours.

We had an awful night; the dawn found us still sleepless and I felt in no state to face the perils of the desert, but the attempt had to be made. Ann sensibly decided not to come. The rest of our party

turned up at half past six; and this was an example of such un
Egyptian punctuality that it gave my thoughts an even graver turn
towards the seriousness of our expedition. Yet the party wor
ordinary clothes. The car was small and flimsy and I could not see i
dealing well with rocks and sand. Nor was it large enough to contain
us all. 'All' consisted of the theatre director Bassem, the actress Azza
Alaa, myself and Saïd, at least for a mile or two. We took him to the
'taxi station', wished him a pleasant journey and turned to our own
more dangerous one. We picked our way through Qena which is a big
city of extraordinary ugliness. A side road took us out into the plain
It was bare as the plain of Akhetaten. Bassem's car was making heavy
weather of its load and I wondered what would happen in more
difficult country if the car gave up. There was a railway track by the
road, but after a while there were no rails on it, only stones. The hills
drew in to the road on either side, low and certainly not very
impressive. Now and then huge trucks rumbled past, coming or
going. At least their vast tyres fitted them for the desert. We came to
and passed a petrol station. A very small tree, carefully watered,
grew by it. The track for the railway vanished.

This was ridiculous. The road was very nearly flat with only the
merest suggestion of ascent about it. It wound and bent and wriggled
but not excessively. We passed two shacks and some machinery
which might have been an oil rig. Near the shacks was a patch of
carefully watered vegetables but with no apparent source for the
water. I was able to consult the map easily, for our ride so far was
smoother than the ride in the boat. The temperature was comfortable. In the map I could make out 'Bir–' something or other. 'Bir'
means a well.

We wound on between rounded hills which did not seem to get any
more impressive. We were in Bad Lands and the hills were set in
plains of dried mud of absolute flatness. How else, after all, can mud
dry out when the water is gone? What was evident was the
mechanism of Egypt's occasional catastrophes.

We passed through an area of sand then moved a little more steeply
up into the hills. At last the road was *doing* something. We were
approaching a very mild example of a pass; and here at the pass was
the only striking 'geological event' of the journey. The strata were
upended suddenly, weathered by wind rather than rain into
fantastication like the 'Manueline' architecture you get in Portugal,
at Batalha, for example. We wound down through this fantastication

94

and behold, the Red Sea appeared, quietly, uninterestingly, uneventfully, a flat stretch of the usual stuff and not very colourful either. Looking at it ruefully as we approached I could not discount the possibility that some innocent imagination of my childhood had prepared my unconscious for a sea which was actually red. The road flattened again and we drove sedately to an open gate across the road where traffic police stopped us and inspected Alaa's papers, which were in order. So we drove into Port Safaga on the Red Sea.

It has to be said that Port Safaga is a dreary dump. It is mostly a camp for sailors and surrounded by high barbed wire. It is in fact a barracks. Much had now been made plain to me. There had been a track through the Eastern Desert; but now that track was a first-class military road. By its means Egypt could shift men and supplies to Port Safaga and so station part of her navy in the Red Sea just across from the entries to the Gulf of Suez and the Gulf of Aqaba. But in 1984 most of the harbour installations seemed to be derelict, or so badly maintained as to be useless. Yet the port was ringed with pits for anti-aircraft guns, which were in position and manned, their muzzles pointing eastwards. When Israel and Egypt made peace, work had stopped, leaving the military road for anyone who was curious enough to use it. Only the guns were still manned just in case. Also, and this is another great truth about armed forces in peace time – you have to find something for them to do. So there they were, sitting round their guns, or drilling with indifferent success behind the high barbed wire.

We did an obligatory wander along a shelly beach picking up the odd pebble then drove on again. There was some slight interest after all in these weary miles, these quantities of desolation, this emptiness. It was like space travel in that there was a point not to be grasped. One was doing something and nothing.

Back in the car we turned inland again to make our way by a different track back to the Nile Valley. We came to a gold mine, unmarked on the map, and modern. It had been closed down by Nasser like so many other things. He closed it down because it was foreign owned. The watchman at this place told us the old Roman mine was further on, by the next well. So on we went and the village of Bir Umm Fawakhir, a single house on the side of the road and a shelter for a policeman on the other, sat more or less in the middle of yet another mud plain. A hundred or so yards away was a stone structure something like an air raid shelter and I thought this was a building put up by the Department of Antiquities to house the ancient Roman well. Sure enough, it sheltered the well but the Romans had put it there and left, it seemed, earlier in the day for there was nothing at all to indicate the age of the building. We bough preparatory orange juices at the house which acted occasionally as a café then walked over to the well. The well of Umm Fawakhir is a most impressive structure in a downward sense. The bore is about five yards wide and more than three hundred feet deep. This central shaft is surrounded and strengthened by masonry and at one side there is another shaft, impeccably cut in rock with a winding stair from top to bottom. Every fifty or so feet down a large opening between the shafts gives light to the feet of the intrepid and increasingly weary traveller; for to go down is almost as wearisome as to come up, which I did myself after getting no more than halfway down. I do not claim to be a connoisseur of wells but certainly this was an unusual structure and splendidly built. Alaa, who went all the way down assured me there was still water at the bottom. He also said glumly enough that today in Egypt nobody could build anything as good as that. In fact, of course, the Egyptians didn't build it, the Romans did. I saw, too, the reason for the massive wall the Romans had built at the top. A flash flood would fill the well with mud if that wall wasn't there. We went back to the café since a well is a well is a well however splendidly built and had some tea brewed, I should think, from Roman water so to speak.

I still had to see my ancient gold mine and the slave huts. The son of the house was a small, good-looking but dirty boy. Evidently water was for drinking. He wore an immense turban and one side of his face was badly bruised. He had run into some rocks while chasing an antelope on his bicycle or so he said. However, he would show us the gold mine and the huts. We drove off down the road. The boy declared we must go further on then further. I doubted the wisdom of this but the boy was now in control. After a mile or two he bade us stop. Instead of gold mines and huts I found we were now to inspect graffiti, which were not what I had set out to see. However, there's no denying they were interesting enough. Some were 'Pharoni' – hieroglyphic records of the regiments which had been stationed there in the reign of such and such a pharaoh, all as untouched as the well and done earlier that day, in the cool of the morning, perhaps. They seemed to me – and this, of course, is a matter for Egyptologists – to be less literate than the many we had seen years ago at Aswan on the

ABOVE: The *Hani.*

PREVIOUS PAGE: Two huge sandals came up the river before a following wind. 'I thought to myself that these graceful sandals with their simple, elegant lines and single, huge sail were going to be one of the consolations of the trip.'

BELOW: El Maragha. 'The stone-and-concrete apron fronting the cornich was so old it was cracked everywhere. There was a low wall and a proportion of the population lined this to watch the show.'

ABOVE: The Fayoum. 'You approach first a grey-green line which broadens, unfolds, becomes a brighter green and then you are quite suddenly in a land that seems even more fertile than the Nile Valley.'

BELOW: Bahr Yusuf. 'I had promised myself such a thrill at seeing it; but now I had been looking at it for twenty kilometres and made it so ordinary to myself that my promised *frisson* was entirely lacking.'

ABOVE: *Calèches* at Luxor. 'The vehicles shine now with intricate brass [...]
a-glitter in the lights of the corniche. Some are real museum pieces,
elegant even in their showiness.'

BELOW: 'The Temple at Luxor had not improved, I thought. There was st[...]
about the building that ineffable air of having outstayed any welcome
the town was prepared to give it and of only waiting for the arrival of
the removal men.'

ABOVE: The Sphinx. On his return to England William Golding wrote his promised letter to *The Times* about the Sphinx's beard and coincidentally it was returned.

BELOW: The Temple of Kom Ombo. 'As for the Temple, I don't say it isn't a good temple as temples go. Oh yes, it has a good position some fifty feet above the river and twenty yards from it.'

LEFT: Stela from Amarna showing Akhenaten. 'First regarded as a towering monotheist, a mystic, a religious genius, Akhenaten was now argued to be a dictator with a purely material idea of his god, the Aten, the physical disc of the sun.'

BELOW: 'Cultivation still clung to the east bank under the cliffs, but only just.'

ABOVE: The Blessed One with his
wife. 'The tomb paintings make a
glamour point of the eye more
than anything else.'

RIGHT: Queen Nefertiti.

LEFT: 'Rushdie spent most of the afternoon with Alaa's head in his lap, reading aloud in Arabic what Alaa called "A tale by some Lebanese idiot".'

BELOW: Saïd, Ann, the author, Rushdie, Akhmet with Shasli in the wheelhouse. Ann is doing her best to bear up while the author is determinedly cheerful.

BOTTOM: Burning limestone.

ABOVE: 'The cliff of limestone reached up about six feet above the gunwale of the tram. The steering position – but this is customary and a definition of "tram" – was right up in the bow.'

BELOW: 'The tram to which we were hitched was loaded with the soft limestone of the mountains over to the east. I knew it was soft because I broke a piece off the cargo and crumbled it easily between two fingers and a thumb.'

ABOVE: Selling fish from a boat.

OPPOSITE: A boy climbing the mast of a felucca.

RIGHT: 'The *calèche* drivers had brought their wretched horses down to the water to clean them. It was impossible not to wonder whether the horses were acquiring new diseases or merely exchanging old ones.'

BELOW: River police station. 'The place was on the slope of the levee with two shacks, some ramshackle boats and a dozen young men who were dressed in seamen's uniforms which were ragged and dirty.'

TOP: 'Here in this potters' field, all the houses were houses of pots because they were built of them. They were not built of sherds. They were built of whole, or nearly whole pots.'

ABOVE: 'In all those superimposed rows of pots that went to make the walls of houses there would not be one without some ventage of air from within. Here, suggested Ann, was the original cavity wall.'

OPPOSITE: 'In one of the huts a potter obligingly performed his dextrous bit of magic which never fails to satisfy the beholder and perhaps the practitioner too; how the seed of clay grows, buds, flowers, fruits and collapses.'

ABOVE: The Great Pyramid. 'Certainly the greatest of them all, the pyramid of Cheops is anonymous in the sense that there is no inscription giving it to him.'

BELOW: The pyramid of Meidum.

RIGHT: Hypostyle hall at Karnak.

BELOW: Hatshepsut's Temple. 'It is one of the few "Pharoni" buildings which acknowledges the presence of the landscape and fits humbly into a gigantic cliff which it can imitate but not out-do.'

LEFT: A sandal on the Nile with a 'balancer' out to starboard.

BELOW: 'All the way up the Nile I had seen women coming down to the river. They had not just fetched water, they had done the washing they had scoured dishes, in fact I could not begin to number the things I had seen the women doing.'

rocks of the island of Sehel. Some were graffiti in Greek and Latin, records of tourist names mostly. Here and there among the others and sometimes over them, were modern scratchings, and it wasn't much good talking about vandalism with three thousand years of it staring us in the face and an infinity of rock all round. When is a door not a door? When it's a-jar, said the child's riddle. When does vandalism turn into archeology? Later in the same day as far as I could see. But tourists! Had they felt the same silly urge to make a connection between the Nile Valley and the Red Sea, even remoter in their time – well, earlier in the day – than in ours?

The boy wanted to show us more graffiti further on but we stuck and said it was the gold mine and the slave huts or nothing. So the small villain had us turn round and drive right back to Umm Fawakhir's Roman well, where he got out and pointed. The huts I had wanted to see were no more than two hundred yards away. I walked over to them, but the boy now wanted us to see the House of the Count or the White House. This was built and inhabited once upon a time by the owner of the modern gold mine, but the owner had 'gone away'. We refused to visi. it so the boy turned away saying that the huts and the mine I had wanted to see were a mile up the valley but there was no point in looking at them. They were just the same as the ones we could see in front of us. He then withdrew with such money as we gave him, much of it in sheer amused exasperation and be it said admiration. He had used authority very expertly and should go far if he doesn't break his neck chasing antelope or get himself murdered by a tourist. The most memorable bit of that desert crossing was after all the magnificently built well of Umm Fawakhir. A day in the desert, even on a highroad, makes you understand what a well is.

So we drove another forty miles by way of the well of the Hammamat and the well of El Laqeita, I trying to get the Arabic 'q' as far down in my neck as I could and only succeeding in making myself feel I had a sore throat. The Kaffir click or the implosive 'p' are nothing compared to that 'q'. But then we emerged from the desert into green and gold, ripe sugar cane and palms, crops inset with shining water. Now, coming from the brown world of the desert with its tumble and jumble, its dried mud and casual drifts of sand the extraordinary neatness of crops in Egypt was startlingly evident by contrast. In Egypt a man puts by habit all that neatness into his crops (no matter how small the patch) which an Englishman or a

Dutchman puts into his front garden. It was fifteen or so miles back along the river to Qena and we reached the city by 3 o'clock in the afternoon. This early arrival will show more readily than anything else how easy is the trip through to the Red Sea. Still, if you are a European who regards green fields as the normal way things are, the trip is worth it for the experience of dryness and the discovery of the significance of a well.

That wonderful well of Bir Umm Fawakhir! It was an investment, of course. Now it served one family and one policeman. But then, when the investment was made it had served the gold mine. Calculations must have been made which do not resound loudly in classical literature. So many slaves, they must have muttered, consuming such and such a quantity of water. But there are flash floods. So it must be a safe and secure source of water in all conditions no matter how deep we have to dig for it and no matter how elaborately we have to cut masonry and fashion a waterproof wall at the top. No water, no gold. Bir Umm Fawakhir was the equivalent of an oil rig. It was not even like those relics of imperial rule, irrigation, dams, railways, roads, which confer some benefit on later generations when the taskmasters have gone and when law and rule, the greatest benefit of all, have collapsed into riotous chaos. When the gold mine was worked out the reason for the well disappeared with the slaves, who were worked out with it. The worst of all fates for a male slave was to be made a mineworker. In the passion for ore, all human feeling was consumed and the slaves were worked to a death which must have been a release from desperate hardship and constant danger. So the ancient well remains there, in working order, perfect, a more vivid and harsh reminder of greed and indifference than any statue of Ozymandias.

When we got back to the river front we found that Shasli had shifted the boat. Apparently a large tourist boat had passed at speed, made considerable wash and we had bumped the steps. *Hani* did not need any more tribulations and Shasli had wisely shifted her round the corner fifty yards away from her first berth and tucked her up more or less out of the reach of wash. The kingfisher was still busy, looping and flirting and diving round her. Ann was sitting on the upper deck in the sun and restored to herself. Rushdie however was still on the sick list.

The car had stood up well to the journey and everyone was in favour of another trip for the next day when Ann would be fit to come. Yet though the car had stood up well, it was frailer, if not older, than we. A gentler and not as lengthy drive seemed indicated. We asked if we might now see something of the life of the local fellaheen.

9

Bassem and Azza called for us at a quarter to seven next morning. Ann, Alaa and I embarked in the little car and we drove off through Qena. It was to be, I found, a day of pots. This is not quite fellaheen; and I never succeeded in persuading the Egyptians I met that I really *did* want to meet men with half an acre and no cow. Perhaps they knew better than I how impossible communication would be, even through an interpreter. Either that or there are none of the examples we had heard so much of, of men, women and children hardly able to live. Did my conductors feel shame at poverty and wish to conceal it from me? Did they feel, as well they might, that it was none of my business since I was in no position to do anything constructive about it? Pots were for craftsmen, not peasants.

We drove first of all to a field of pots. Was it not in a potter's field that Judas hanged himself? In my small experience he would have found it difficult to find a convenient tree for this field was treeless, grassless and bare as the desert. It was in the outskirts of Qena and visible first by the mountains of sherds that had built up over a period of many years. But as we parked I found the phrase 'The House of Pots' spring into my mind. I don't think it comes from the Bible. Perhaps it's somewhere in *The Arabian Nights*, but wherever it comes from it is notably explicit. Here, in this potter's field, all the houses were houses of pots because they were built of them. They were not built of sherds. They were built of whole, or nearly whole pots. Some were houses for living in. Whether you worked at the wheel or the furnace or more menially pounded clay into a consistency which your betters could fashion as required, you had a house of pots. These were flagons, which would hold, I suppose, four or five gallons. We were introduced to the manager of the pottery and I asked at once how they came to build houses out of pots instead of mud brick or burnt brick, since the field was obviously prosperous. The manager explained that they only used pots which cracked or were holed in the firing. If they used whole, unblemished pots built into the wall the change of temperature between day and night would cause them to explode. That was why, as we would see

100

if we looked closely, that in all those superimposed rows of pots that went to make the walls of houses there would not be one without some ventage of air from within; not through into the house but from within the pot. Here, suggested Ann, was the original cavity wall. It seemed ideal for the purpose, cool in summer, warm in winter, and smoothing out the difference between day and night. With a thatched roof, the pots made as good a house as you would wish unless your ambition was a villa. True, these houses were after all no more than huts; but their unusual construction, their irregularity and necessary individuality, together with their grouping into a village gave them great character if not charm. After all, except in rare and catastrophic floodings when no building could be guaranteed to stand against a torrent of muddy water sweeping down from a wadi, they were good enough in that climate under a sky so seldom clouded. For all these huts were roofed. That is a most important point. They had good, wooden rafters and above the rafters a thick layer of sugar cane reed. Ten years before, seeing houses, or huts rather, without roofs I had supposed it to be because in a rainless area roofs are unnecessary. I envisaged the happy Egyptians or Nubians as we had increasingly to call the people in this area and further south, sleeping in their huts under a starry sky as the Bedouin were supposed to have spent their nights crouched by the camp fire under bright constellations, busying themselves in the invention of astronomy. But no. Anyone, Egyptian, Nubian, Bedouin, will get himself a roof if he can even if no more than a canvas one. Even in the boat we had found how, after a hot day then sunset, a clear sky had let the heat pour away upwards and leave us shivering. Yet we had a wooden deck between us and the icy points of the stars. How much quicker then, how much deadlier must be the flow of body heat from poor devils insufficiently fed at the best of times, lightly clothed, and with not a cloud in the sky to give them cover! Where the Nubian or Egyptian has no roof it is because he cannot afford to get himself one. Wood has always been expensive in Egypt. There are no forested borderlands. It is all either farm cultivation or desert. Yet so poor must be a proportion of the fellaheen they cannot even afford the few pence for a load of river reed or cane to heap across the odd corner of a mud hut. Such poverty is difficult to credit; and it was *that* side of Egypt I planned to reach without, I had better say straightaway, succeeding. Here, the thickly roofed houses of pots were a sign of great prosperity. The

Egyptians have always been justly famed for their mastery of stone; but their natural, their inevitable homely craft is with clay or mud.

In one of the huts a potter obligingly performed his dextrous bit of magic which never fails to satisfy the beholder and perhaps the practitioner too. How the seed of clay grows, buds, flowers, fruits and collapses; it seems to perform of itself, the potter's hands merely serving to support and show it off as a mother will show off her baby. We tore ourselves away or were torn away and visited the huge kiln which was also constructed of pots, at least on the outside. We saw the ancient hill constructed of pot fragments, so that remembering 'Cocking-Troop' and 'Ceramicus' I asked if it had a special name but as usual, Arabic was not all that forthcoming. It was called in Arabic 'The Heap'. I had been told that Arabic has so many alternative words for things – sixty, I seem to remember for a sword – that the learner is instantly lost among them, which is one reason why I had never even begun to learn the language; my experience in Egypt led me to think that the words are so common as to start life threadbare. We also saw the well. There was no stone about this one and no steps down. But it gave us our first glimpse close-up of that other indigenous Egyptian ability, the working of wood when they can get it. For the windlass had no metal at all, neither bearings nor handle. The bearings were wood but could stand an enormous weight. The drum round which the palm-leaf rope was wound was a cage of battens stuck into or through each other. It looked flimsy, crazy and as if it would come apart at any moment; but it was at once ancient and efficient. This mixture of the haphazard and efficient, the apparently ramshackle, is typical of Egyptian peasant craft. It does not occur to them that a pleasantly symmetrical piece of primitive machinery would be more agreeable to work with. Let the thing do its job; and there was no doubt that its job was precisely what this thing could do. For as we watched, a man turned the cage and wound the rope up. There appeared on the end of it not a bucket but a basket with about half a ton of clay in it which had needed to be kept wet and cool through the night. So we said our thanks and left them at it, having taken photographs this time with a film that actually was advancing.

We drove then, first through more suburbs of Qena and then by a complex of smaller roads to the village of Garagus. It was like every Egyptian village I had seen and was to see; not so much dirty as untidy, for who minds a bit of dried cowdung and dried straw about the place? The hot sun of the near-tropics had disinfected every-thing, or so it seemed. The houses were quite clearly built and intended to stay up until they fell down, which some of them had done here and there all in one piece but more often bit by bit, a wall cracked open, a gap, a scree of white rubble which seemed the hallmark of village life outside a house or indeed, inside it. Mark you, this is not dirt. It is clean rubble and the inhabitants seem to take the rubble for granted and it never occurs to anyone that rubble can be shifted. There were as usual crowds of children, all cheerful and interested in the strangers, crowds of grown-ups and, as it seemed to me, even bigger crowds of assorted animals. It seems that Egypt is fertile at every level. A village would be a town anywhere else and not just the capital but every city in every province is bursting at the seams with a population the average age of which seems far younger than our own. Either I had too little diagnostic ability which is very likely or the signs of the celebrated Egyptian diseases were nowhere in sight.

As I said, it proved to be our day for pots. We were met by a potter who seemed no different from any other villager. He wore a galabia and close turban. He was a Coptic Christian. He took us down an alley to his workshop. As we passed down it a fly took off from the wall on our right, circled my head then settled back on the wall again. I say this because it reminded me of what had been missing in our experience. The famous, the notorious flies of Egypt had been absent. Now it was towards the end of February but we were, on the other hand, not so far from the tropics. I realized with confusion that we had seen no flies and precious few other insects, including the infamous domestic ones. The air had been clear of the swarms which had been alleged to haunt the head or other part of every living creature. I could only guess that this was the result of use and over use of DDT and other inventions; so that if there are few flies and fleas it is the obverse of the coin that has the decline of the Farmer's Friend on the other side of it. I saw the same thing happen in Greece twenty-five years ago. What a balance to have to keep! Meantime the rare fly had settled back on the crumbling, limewashed wall and we had entered the potter's workshop. He had many objects on his shelves. The floor was concrete, not rammed earth, and the shelves were of valuable wood. More than this on one side of the alley which I now perceived to be a dead end and the potter's personal property rather than a passage, he had an electric furnace. The whole place was his and his galabia and turban were marked with dried clay to prove that he worked there. He had a few words of English but more of French. Chairs were produced and tea. Explanations began but were confused. He talked about the fathers. The village was more Coptic than Muslim. He showed us his stock. The crowded groups of pottery on the shelves contained Christian saints and crosses; not the western or eastern cross but the ancient Egyptian one, 'Pharoni', the symbol of life, the ankh, the cross with the loop at the top. There were many pots and jars and figurines, some made with great deftness. Apart from the ankh there was nothing particularly Egyptian about the technique or the matter. All the objects were in raw, red clay and waiting to be dipped in a slip and refired. The translated or partly translated conversation confused me. At first I could not understand the frequent references to 'the fathers' and 'the strangers' but soon certain things became clearer. There had been a settlement in the village of Jesuit missionaries. Thirty years ago some 'French strangers' had arrived and stayed. They were potters and, at the Jesuits' behest, it seemed, they started to teach the locals their skill. So this then was not indigenous. Hence the un-Egyptian styles to say nothing of the few words of English and French. Saïd, for that was his name, explained that the 'strangers' had 'gone away'. They had sold all the equipment of the school to the locals. And then? The locals had continued to run the school. Was Saïd part of the school? No, he was not, not any more. He liked to be his own master. He had set up on his own. He had had an apprentice but young people today were very difficult. Meanwhile, would we choose whatever we should care to carry away from his stock?

It was the inevitable present-giving, and very difficult. You do not want to take something of value and in any case are never going to be able to fly the stuff home, let alone carry it around Egypt; but what to do? I took refuge in the dishonesty of praising enthusiastically the smallest and cheapest object in sight. It was an ankh in red clay. Saïd rushed away and came back with a duplicate but one which had been dipped and fired in blue slip. I have it on my desk as I write this and can just decipher the name 'Garagus' on it. 'A present from Garagus', then, or from ancient Egypt, blue colour and all, courtesy of the Jesuit fathers, and the strangers.

Saïd led us away to see some of the other local crafts. He introduced us to a carpenter who took us into his house where his daughter was weaving carpets on a loom. She used very thick material and her carpets were heavy. At least, I thought, we would not be forced to carry a carpet away with us! She explained that some of her patterns were traditional but not all. She had been encouraged to follow her fancy. So some patterns she thought up herself. Others she took from pictures she had seen, ships or planes or cars or actions which looked interesting but incomprehensible in the newspapers she could not read. I asked who had made the loom, and of course it was the carpenter. He hurried us round the dark rooms of his house, all three of them, and showed us the furniture piece by piece. Like God he had made everything. I think he had made the house. Next he led us away to a kind of den or alley which ended in a pit. There was a loom built over and across the pit. A woman sat under it. The loom was built in the same way as the windlass of the well at the house of pots. That is, it was built of adzed rather than sawn timber, joined with mortice and tenon and trenailed. It was functional and since the tolerances were much narrower than those necessary for the windlass, altogether neater and more elegant. This elegance, as if by nature, had transferred itself to the woman. She was middle-aged with a naked, aquiline face and splendid nose jewel of silver. Her hair was covered with a purple veil, her dress was green and red and purple, there were silver bangles on her arms and ankles. She squatted in the pit under the loom and made motions of pass with her dark hands so that the loom performed its magic before her. Huge skeins of dyed silk hung on a beam above her head. The colours looked gaudier, more brilliant if you like, than vegetable dyes to me, but I was not informed enough to be sure. It would only have needed vegetable dyes to complete this exquisite picture of a craft where the wood and the thread and the woman and everything were local. I asked where they bought the loom and got the answer I was expecting. The carpenter had made it. By now all of the village who could had crowded into the alley and were pressing forward to the pit. This was an exchange of interest. We were exotic to them and the weaving in these circumstances was as exotic to us. Everyone was happy. Alaa and I produced our cameras and the difficulty was to prevent people posing. Nobody wanted to look natural but like people who are having their pictures taken and are therefore important. As I backed away from the alley and the pit I was bidden to look in a door. Here squatted a very old woman and she was spinning thread. Once more her machine was an example of the carpenter's work. It was pinned together. Take a heap of kindling,

105

sharpen the ends, bore some holes then stick the lot together and you have a machine for producing balls or long skeins of thread out of a mass of coloured wool. It was again something that had to be seen to be appreciated, believed. Surely all this stuff appears as by nature (or electronics) on the shelves of a shop! Yet no, for here it was, straight off the animal's back and then by way of the old woman's hands and then by way of the magically passing hands of the carpenter's daughter and – hoopla! Here there was a carpet, a magic carpet. I shall never stand on a carpet with the same indifference to it again. I asked the carpenter and the village generally – who had followed in a flood – how long the village had been weaving and where they learned it from and everybody laughed. This whole set-up went straight back to the pharaohs they said, for that is how I translated the cries of 'Pharoni! Pharoni!' and romantic or not I was prepared to pocket my scepticism, confused as I was by the history of the pottery, and believe them.

Now Saïd reclaimed us. He took us to the school where he had learned the craft himself and introduced us to his master, Mustapha. He had four apprentices. He had had more but they had left. The school was dying. 'Dying,' I asked, 'really dying? Coming to an end?' It was all too true. Mustapha spoke good French and was downright about it. The impulse had come from the Jesuit fathers and 'the strangers'. It had been a very strong impulse. He showed us the excellent buildings, the elaborate machinery, the two furnaces and western style potter's wheels. Now there was no more impulse. These were the last apprentices. Soon there would be no one left at all to carry on the work.

I had to accept what I could not understand. Without the foreigners, the Jesuits, the place would die. One sensed a strange malaise as if some injection of will was necessary year after year. I thought of the houses I had seen, left unfinished, the plans all made and elaborated but unrealized, yet treated as if they had been accomplished. What was it? Had I found something or only imagined it? Does the foreigner with however good a will simply force on the mild and indolent fellah twentieth-century culture he does not want and does not need?

The storeroom of the pottery was filled with objects. Yes, sometimes it was sent down to Cairo and sold. What would I like to take away? There were many amusing figures but they were elaborate, too elaborate for me to choose as presents. St George on his horse thrust a spear down into a writhing devil. There was something curious about the devil.

'Mais Monsieur, votre diable est feminin!'

'Eh, Monsieur, pourquoi pas?'

Once more I chose the smallest thing in sight, a tiny pot which was pretty enough. We said our thanks and went away. What would we like to see next? Well, since this was predominantly a Coptic village I would like to see a Coptic church. This was easy. The Coptic church was a house not much bigger than the others and built into them, or they into it. Everything was limewashed and flaking. We went inside, the Muslims of our party waiting courteously outside. The little church was notable mostly for at least a dozen pictures, holy of course, and all of which had been executed locally. A good half of them were of woven material. Unconscious of or indifferent to the fact that the Vatican had pronounced St George a non-person, most of them were of him and his dragon, or devil. Unlike in pottery, the weave of the material was too coarse to reveal the sex of the devil or the saint's victim which is what it/he/she looked like. I had the uneasy feeling that St George was spearing a maiden rather than rescuing her, a Perseus who had got his maiden and his sea-monster mixed. From this I deduced far too much about the status of women in Upper Egypt. Egyptian males are still in that splendidly innocent stage of feeling that if women are given a limited role in society *it is for their own good*.

I asked if there were any more churches about. Of course, said Mustapha, there was the Catholic church with the clinic attached. This was news. Apparently only the religious part of the missionary effort had been dispensed with. We walked to the church outside which children of the attached school were having a break and playing football. A nun from Naples who spoke perfect English took charge of us and showed us the church. To my amazement, in the sanctuary, there against the wall, behind the altar was another example of the Coptic cross, the ankh, and made, I dare swear, by Saïd in his little pottery. It was all pink clay and faint blue slip like the small one I had still in my pocket! I began to question the nun. Yes. This was a Coptic church and a Catholic church. It was officially the Coptic-Catholic church. They were not only in communion but united. They used part of the ancient Coptic language, Ancient Egyptian, in fact, in part of their ritual. I began to understand and admire the worldwide and infinite subtlety of the Catholic Church and its straightforward political sense. It was the meekness of the dove and the wisdom of the serpent. Put at its lowest it was a case of 'If you can't beat'em, join'em'. Oh, I've no doubt it was all wrapped up in a language of the highest spirituality. In effect, it ducked Nasser's too inconclusive blow. The Coptic Church was founded by an apostle and therefore acceptable. There were far too many Coptic Christians in Upper Egypt for Nasser to risk offending them. Therefore, join the Coptic Church! The Coptic-Catholic Church stayed and provided the village of Garagus with a school, a clinic and a church.

We came away and walked for a while in the environs of this 'village' of seven thousand souls. We passed an old man sitting by the roadside and Alaa said that he was one hundred and thirty years old. It must be a very good clinic. The fields round about were beautifully planted and you got the feeling that the difficulty would be to stop things growing rather than bring them on. Even the clover was standing up in great green bushes rather than behaving as plants of a proper creeping habit. As for the palms they seemed to soar away up out of sight so that all we had was a green sky.

I thought now that we had done our day among the fellaheen. Indeed I was beginning to feel that either there was no such thing left as a poor fellah or that they were being concealed from me. We walked back towards the village. We were surrounded by the most bursting fertility imaginable. There were groves and avenues of massive palms over wheat, sugar cane, clover, spinach, onions, beans, kale, cabbage and a dozen others that I could not identify.

Where, oh where was the filthy dirt of place and people which books and some American friends had promised us? Was I, by their standards, just as dirty and so unable to appreciate Egyptian dirt? In the village the two of us agreed we were at ease. Yet we knew of some sociologists who had given up after two days and gone back to their universities rather than put up with the 'squalor and filth' of an Egyptian village! True, things were untidy, but broken down rather than decayed or rotting. A square of about twelve yards on each side contained old women, children, chicken, dogs, a cow, two donkeys and a camel. The road was uneven with heaps of dust and rubble which the bright sun had dried and disinfected. The whole village was like a place that had been lightly bombed and shot up and left to recover by time and sun, the inhabitants being content to accept the

108

result whatever it turned out to be.

I expected us now to return to the car, but no. Saïd, the first of our two potters was to give us a meal. We were, therefore, to be subjected to the ordeal which Mr Fisher of 'Fisher's Island' had refused. We turned into an entry between two houses which I thought was a way through. When I saw that the way was blocked off I began to retreat but Alaa hissed, 'It's his house!' I stayed where I was. The narrow, roofless entry was at once a living room and a kitchen. A long, low table stood on the right-hand side. Women, children and, it seemed, babies, were cooking at it. On the left, the other side of the entry, steps led up to the further roof. Beyond the steps was a low door through which we went into comparative gloom. Here were three beds arranged against two walls and Saïd pushed a table into the angle between two of them. He, and a young relative brought chairs. Opposite the table on the other side of the room was another bed. But this was of solid brick and heaped with all the junk from a pottery. At one end of the bed the junk had cascaded to the floor and spread there, forming the usual scree of rubble, which added to the unevenness of the earth floor and took up perhaps two square yards of it. We sat round the table on chairs and beds and two young men, perhaps of Saïd's family, brought a basin, a ewer and some napkins. One held the basin while the other poured water over our hands in the biblical manner. He and they then brought in food. It was a huge spread. There was a great bowl of chicken, sauces, soup, pasta, sunbaked and oven-baked bread. We ate as well as we could in the unfamiliar way. Saïd brought a single tumbler full of water and set it on the table. Ann and I contrived to avoid it without attracting notice. There was sweet tea, which we drank.

All this sounds attractive, and it was. But the surroundings were not. It was not a case of ordure but of 'ordures' in the French sense, junk and waste, rubble, cracks and stains and asymmetry. It was not shit but the indifference and the untidiness of whole generations. That brick bed was covered with a load of broken pots, dried lumps of unfired clay, rusted implements and a scree of dusty rubble which had not been touched since the Jesuits left. In the village we had seen that nothing was ever repaired if it required the minimum of technology beyond the local skills: naked wires hung loose; sockets pulled out of a wall stayed that way. We said our thanks and walked out into the entry where the women had waited until we had finished our meal in order to eat what we had left. This sounds worse than it was since by the laws of hospitality Saïd had provided us with far more food than we could possibly eat. He had also entertained us with a discourse on hospitality. Perhaps he thought, being foreigners, we needed it.

We washed at a hand-pump in the next alley. These pumps, raising water from a few yards down will make an enormous contribution to the improvement of the country's health. Perhaps they were the reason why we were not in fact seeing as many obviously sick people in the village as travellers used to claim. In Garagus the children were mobile, cheerful, looked healthy, and apparently might live to be a hundred and thirty! The incidence of sickness had seemed to strike more severely among our crew than the villagers we came across ashore. But it was too small a sample for statistics even if I believed in them. A more cogent observation was that during my lifetime there had been a force at work which I have never understood and never heard identified. It is an anti-economic force which has made nonsense of predictions. As a country gets poorer it becomes better off. We are poorer and better off. So are France, Italy, Greece and Egypt, countries on which I have tried, so to speak, to keep my eye. This is a paradox in action. Or perhaps the explanation is that economics as a theoretical study, passionately engaged in, argued, fought over, deeply examined and massively documented will one day join the list of other studies with a like relevance to the truth: phrenology, palmistry, flat earth geography, and haruspication, the divination of the future by examination of entrails.

We walked back to the car. It was early evening. Children, men and women were sitting on the hard, dry earth of the street. They were all weaving mats and twisting rope from the dried leaves of reed. In some places old bits of machinery lay round them where the machine had, as far as one could see, lain down and died. Machinery, it seemed, was at greater risk than people. Perhaps Bassem's car had caught an infection? We walked towards it. We were privileged in the company of local people so the inhabitants observed us courteously, with a mild and perhaps amused curiosity. No one seemed to wish us ill, from the man who was a hundred and thirty years old to the little girl, called so exotically 'Rosalind' after Mrs Jimmy Carter. The *otherness* of the village was in its casual attitude to things, to physical objects, and it was made most striking by that same spirit of indifference to untidiness so complete as to be raised to a fifth

110

element, a gentle chaos. We said goodbye to our potter host and bumped away in the failing car under a sunset that covered the whole sky. When we came back to the boat and entered our cabin we said nothing to each other for some time but sat opposite each other on our two bunks; and then we both confessed that the same thought had struck us as we entered our spartan but crowded cabin; what neatness, what cleanness, what utter luxury we have the good fortune to live in!

From Qena to Luxor is about forty miles. We got away at 6 o'clock in the morning and the air was bright. The Theban Hills rose higher and higher. Shasli was pushing the boat again and the engine was dancing in its bed, the propeller shaft doing a Dervish dance. There was no question of getting used to the noise. Noise and vibration were one and the same thing so that you could not tell if you felt the constant shudder through your ears or your feet. It encouraged us to go on deck. The usual north wind was blowing, but now from astern. Above Qena the river turns back on its course and '*bahari*' really is north. The sun rose higher and almost immediately we were in subtropical weather again. Suddenly we were both of us overwhelmed with a positive lust for Luxor, hot baths, clean sheets, leisure, space, privacy. We went below for all the dancing deck, got down a large suitcase, filled it with laundry, changed into clean clothes and put others in a second suitcase. We planned an orgy of cleanness and prayed that the boat would hold together at least long enough to get us made fast alongside in Luxor and a bit of our own kind of civilization. Then we climbed back on deck, not so well wrapped up this time and willed the boat forward. The Theban Hills closed in on the right hand. A large sugar factory appeared on our left. To the right again and moored in an elbow of water were two very large tourist boats. They might reasonably be called ships. They were both burned out. On one, the upper deck had crumpled and collapsed. The other was all in one piece but burned and stained everywhere down to bare metal. It looked like a child's toy that has accidentally fallen in the fire and been raked out next morning with the ashes. I thought them a poor advertisement for the tourist trade and wondered why they had not been towed away – they were both afloat – and put in a shipyard or breaker's yard, but no one could tell me. Alaa said they had been set on fire by electrical faults. He also said there were no casualties.

Luxor was barely recognizable. The corniche was hidden for a mile by craft of all descriptions, but tour boats, of course, predominated, sister ships to the ones burned out and I wondered what their passengers made of the spectacle. The smaller craft were a nondescript multitude; ferries, open motor boats, a private yacht or two, launches of the river police, feluccas of several sizes. There were also the big sandals which would take those people who had the taste for it and the leisure still further up the river to Esna, Edfu and Aswan. But those sandals as I remembered seeing them years before were only the same as the working ones of the lower river in build. Not for them the worn paintwork, the patched and tattered sail and ragged crew. Here the crew would consist of one elegantly galabia'd *Reis* with a small boy for his total crew. The boy would be done up to kill. As like as not he would wear a rose-coloured galabia and a rose-coloured turban to top it off. Clothed thus, he would enchant and appal the tourists by climbing to the very tip of the tall and slender yard by means of wooden footholds conveniently placed. I suppose his function under sail was to serve the indolent tourist with sherbet or beer or wine or anything else he wanted. As for the foreshore itself, today when we had tied up by the police station to a pontoon, we found it had been worked over extensively. Here and there were attempts at ornamental planting; but most of the actual slope of the corniche was now occupied by restaurants and cafés and night clubs. It was a considerable change brought about in ten years. But we did not stop to examine it. Once made fast, we rushed ashore with a perhaps impolite haste and hurled ourselves into the Old Winter Palace Hotel. We told our Minder the crew could do what it liked for a day or two as far as we were concerned and then did our best to forget the boat. We found a room with a view of the Nile and the hills. It had a bathroom where the water did not have to run for more than five minutes before coming hot. We had midday baths.

It was a long bathing time and a long lunch. We emerged at last and wandered for a while. There were new hotels, high-rises that dominated the corniche and the temples. We declined tickets for the *son et lumière*, good though it was said to be, and spent most of the day sitting behind the hotel in the garden which is now very well looked after and pleasant. Here, in the sun, sheltered from the wind and watching bees among the February roses, hollyhocks, pansies and tobacco plants, thyme and sweet peas it was possible to forget the Nile. This was in fact one of the things for which our Victorian predecessors had come.

The other thing they had come for was health, here in the Old Winter Palace and up at Aswan in the Old Cataract Hotel. It was extraordinary. People with 'weak chests' or, more critically, people 'in a consumption' came to Luxor to get well, if they were fortunate and privileged. But if you talk to the European women who live in Luxor today – archeologists or wives of artists and archeologists – you find they constantly suffer from chest complaints, which only clear up when they leave. The first time we were here, Ann went down with a severe cough. All the European women in sight rallied round. Without exception each one had had the same cough and each one had her own remedy ready in a bottle. The idea that anyone ever went to Luxor for his or her health and found it there seemed preposterous to me. In Upper Egypt when the wind blows from the north it is cold. When it blows from anywhere else it is full of dust. I believe that those people who brought a 'weak chest' or a 'consumption' here simply died of it, the poor things, so far from home.

This time, however, we were both in reasonable health. Before dinner, we went for a stroll along the corniche again. The Temple of Luxor had not improved, I thought. There was still about the building that ineffable air of having outstayed any welcome the town was prepared to give it and of only waiting for the arrival of the removal men. The dark brown stone has the same influence as the famous 'dark brown poetry voice' and the whole thing has not even such a doubtful claim to attention as the Temple of Karnak's gigantism. There are three things which have improved in Luxor. One is undoubtedly the *calèches*. At last, the oriental love of decoration and finery has found a proper object. The vehicles shine now with intricate brass all a-glitter in the lights of the corniche. Some are real museum pieces, elegant even in their showiness. The horses seem less decrepit and are furnished with *parures* of brass and perhaps silver. Another improvement is the complete absence of the bakshish boys, who used to make such a bore of themselves on the corniche whenever they saw some obvious tourist. The third improvement is the new Luxor Museum. If you are pressed for time in Luxor, don't bother about the Temple but concentrate on the museum. It is the best Egyptological museum I have ever visited. The objects seem to have been selected as much with an eye to their aesthetic merit as for their archeological importance. They are splendidly placed and expertly lighted. It is worth insisting that for the visitor to Luxor the museum is a 'must'.

Clean, well fed and clothed, we looked in on the boat as we passed it. We found Bassem and Azza together with another Director of Culture had turned up from Qena. Their car, still mobile, was at our

114

disposal for the next day. It was strange to realize what a trivial matter the forty miles between Luxor and Qena was by road rather than river. We arranged forthwith to cross the river and see a couple of things in which I had become interested though they are not on the standard itinerary. I only hoped that the increasingly fragile car would be up to it. However, the main road on the west bank is good. We went back to the hotel to find our room agreeably scented by a bouquet of red roses which probably came from the hotel garden. Then we went to dinner. There was no doubt about it. Tourism in Egypt was a little *down* in the year 1984. There were many empty tables. After that we were both glad to turn in between beautiful cool, clean sheets.

We got up at twenty past seven and checked the laundry in. Breakfast came within minutes of my ordering it. The Old Winter Palace Hotel is much improved and should be preserved among the other archeological treasures of the place. There was fog over the Nile though it was clearing away by 9 o'clock. I couldn't tell what kind of fog it was but felt sure that dust was a component. It looked like smog. Smog at Luxor! It made me feel that perhaps the year 1984 was a significant date in a wholly unexpected way, the year when the world had reached a critical point and that the whole atmosphere of the globe had changed in one night to reveal its pollution – changed suddenly, as the colour of a liquid changes in a titration. However, by the time we were ready to go out the fog had disappeared and I had forgotten my strange fear. For this day was important to me; and the reason stretched back, to refer to and perhaps include consideration of so many things: the red bricks that used up rich soil and the mud brick so readily available; the immemorial angle which did not exist; the crazy Egyptian building; many things. Let it all emerge as the account goes on.

We went to the car and found that there were now only five people to be accommodated in it, Ann and I, Alaa, Bassem and a new person, one Hassan, who had been seconded to us as cultural persons from the Department of Antiquities. I was a little amused at this for I intended to slant away from ancient monuments and was even prepared if necessary to ignore them altogether. We set off and crossed the river by the antique car ferry. I asked to be driven not to the Valley of the Tombs of the Kings but sidelong, to the edge of the Theban Hills near it. There, clinging to the irregular slope, among holes, ledges, crags and fields of broken stone, is the village of

Gourna where the Gournawis live. They are among the most interesting people of Egypt though not necessarily the pleasantest. They are descendants of medieval tomb robbers and have lived there as a group since the thirteenth century. It would pitch the description a little too strong, to describe their trade as a kind of necrophilia. However rumour, a strong rumour which has the backing of many professional Egyptologists, credits the Gournawis with knowing far more about the graves of the West Bank than they are prepared to say. Rumour, a strong one once more, declares that *objets* have appeared and continue to appear on the market which cannot be accounted for except by the existence of tombs which the Gournawis know about, despoil selectively and keep to themselves. Above all, rumour claims that in order to keep the secret of these tombs the Gournawis have built houses on them and live there, with the family fortune tucked away in a kind of ancient cellar. The more I had read about the Gournawis the more interesting they seemed, since it appeared that for an assured income they were prepared to sit it out, generation after generation in conditions of deprivation and squalor. There was something more. They had been the subject of an experiment and as far as I knew the abandoned apparatus of that experiment was still lying on the west bank, near the Singing Stone of Memnon. Now, with Alaa to interpret, I wished to talk with them. Huge moral questions and hypocrisies were involved. I did not expect to learn much, merely talk to a character or two and get a feeling for the place. Even that was a lot to expect but it was worth a try.

So up we drove in that extremely dead piece of land, rock, rubble and dust. Once again, while Ann and I had been luxuriating in the Old Winter Palace, Alaa had contrived to do some spadework and knew which among the houses to approach. There were perhaps half a dozen which by their gaudy advertisements were seen to be those where replicas of famous *objets* were made and sold. Each of these houses, of course, was *rumoured* to produce at an appropriate moment an 'original' offered secretly and illegally for sale. We were ushered into a house and seated in the guest room where a low divan ran right round the wall. We were given tea while someone went to fetch the Head Man of Gourna. He was large and imposing, wore the usual galabia and turban and wished to give us food which Alaa was able to decline on our behalf without it seemed, giving offence. The Head Man asked us out into the main passage of the house and caused chairs to be brought. We were given an exhibition of how to work alabaster by a craftsman. More tea was brought. The Head Man proved to be a Hajj which originally meant someone who had made the trip to Mecca but now was applied to any elderly man of sufficient dignity. Perhaps air travel has cheapened what was once a distinction. The Hajj asked me what I wanted. I told him I had heard many things about the Gournawis and their difficulties. Could I ask the craftsman some questions? The Hajj agreed.

'Where does this alabaster come from?'

'There is a place five days' journey by donkey into the desert.'

'Is that where the pharaohs got their alabaster?'

'I don't know.'

'Is it a difficult journey?'

The man shrugged, spreading his hands.

'Well, could I go there; or rather could this young man Alaa go there if he wanted to?'

'Yes. But only if someone went with him to show him the way. It is not an easy journey. In the season of the *Khamsin* it is dangerous.'

'Do you always use this steel tool?'

'I always use this tool.'

'We are told that the pharaohs had no steel for tools. Do you know how their pots were made?'

'I suppose they used other things. Wood. Stone.'

'Who fetches this alabaster?'

The man giggled.

'I do.'

'Is the mine secret?'

He giggled again.

'No.'

'You like it in Gourna?'

'Of course.'

'There is not a single growing thing for miles, not even an onion! Everything has to be brought from down by the river. Here. . .'

The Hajj interrupted.

'Things would be better for us it if were not for the government. They hedge us round.'

'The government wanted you to move years ago. There was some sort of village built for you back there, down by the river. It is fertile land. Yet none of you would go. Or if some did, presently they came back here where there is nothing and left the new village empty.'

'That was long ago,' said the Hajj. 'Also the houses were inferior.'

117

'How?'

'They were made of mud brick.'

'What is wrong with mud brick?'

'It is for very poor fellaheen.'

'What sort of houses would have persuaded the Gournawis to move?'

'Proper houses,' said the Hajj. 'Houses made of concrete and red brick like in the cities and towns. Not mud brick.'

'I have heard it said that you were unwilling to move because you would no longer be able to carry on this trade.'

'What trade? What trade do you mean?'

'This one, the making of objects in alabaster.'

'We could have carried on our trade anywhere. The tourists would have come to us. But, in fact, the government is moving us now. To proper houses.'

'I had not heard that.'

'They are already building a school for our children.'

'When will it be finished?'

'Who knows? They've been talking about bridging the river for the past fifty years. Come, I will show you the school.'

Ann, I, Hassan, Alaa, Bassem and the Hajj piled into the little car. We set off across the empty plain. It was the top of an *armant*, a geological formation named from another just like it to the north. It was a mile or two square and lifted up – lower than the Theban Hills but still higher than the fertile plain by the river. There was no soil anywhere. Except in the actual path it had been dug into a series of exploratory pits. They were ancient burial pits, I think. The plain itself, the holes and the path were thickly strewn with lumps of rock up to a foot in diameter. It seemed to me that nothing but a tracked vehicle would be any good in such a wilderness which was a less penetrable terrain even than those of Beni Hassan or Tell el Amarna. Bassem drove straight into this appalling mess. The car lurched and bumped, rocks struck the sump and burst like bombs. The exhaust fell off. Bassem and Alaa descended and tied it on with string. The car bumped a little further and the exhaust fell off again. At this, even Bassem admitted defeat. A quarter of a mile ahead of us there was indeed a skeleton building of concrete with a few red bricks showing. It was right in the middle of the wilderness of stone. It was the school with no sign of any building activity near it. It was not finished. It was hardly begun.

'How long has the government been building this school?'

'A year.'

'How will children get there?'

'A school bus!'

'Through all this?'

The Hajj waved expansively at the wilderness.

'All this will be cleared.'

It was a task to be equated with building a pyramid. There seemed nothing more to say.

We bumped back to Gourna, thanked the Hajj and said goodbye to him. He gave us his parting explanation. 'We would be willing to leave here at any time. We know the government wants us to leave. Every year they think up regulations to make life more difficult for us. We are not allowed to build anything new and we cannot alter anything already built. The government forbids us even to dig a hole for a privy. All we can do,' he spread his hands and smiled expansively, 'is to wait for them to build us a new village of red brick and concrete round the new school.'

It all seemed very calm. It seemed what is sometimes called timeless. The Hajj strolled away to his house. The young man Hassan bought buns. I took a long look at Old Gourna, scattered haphazardly as tombs might be scattered against the layered hill. It was evident that some of the 'houses' were hardly even huts. They were more like minimum structures put up to stake a claim. The village was rich by Egyptian standards yet some of the building was more hopelessly ramshackle than anything I had seen in hundreds of miles of travel. It was impossible not to wonder what these dusty shelters hid. It was a strange complex of forces into which I had tried hesitantly enough to force my way. In one direction, where the village was linked by rumour with the whole international world of smuggled antiques or faked antiques, I would make no progress, could not expect to. That was a blank and impenetrable wall. In any case, I had no very strong feeling for either side in the argument, believing that faking antiques is illegal rather than wrong. But in the other direction, and this was the one which really interested me, the intransigence of these few villagers of Old Gourna, or if you like, their refusal to be driven forcibly from their homes, had affected the whole country. It had been one of the factors which had ruined a great enterprise in Egypt. It had set back the work of a man who might have changed all those crazy buildings with their erratic angles, their staring red brick, and hideous inartistry. There had been a stubborn war waged round that layered hill where the ignorant and greedy Gournawis clung to the only thing they knew. It may be that to move them would not be worth the trouble even in archeological terms; the discovery of the odd tomb probably already exhausted of its treasures. But the Gournawis must have been helped in their resistance by men higher up, by men of power, men with much to lose, men who were expert in manipulation of the vast delaying power of Egyptian bureaucracy.

Alaa said, 'Where now?'

'I want to go and see what there is left of the work of Hassan Fathy.'

11

Hassan Fathy was, and is, at the time of writing, a member of the Egyptian upper class. He had, he says, two dreams in childhood: one was to sail round the world on a yacht with a full orchestra; the other was to build a village where the fellaheen could live in comfort, beauty and cleanliness. His father had large estates but disliked the country and avoided it. Hassan Fathy himself claims that until he was twenty-seven he never set foot on his father's estates. However, he studied architecture and when qualified was given the job of overseeing the building of a school at Talkha, a village in the Delta. He says that the squalor of the place haunted him. One of his father's farms lay nearby and he went to look at it and was appalled by the experience.

He determined to design a method of building that would be available to the peasantry. It would have to cost next to nothing. Burnt brick was too dear, and, as we had seen, by a fortunate coincidence, red, burnt brick is ugly. So Hassan Fathy experimented with sun-dried mud brick and found, as had been known for thousands of years but had dropped out of architectural practice, that as a building material in a dry climate it was unbeatable. What was more, in Egypt every peasant had an infinite supply of this same stuff lying in his own fields and on the river bank.

Hassan Fathy knew that mud brick would not use up the valuable red clay of the Nile Valley. Theorist that he was, he began to philosophize about the building of simple houses out of mud brick. To build so was to be connected with the simple things, such as sun, water, earth, was to create a home aesthetically from the very elements among which a man lived.

However, when it came to putting this aesthetic proposition into practice he came up against an apparently insurmountable difficulty. He built country houses in mud brick, but for the rich! These houses were very little cheaper than those made of brick. The paradox lies in the unique nature of Egypt herself. She is always short of timber. We had seen the wretched attempts at roofing that the poorer fellaheen make with bundles of river-reed laid across the crumbling corners of mud shelters. Fathy's houses were only for the rich because the wood for ceilings and roofs was so expensive. What he had tried to work out for the very poor was in danger of becoming an up-market fashion for the rich. How, then, even if the peasant built his walls of mud brick was he to afford the wood, the rafters, to lie across them? Sometimes even the few pence necessary for buying and carrying reeds was beyond him. The rafters might as well have been made of gold. On top of that, World War II came and wood in Egypt was wholly unobtainable.

It sounds ridiculous; but Hassan Fathy rediscovered the arch. He found arches functionally alive and well near Aswan in Upper Egypt, at the First Cataract in the Nubian village of Garb Aswan.

Now, with the arch revealed as a viable construction in mud brick the problem of the expensive, wooden rafters was solved. He determined to preserve what was good about this method of building and get rid of the squalor, the roofless hovels in which men, women and children shivered all night and died of cold if they were not already poisoned by the filthy waters of the Nile and its canals.

Then he had what must have seemed a great stroke of good luck. A Royal Decree expropriated the land on which Old Gourna stood as the result of a tomb robbery so blatant that it could not be ignored, even in Egypt. A ministerial decree followed, which expropriated the very houses of the village so that the Gournawis would be forced to move out of the ancient graveyard. One million Egyptian pounds was the estimate for building them a new village by traditional, that is, concrete and red brick, methods. Hassan Fathy had proved that mud brick was cheaper. He was appointed architect, a committee chose a new site that was well away from the tombs and on agricultural land down by the river. The land was purchased from the owner of it by order.

His ideas, like his intentions were so good! From the other side of the Red Sea he imported the system of ventilation of the mud hut by convection, which cools the air. It is the system of wind towers or those wind funnels which were once used in the days of sail to ventilate sailing ships in the tropics. He was going to dig a lake to keep children out of infested waters. He would organize the houses round communal squares because that is how an Egyptian peasant *feels* society even if he cannot say so. In this new village which was to be populated by seven thousand mainly illiterate people he built a theatre. There was, or there was to be, a Coptic church, a Turkish bath, a police station, a dispensary. There was to be a women's social centre. There was a market place, a *khan*.

How much was ever built? In his book on the subject, there is at times a certain vagueness of tense which reminded me of the Secretary General. Certainly the photographs that remain show a great deal of charming and gracious building. But he was not dealing with the average Egyptian peasant. He was dealing with Gournawis on the one hand and people who wanted control of a million pounds on the other. He was hindered at every turn by the government, by the contractors, by the workmen and not least by the Gournawis, who after a while became active in sabotage. Hassan Fathy built a dyke to protect New Gourna from the seasonal flooding of the Nile. Despite all the delays, the bribery, the malice, the ignorance and sloth he was getting forward a little. The Palace became interested, a thing in those days of great moment. He was summoned to explain his theory and practice to the King. On his way back from the palace he saw a poster, 'The Great Mire'. It was only an advertisement for a film, 'but it gave me a nasty feeling'. A message was waiting for him when he returned home. The dyke had broken and mud brick New Gourna was flooded. He hurried back to Luxor. He found that a deep wide trench about eight metres across had been dug through the dyke. He found that the Gournawis had refused to work on the dyke and when 'driven to it' had widened the breach with their feet rather than help repair it with their hands. As Fathy says, everybody obeyed the heads of the families and they were tomb robbers. 'They had no intention of giving up their nice, profitable squalid houses in the cemetery with treasure waiting to be mined under their floors to move to a new, hygienic, beautiful village away from the tombs.'

New Gourna is immediately recognizable. It is signed all over by Fathy's particular vision. There is everywhere the sophisticated use of mud brick, use of the vault and the dome. There is a sense of grace and fitness.

We were invited into one house. The owner, or rather one should say squatter, for only Gournawis should live here and this man was from Cairo, showed us first into one of the rooms which were Fathy's architectural unit, his invention. It uses a vault for a ceiling, not a simple arch but half of an ellipse. Such units could be multiplied to taste. They could, literally, be made by a man from the mud round his feet. Here there was a row of four units faced by another four. One unit might be the home of a poor man. It needed no wood. If he prospered he could join a second unit to the first. Not all these eight units were occupied as far as I could see. The one we entered had much lumber stored in it. Our host led us into another part of the house. This was a courtyard with six palm trees and a hand-pump for water. He led us up stone steps in the wall to a flat roof level with the palm fronds, where the Colossi of Memnon looked across a field at us. There were tourists gathered round them but none looking at New Gourna. This roof, which certainly needed rafters or it would not have born our weight, was delightful and a place to sleep during the day in hot weather perhaps under an awning. The house expanded from the original units was unquestionably more fitted to an extended family or a prosperous man than to a poor fellah. The way led round three sides of the top of the courtyard wall to a kind of penthouse, a small sitting-room – best room, probably, for it was filled with the family treasures. The wife and her sister (or perhaps second wife) welcomed us proudly. They showed their treasures, the suite of furniture gaily decorated, a rosewood side table, a richly boxed and bound Koran, pictures and knick-knacks. It was the opposite of Hassan Fathy's ideal but all the garishness of the room could not spoil the quiet beauty of the courtyard with its palms and the ingenious idea of a walkway round the wall of the court. We were given tea in a matching set of porcelain cups and saucers. By fellaheen standards our host was wealthy.

Between the Fathy houses and the Colossi of Memnon the authorities have built a new school. For an institutional building in concrete and rendered brick it is not so bad – dull, uninspiring but neat. It does at least have vertical walls and more-or-less exact right angles. Two hundred yards from it is the original school that Fathy built entirely of mud brick. It is a coherent, modest and attractive complex. Indeed, for me at any rate there is so clearly a special and indefinable grace inherent in a Fathy building that I have been at a stand, trying to decide how much is the material and how much Fathy. My conclusion is that the material is the style is the man and the choice of it his individual genius. Nevertheless, his school has been abandoned. The authorities made a claim that one wall suffered from rising damp and had water under it, a most unexpected phenomenon in an Egyptian flood-plain. However, since the high dam at Aswan has been built the plain does not flood. Yet the authorities in a gesture either of monumental sharp practice or stupidity at once abandoned the old school and built the new one with a speed only to be explained – it was after all in Egypt – by their extreme relief at getting rid of a complex worthy of its setting!

Fathy's achievement at New Gourna fell so far short of his ambition for it that he considered New Gourna a failure. I do not see how it can fail as long as what he built is visible among the other monuments of that extraordinary plain, with a clear message for those with ears to hear.

There's no doubt that we were getting choosy in the architectural sense. There are many acres of interesting architectural junk strewn round Luxor, and for my money, not many successes. Now we turned away from Fathy's mud brick 'failure' towards the other masterpiece in this wilderness of carved and uncarved stone, Hatshepsut's Temple, lying in its horizontal and ascending layers against the cliff.

It is one of the few 'Pharoni' buildings which acknowledges the presence of the landscape and fits humbly into a gigantic cliff which it can imitate but not outdo. The pyramids of Giza and the pyramids of Zoser and of Meidum are the others. The pyramids of Giza admit the necessity of a certain grossness in that illimitable space where anything smaller would be pitiful. Moreover as you watch the cliffs of the Eastern Desert move past you between Cairo and the High Dam, hundreds of miles to the south, you see time and again the very shape of pyramids suggested in the natural angle of rest of the stony screes. Sometimes, indeed, corries will diverge from the top of a cliff and make an angle a thousand feet tall which is that of the great pyramid. The best of Egyptian architecture learned from nature and followed it. So now, in the Temple of Hatshepsut the other physical component of the barren land, the layered quality of alluvial rocks, was imitated and reduced to a geometrical suggestion of it. This was a woman's approach, and sympathetic.

We drove towards the Temple, or perhaps it would be better to say that we now clanked towards it. Bassem's car was like a boxer who has unquestionably lost the fight on points and may now not go the full fifteen rounds. When we arrived in the area before the Temple precincts which was devoted to tourist trinkets Bassem discovered that the car would no longer move in reverse. This was awkward since at the same time Alaa found that tickets for entry to the Temple were only to be procured a mile or so back along the road by which we had come. He, Bassem and Hassan contrived to get the car round by sheer muscular force while Ann and I waited in all the privilege of age. Hassan, who spoke no English, found friends and talked to them. Alaa and Bassem clanked off to get tickets. Ann and I sat side by side in the sun on the low wall of the *temenos*, though its position is dictated more by reproduction *antikas* than sanctity, and waited. We were visited by a procession of sellers of *antikas*, which was a rewarding experience. Taken all in all they went the full gamut. Conspiratorially and in succession they produced *genuine* objects! The first produced from his sleeve the clay head of a noble which he pointed out was genuine because the dirt was still clinging to it. The next tried us with a too large soapstone scarab in which the cuts of a steel saw blade were clearly visible. After that we were offered any quantity of blue beads, which by sheer coincidence I happened to know were exported from Germany and strung in Luxor. The best way to deal with this salesmanship is to treat it as a joke which you are sharing with the seller. The final effort and, in my view, much the most effective came from a man who positively sidled up to us. He came close, secretively produced from his robe a six-inch square of *cartonnage* with the edges authentically broken but leaving in the middle sufficient space for the pharaoh and queen who faced each other there. The man thrust this in my face and hissed: 'Smell mummy!'

The car had been gone a long time. We wandered off and looked at more objects. When the car came back nobody wanted to visit the Temple, not even us. There is a psychological limit to what you can see, think, appreciate, in one day. However there the tickets were so in the two of us went for a short and unhappy visit. Half the temple was out of bounds because of Polish excavations or restorations – the temple is very heavily restored indeed – and I had a brief, pointless shouting match with a guide or guardian of which I am now ashamed and cannot account for. So we came back, feeling that the Temple of Hatshepsut is best seen from a distance where its relationship with the mighty cliff above it can be appreciated. We found that the car had disappeared so we went to the Thomas Cook Rest House for orange juice after orange juice, and the car came clanking back again. They had had a puncture on top of everything else. What else did we want to see?

The orange juice had been somewhat restorative. When I explained that I did not want to go to the Valley of the Kings, every face seemed to light up. But I had never been to the Valley of the Queens – faces fell – and we must subscribe to the equality of the sexes and the right of women to have their graves gawped at; but that would be all, I promised. After that we would call it a day. So the car with its tired load creaked and clanked through the stony landscape under the wonderful cliffs, then climbed into the Valley of the Queens, which had not a tourist in sight and only a solitary ticket collector. All the tombs were closed except two, which we visited dutifully. One was full of really lovely wall paintings, though I, at least, seemed to be seeing them from a great distance. The other tomb wasn't worth being buried in. I have forgotten which was which. However we had visited the Valley of the Queens.

The car when we moved off was now making much the same noises as the boat's engine when the bearings 'went'. Where there was a slight descent in the road it moved quite well though noisily. I think the exhaust had fallen off again and not been replaced. A tail of smoke – surely the emblem of Golding in Egypt? – was polluting the air of the Valley of the Queens. It was fortunate for us that the way to the ferry was almost all downhill, because a couple of slight ascents demonstrated that the car was within minutes of its end. It was like pushing a current and the smoke blackened. One might almost have expected to see a police car emerge from it with Saïd waving a bunch of dusters. There is nothing quite so inducive of frivolity as a day among the tombs. Slowly, carefully, Bassem manoeuvred the car to the ferry. He stopped and the car continued to shudder. We descended. Alaa explained that we two had better go on across. They would wait with the car, as not being reversible, it would have to be pushed on and off the ferry. We are of the age to accept this kind of get-out gracefully. In a sentence, aware of the trauma that faced them, we left them to it.

The day had been unaccountably exhausting seeing that we had walked so little. We made full use of the comforts of the hotel. We bathed, dined, sat on the garden terrace, where the scent of the roses ascended to us through the warm evening air. The Egyptian experience was becoming more and more *various*. How to get the lot under one hat? There was a great defect in width of sympathies, I thought. I could not spend any time in the Old Winter Palace without returning in imagination not to ancient Egypt but to the Victorian and Edwardian days when these quaint and spacious hotels had been filled with people so, so . . . *different* ! Then there was the new museum with its solitary mummy, which stirred in me childhood terrors and fantasies. The temple next to the museum was being eaten slowly, but not so slowly, from the ground upward by rising salts from that filled canyon with its clays and earths and pebbles and gravels and evaporites. And Hassan Fathy with the key to a better Egyptian life there in his hands but frustrated at every point by the very Egyptian-ness of the Egyptians. . . . There were the Nubians, too. I wanted to see the villages, meet the Nubians; and they would add another tangle.

Next day I had come to myself again. Bassem's car was in dock. The crew of *Hani* were either visiting their families or holed up with the propeller shaft and trying to fit a rubber collar to it! Ann felt she would like to spend the day in the hotel garden. So I hired a car for Alaa and myself and set out briskly once more, to fill in a couple of gaps. I had never seen the temple at Kom Ombo, and though by now I was not a temple-fancier, that one was said to occupy a particularly spectacular position at the water's edge. We could, I thought, combine this with a visit to one of the Nubian villages which had been built for them when the rising waters of Lake Nasser covered their homes. I had seen one of the villages from a distance. Now, with Alaa to interpret, I thought I might be lucky enough to find someone I could question. There are several of these villages and the nearest though not the largest was Kalabsha about a hundred kilometres up river from Luxor. We set off at about 10 o'clock. The first point of interest was another phosphate factory like the one the other side of the desert on the Red Sea coast. So they will use artificial manure to replace some of the silt that no longer covers Egypt but settles on the bottom of Lake Nasser. The balance sheet for the High Dam and Lake Nasser is still being drawn and no one knows what the result will be, but my guess is that it will be a close-run thing. Lake Nasser is terrifyingly big. If the dam burst or was broken deliberately the Nile Valley, that is to say Egypt, would be scoured into the Mediterranean. As it was now it covered the homelands of hundreds of thousands of Nubians, who had all had to be settled elsewhere.

At Esna we saw the famous camel market. Hundreds of camels were being sold, some for work but most for slaughter. There were trucks waiting from as far away as Cairo and Alexandria. In common with all Third World peoples these traders and their customers had little thought for the camel's comfort. The worst sight I saw this time was two camels roped down in a truck too small for them so that they could neither stand nor kneel. However I suppose the feeling, or view rather than feeling, was that they were meat already.

A little further on we came across a huge herd (if that is the appropriate collective noun) of camels being driven north. They had made one of the longest herding treks left in the world, all the way through the desert from south of Khartoum. The escorts were a number of genuine-seeming Sons of the Desert who could have ridden straight into a story by P.C.Wren. They all rode camels and flourished long sticks as a substitute for the long rifles which had been taken from them at the border. Their leader was a really magnificent sight. He and the camels were enough to stop the traffic though they were off the road. Soon there was a row of car-people busy photographing camel-people. At this, the magnificent leader rode forward, shouting insults at the photographers. He was a noble savage, and he scared everyone back into their cars.

We reached Kalabasha at about 12 o'clock. It is really a collection of ten villages grouped round a central, mainly administrative nucleus. This complex was set up by the Egyptian Government in 1963. We were lucky. The day was the Prophet's Birthday, everyone was on holiday and the Mayor, or President of the whole area, was very willing to talk. We sat in his office and were given tea. Several members of his council were with him, one a schoolmaster who spoke fair English. I asked what proportion of the population was too young to remember Nubia. For no one under twenty could possibly remember the move down the river to a new country. The President replied that there was indeed a large number of inhabitants who could not remember the land of their fathers but he had no statistics immediately to hand. However, I had noticed had I not that they had plenty of children! I had indeed. Kalabsha seemed even fuller of children than an Egyptian village. I asked if the older people remembered their villages with regret, seeing that the government had built them a brand new one. Oh yes, said the President simply. The older people did remember their villages with much regret. But then the waters had risen – he paused, made a wide gesture – had risen and risen and there was nothing to be done. Nothing. The schoolmaster agreed. He said it was a great pity but nothing could be done. You could not argue with water; and then, there was the government. He and the President agreed solemnly. Yes, there was the government. They made no criticism, just acknowledged the existence of the water and the government. I asked if they had had water piped to the villages in Nubia. No, said the President. The women had fetched water from the Nile. But I was right to ask that question. He knew what I meant. The government had been good

130

and they were very grateful. Kalabsha as I had noticed had water piped into the town and the villages. It came from the water tower at Kom Ombo and had been purified. There were many stand-pipes and some people had water piped into their houses. I said that I appreciated what a blessing pure water was. All the way up the Nile I had seen women coming down to the river. They had not just fetched water, they had done the washing, and had scoured dishes, in fact I could not begin to number the things I had seen the women doing! This made everyone laugh. Well, said I, what I had seen was that the waterfront was a meeting place for women. It was partly a place for work but quite evidently it was a place to gossip and tell the news, a place for children to play where their mothers could watch over them. It was a most important place in a woman's life. Did not these stand-pipes and this water piped into the houses, though in themselves benefits, did they not mean that the women lost something by it?

There was more laughter. Women were women said the President, and Nubian women would find somewhere to gossip no matter what. The only difference was that now they made groups at the stand-pipes or at the door of the house. All that women had lost was the labour of bringing the full pots back from the river. Then too they had a large community hall where the women met when they wanted to. Did they want? Oh yes!

I asked what the population did in the way of work, skills and professions. Fifty per cent, said the President, were craftsmen of one sort and another. Twenty-five per cent worked on the land that the government had given them. Had they enough land? No one ever had enough land! But really, the government had not given them enough. Besides they did not live on or beside their land. The lucky ones had only a kilometre or two's donkey ride to reach their patch but the unlucky ones had to ride as much as seven kilometres. In any case I could see the desert close at hand could I not? There was simply not enough land to be farmed near the complex. In fact some of the old people had already left Kalabsha and gone back to the high land near where their villages had been and were living there. Contrary to what one might expect, many of the young who had never known Nubia now wanted to go back there.

I asked if this was a large factor in Nubian life. Yes, said the President, there were already two Nubian societies trying to get people back to Nubia. It was difficult, though.

But surely the land was drowned? Lake Nasser was hundreds of miles long and many miles wide! Oh no, said the President, the place was not what it looked like on the map. There had been much fertile land in Nubia and even now there was much left. In a sentence, here they were constricted. There the land was so wide there would be room for all. They had not been given enough land. That was the root of the problem. I should contrast them with the Nubians who had been shifted into the Sudan.

I began to realize that the Nubians had not just been shifted from one part of Egypt to another.

'The Sudan? You think of yourselves as Nubians rather than Egyptians?'

There was a silence. I had to break it myself.

'I beg your pardon. Of course you are Egyptian and Nubian too as I am English and British.'

All the same it was becoming clear that the Nubians had a profound sense of national identity. The move had not been a migration but a diaspora.

'Well. What happened to the Nubians shifted into the Sudan?'

'*They* don't want to go back. *They've* been treated properly and given as much land as they need.'

As I looked through the doorway I could see the desert, just across the road. Curiosity and also an urge I could not understand had led me here to ask my impertinent questions. Was it a hangover, some far-off touch from the days when a quarter of the world's map was red? The strange thing I was beginning to find as well was that Nubians – and this included, indeed started with Saïd, the old man in the boat who told me about Fisher's Island, and whom I should remember to the last days of my life, waving his idiotic bunch of dusters in the police boat – the strange thing about Nubians was how immediately likeable they were. It was happening here. They were all cheerful even when talking about their shoddy treatment. It was not a complaint but a statement of fact. It was all embarrassing. If I asked myself what I was doing here, I had to reply that I was trying to interview people – I, who had never liked interviews and had come finally to invent the sourest apothegms – 'Always treat an interviewer as a guest; but remember always that he is not a guest.' – I who tolerated interviews only as part of a writer's job! This was tit for tat with a vengeance. How many interviewers had I embarrassed, or refused to see, put them off? Yet the President and his three old councillors were cheerfully smiling and I would have gone so far as to say that they accepted me as having a *right* to ask questions. Perhaps they were wearily accustomed to government people coming for statistics, sociologists on the prowl, anthropologists trying to integrate, camera teams looking for new angles – perhaps I was only one more fly in their ointment.

'I have another question. It may seem foolish.'

'Please.'

'There is fishing now in Lake Nasser?'

'Yes. Much.'

It was a technical question really. There was no reason why they should be able to answer it.

'You used to fish in the Nile. Now Lake Nasser in many places is many miles wide. When the *Khamsin* blows there must be waves more like the ones we have near Great Britain – sea waves. To them, the waves on the Nile would be ripples. Was this thought of? Are there boats now that can cope with that sort of weather? Were your people taught?'

There was another pause. Then the schoolmaster answered in his careful English.

'They are not yet ready. As far as I know there are not new big boats. But with the old boats, those of the same size as before, they fish near the land. There is flat water near the land in the bags.'

'Bays. I think you mean bays.'

'Yes. Thank you. In bays and inlets. There are many inlets.'

All the same I would have made a bet that the first ten years of spreading water had taken its toll.

'There must have been many accidents, many losses.'

'No. Nothing like that.'

But the President was speaking again.

'There is a thing. I wonder – can you help?'

'Please.'

'All we want is a way to go back if it is only for visits. We want a decent road up past Aswan through the desert to where our homes used to be. A bus road. That's all we want.'

I thought of the good road, the two roads through the Eastern Desert to the Red Sea, the military roads.

'There is a kind of road to Abu Simbel isn't there?'

'But a bus road. That's all we want. So that sometimes when people want to go back. . . .'

133

'It is a request, a plea, a demand, that has to be made to men of power.'

There was much nodding and sounds of agreement.

'I have no power. All I can say is that what I write may be read by men of power, though I do not know if they will nor what they will make of it. But I will write what you say in a book. I will say that the Nubians of Kalabsha ask for a decent road back to where their homes used to be. It's all I can do but I will do it.'

You would have thought by the happiness and laughter that the road had been built there and then. We all shook hands with each other.

It may have been silly. Yes, perhaps it was. Nevertheless I record here a plain statement of what my Nubian hosts want and hope it may be printed in a book with a photograph of Kalabsha – and perhaps the President and his council – on the page facing. *Does* this kind of thing ever do any good? The long and complicated levers of power have never been accessible to me. I have never known even where to look for them.

Now the party showed us round. We saw a craft centre where a young lady as black as a piece of coal and far shinier presented me with some colourful raffia work. There was a reading-room full of children with plenty of books. The President explained that they had two languages, Arabic and Nubian. But Nubian has never been written down. (Forward, the Bible Society!) The children had to learn to read and write Arabic. In the home they still spoke Nubian.

We gave the President and the schoolmaster a lift to the next village where he introduced us to families in two houses and explained that we had already been given tea. So we were only given soft drinks. The houses were simple. The walls were rendered so I was not able to find out what was underneath but they didn't seem to be built of mud brick. They were simply furnished too. There was none of the heaped-up gear I had seen in the other houses, none of the rubble, none, you would have said, of the poverty. The people and the children were happy. It seemed that this happiness was an act of God as far as Nubians are concerned. They are happy no matter what. The children were charming, unafraid and playful. It was of course a holiday, nevertheless everyone seemed genuinely glad to greet a stranger.

So we took photographs, said our inadequate thanks and left. On the way we found that the camel drove had been, as it were, tapped

134

all along the road. Here and there were trucks still loading camels, their owners having forestalled the Esna market further north. Getting a camel into the first truck he has ever seen looked like an all-day job. It should be noted that the camel market was at Esna-on-the-Road. The rest of Esna is a large city with a barrage on the Nile but the main road avoids it.

At Kom Ombo-on-the-Road we turned off towards the Nile. Indeed if it were not for the riverside temple tourism would ignore Kom Ombo altogether for it is a manufacturing town and even dustier and uglier than Qena. We reached the temple and paid for tickets then went in. We – I was about to say we were unlucky, but the word would have been a foolish one. The bad luck was or had been somewhere else. We found that the end of the temple away from the river was out of bounds. It looked like a play being performed. *There* was the high façade of the temple and *there* on the top was a brilliant cast. They all wore brilliant uniforms up there, and in Egypt uniforms for top people are very brilliant indeed. Alaa found from a tourist guide that a tourist had fallen off that façade and been killed. When? About twenty minutes ago.

The speed with which a crowd gathers in Egypt! And this one, gathered by car from every quarter! The poor creature's body was being given more attention than a VIP.

'Man or woman?' I said that because somehow I had assumed it was a man.

'He doesn't know.'

I had a sudden shuddersome awareness of fate, bringing him – yes, I was sure it had been a man – bringing this man at his own considerable expense to Egypt for a holiday – all the excitement of travel – getting him here to the temple – had his wife come with him, or had she stayed in that tour boat moored out there? *No*, dear I don't think I'll come – another temple – I've a bit of a headache. And he, solicitously, oh then I'll stay, keep you company! But she wouldn't have that and neither would fate, taking him by the hand, leading him up to that high platform above the façade. . . .

The trouble with a storyteller is he can't even grieve without watching himself grieving. Why expect truth from such a creature?

As for the temple, or what we were allowed to see of it and what we were inclined to see of it, I don't say it isn't a good temple as temples go. Oh yes, it has a good position some fifty feet above the river and twenty yards from it. There were working sandals out there in the river and alongside the scree of broken stone which leads down from one end of the temple to the water. It seemed odd to be looking at sandals from that angle. They looked smaller and had nothing to do with the temple. It seemed inadequate, the temple I mean. What is an adequate temple? After all, there were the hieroglyphic inscriptions, walls of them. The entrance looked Ptolemaic. Sebek (Sobek, but what's the odds?) appeared to share the temple with Horus. I found myself remembering the place named 'Horus' in a certain Egyptian city and wondering if that's what it was. This end of the temple – the Ptolemaic end – was much lower than the other end where the gaudy uniforms were now dispersing.

Alaa asked if I wanted to climb up to the top of the other end where the unfortunate tourist had been killed. I shook my head. We watched the Nile for a bit, I sitting on the low parapet above the scree of stone. Here the Nile was narrower and the current faster. Our boat would never make it, I was quite sure. I began to agree with myself that I had seen enough Egyptian temples, one time and another. It was that complete *emptiness*. How long ago did the rite of deconsecration evolve? Was it no longer ago than Christianity? And there was much restoration and reclamation going on. I thought to myself why can't people let monuments decay naturally? They rebuild temples but let Fathy's school and houses fall down.

Out in the river there was a floating crane with its grab down. I asked Alaa to find out about it, for one rusty corner of a wreck showed above water. It had been a tourist boat he said at last. Unlucky place for tourists, Kom Ombo. Had there been any casualties? No. No casualties. That was the third wreck I had seen in the Nile which had no casualties! But after all, with tourism among the top three money-spinners for the government should we, I wondered, ever have known that accidents *do* happen to tourists if we had not arrived in time to see that gaudy cast on the top platform and been forbidden to approach it? So we drove back in the taxi with utility music going on from the tapedeck. On the way through Kom Ombo we took in some unpaying passengers because as the driver said we were good men and they were good men and we wouldn't mind. So I sat in the utility music and Arabic chat which I couldn't understand and lost a chance I suppose of Getting to Know the People. Instead I was thinking about the temple (having really not bothered to see it) and wondering why temples did not seem much like Rider Haggard's view of them. In him, of course, there is usually a wind that blows for no reason, or a wonderful light and an unearthly voice, high and pure. Then there's the puzzle of a temple dedicated to Sobek and Horus – to a hawk and a crocodile. Of course, say sympathetic historians, people didn't *really* worship a crocodile but the idea of the primeval being in the primeval water, and the hawk is a symbol of the spirit, like the brass eagle which does duty for a lectern in Christian churches. You can get away with any belief provided you split it small enough. For a thousand years Christians have worshipped in the same way a man being tortured to death on the gallows. Perhaps people have to have something to look at. Even Buddhism, which insisted on having nothing to look at, has got so far as having a very elaborate art surrounding the nothing.

So back we went to the Winter Palace. Ann was well rested so we went for a walk in Luxor, agreeing that it might well be the last time we should see the place. It's a bit different, that. You can quite easily accept the idea that you've seen a place for the first *and* last time, but the last time on its own, yes, that's different.

However, we had a stroke of luck which cheered us up. We discovered a newly opened shop which actually sold books in European languages and not just guide books. We stocked up then and there for the return journey down the river. One of the troubles with air travel is that you can never take enough books to read. Sometimes I fall for the old traveller's trap and take one of the great unread Good Books – *Finnegans Wake* or Motley's *Rise of the Dutch Republic*, which of course I can no more read in a hotel bedroom than in my own house. So I still pine for an unread Small Book and read the instructions on my airline ticket or a newspaper several weeks out of date. The ones we bought were Small Books all right so I won't name them but they were PRINT.

It was a subtropical night and pleasant. But there was still that strange haze in the air, now illuminated by the lights of Luxor, or maybe lit from within by some meteorological effect. We went back to bed and so strong was our hunger for PRINT that before we went to sleep we had each read one of our new books, thus wasting them, since they were not worth keeping and we should throw them away. I remember thinking that we had seen plenty of books in Kalabsha but nowhere else.

We had breakfast at 6 o'clock since we wished to set a good example to the *Reis* and start early on our trip back down the Nile. I was depressed by our failure to get further than Luxor. We were now faced by a return at such speed as the boat could attain – taking advantage of what current there was – in order to get the boat back to Cairo without letting down the owner, who had much need of it by a particular date. I thought it possible that if I was firm enough I could hold up our headlong progress long enough to get ashore for a quick look and fairly lengthy meditation at Oxyrhynchus. But apart from that it ought now to be hell-for-leather all the way. We were at the boat by 7 o'clock.

Akhmet was fiddling with the engine. Apparently he had spent very little time at 'his' village. Instead he had spent two days lovingly fitting a rubber sleeve in place of the metal bearings! I was at pains to admire this but privately gave the rubber twenty minutes' wear before the shaft wore through it. Faroz looked a bit pale I thought. However Rushdie had tidied our cabin and it looked neat enough. So we sat and talked to Alaa of this and that until *Reis* Shasli turned up at 10 o'clock. He had spent his two days in Qena and seemed tired and morose. A salacious rumour pervaded the boat to the effect that he had found both wives in residence, et cetera. So we cast off and moved away downstream. In general Egyptians are adept at keeping small engines going by the use of bits of wire, odd wooden pegs and elastic bands. But the boat's engine was heavier than that. I did not think the rubber sleeve was muting our noise much though it may have altered the pattern of our vibration. Then, not a mile from our starting point, the propeller shaft thudded its way through the sleeve and commenced the familiar banging of metal on metal. The only thing to be said for the boat was that it seemed to perk up when facing homeward the way a horse smells the stables and it even managed to produce an extra knot or two as if the favourable current was not only adding to our speed but encouraging the engine. I was still provoked and unable to understand why nobody had got new metal bearings flown up from Cairo. Perhaps, I thought, the engine was so old that bearings for it were no longer obtainable.

138

There came a loud yell from the fo'c'sle.

'It is Rushdie,' said Alaa, frowning and shaking his head. 'He is suffering from kidney trouble. I had better go and see.'

There was another yell, louder this time. The *Reis* turned up the Arabic *Three Blind Mice*. Alaa disappeared into the fo'c'sle. The Theban Hills were sliding past at a quite respectable speed. Really, it *did* seem as though the engine was helped by the current – more speed for the same effort – but that was impossible! Or was there some help from The Shallow Water Effect?

Alaa reappeared.

'Rushdie will be better soon,' he said. 'He has been like this now and then since he was a child.'

What with an exhausted *Reis* and a sick cook we were a ghastly crew. Ann had not been well. Saïd, who would rejoin us at Qena, had been suffering in one way or another and perhaps we should never see him again. The only really healthy people were Alaa, who is never sick, and the two who had bathed in the awful Nile waters, Faroz and Akhmet. I went on deck and found Akhmet sitting in the wind. The useless sleeve, so swiftly worn through had dispirited him.

'Next time,' he said, 'get a better boat.'

'With the same crew?'

'No,' he said. 'Not the *Reis*. Me and Faroz, we're all right.'

It was true they had worked hard, particularly Faroz. So had Rushdie come to that. The *Reis* had only run us aground once, which in a river of the Nile's length and shallowness is pretty good.

The wind was strong, for as we stood north we were adding our speed to it. I went below and into our cabin, where Ann was three-quarters of the way through her second book. What is sometimes thought a vital piece of equipment for the literate (ability to take in a page at a glance) is a serious defect in the traveller. I begged her to slow up but she said she couldn't. I didn't feel like reading myself. I sat on my bunk, therefore, and tried to bring some order into this at least partly crazy experience. How the devil could I get a book out of it? We were retracing our course through waters we already knew. That sameness which had inevitably been part of our experience of the river on the way up would be increased on the way down. On the other hand was the need for speed – *Reis* Shasli had sworn you come down the Nile in half the time you go up it – and on the other hand there was the need for interesting *experience*. Well. There was still Oxyrhynchus.

Now we were approaching the two burnt-out tour boats. Seeing them twice was sheer waste to the practising journalist; it simply got in the way of new experience. Exploration by boat had come to an end. Glumly I numbered the things I had meant to do and had not done. I had meant to reach Aswan and have another look at the High Dam. I had intended to find the Unfinished Colossus this time and had even designed what I should say about it. I had slotted it in with Michelangelo's unfinished sculptures of the fettered giants, had designed an elegant bit of writing about our modern preoccupation with the fragment, the allusive and the suggestive – a generation and perhaps century that believes *a* truth is there, somewhere, but not to be grasped, not to be seen plainly; in fact if we saw in any way it was the Mosaic way, seeing not the face of Truth but his or rather her back parts from our cleft in the rock and covered by her hand or sat on perhaps, perhaps, perhaps. But I had not found the Unfinished Colossus, so that though I guessed how powerful an image of emergent majesty it was I could not say so.

We were close to the western bank, slipping past it at more than ten knots, a headlong speed. Our wash broke against the bank. Here and there it struck a clod out of a little mud cliff or mounted splashily to a foot or so of green. There was a beautiful plot of onions holding up their proud heads. Is there any crop quite as beautiful as a patch of onions? Our wash snaked into it. A young woman who had been squatting beside it jumped up. She seized a stone and hurled it after us, screaming, a good throw, though short. Then she went on making furious gestures after us as we slipped away. She was handsome, her face uncovered. You could see her eyes flash long after the rest of her features were a pale blur. Eyes really *do* flash, at least in Egypt. Once I had received a flash from a young thing through a slit in her yashmak or whatever they call it. The flash had not been meant for me but for a young man. Even so the near miss had startled me. Now here again, flash after flash, oath after oath – not the same thing, no not at all the same thing.

Egyptian women have relied on their eyes for glamour for thousands of years. An undiseased pair of eyes in Egypt must have been rare and a sign of rude health. Even famous, fabulous, poor, boring Nefertiti had one blank eye which she does not commonly turn towards the camera, though she does very well with the other.

The tomb paintings make a glamour point of the eye more than anything else. There was – is – a wall I remembered, it's not painted but sculpted in *alto relievo*, which is an astounding record of delicacy and sophistication. Of course, not realizing that these thoughts on eyes would be forced on my attention I had neglected to go back and check on the wall; but I did remember taking a photograph of it years ago. As you back off from the wall you can see the eyes long after the rest of the figures themselves have become indistinct.

It was a pity about the woman who had thrown the stone, though. One couldn't apologize. And how typical of alluvial Egypt that she had no more than one stone to hand! Her world was a muddy one, for all the Theban Hills and the huge canyon reaching down more than two miles under her. She would never know about that canyon either, or that the slight rise behind her, 'Armant' was not just a place but a geological expression.

Faroz got us a meal as Rushdie was still turned in to his bunk and groaning every now and then. I asked Alaa if he thought we ought to take Rushdie to the hospital at Qena, but Alaa said he thought Rushdie would be all right. Alaa had a medicine chest and faith in it.

At Qena *Reis* Shasli hurried ashore to see his wife, or wives, again. What was left of the crew and on its feet sniggered. Then the old Nubian, whom I had expected never to see again came aboard. Absence had made his heart grow fonder evidently. He was grinning all over his face and shook hands heartily. He produced a length of flexible steel wire, good old man, which he thought would take the place of the jury-rig. He seemed much more cheerful now than anyone else in the boat. Shasli had been gone no more than a few moments when he came hurrying back and climbed into the steering position. His family life seemed to be at some point of crisis but we never discovered what it was. We set off again, this time into the Big Bend below Qena, where west was *bahari* and so on. Alaa entertained us with the saga of Bassem's car. Half Luxor seemed to have been involved in one way or another.

'But now,' said Alaa, 'his car is as good as new.'

We were positively roaring along, the propeller shaft hammering like mad. I was resigned to my impotence. If we dropped the screw on the river bed, well, malesh. If the shaft broke in the bilges and knocked a hole in our bottom – what of it? If he had meant us to have engines in boats Allah wouldn't have arranged the Nile in the way he did so that for most of the year an engine is only useful for the foolish purpose of saving time; and what do you do with this so famous Time when you have got it? For the current of the Nile being for nine months of the year or thereabouts opposed to the wind the two may be balanced the one against the other and so you can perform marvels of dexterity in the slow handling of a sailing boat, making it hang in the current or slide off as you please, go up or down; and in the case of the frequent ferries sometimes use no sail at all, the furled mass of canvas catching sufficient wind to bring you from east to west or contrariwise almost imperceptibly. Then, if it were not for the god-forsaken engined craft that make waves on the river you could cross with no more than a half-inch of freeboard, though the sailing boats and the powered boats get on well enough with a kind of lazy acrimony. *Reis* Shasli, when he wasn't dishing out information or advice or asking for information from the other Riders of the Sea of the Nile, was pretty indifferent to what happened to our wash. It was embarrassing sometimes.

We were back in sugar cane country. There were many trams under way with lighters full of cane made fast to them. Sometimes a tram would be centre to a whole cluster of lighters so that the group looked like some sort of moving island. Halfway round the Big Bend we passed a huge sugar factory which I had not noticed on the way up river. Presumably I had been watching the other bank steadfastly, which only went to show that the River Nile was only half as good – or rather twice as bad – a vantage point for tourism as I had supposed. But this factory was built of aluminium with flashing great tanks for molasses and a deal of river traffic fussing round its feet. Yet such a factory is only busy for two months in the year. Once the cane harvest has been dealt with the factory goes to sleep. It seems wasteful. I suppose in a better organized world, cane would be trained in from other seasons.

It was about here, my eyes having been opened in Qena, that I discovered that the Nile Kingfisher, though rare enough, is not as rare as I had thought. Each stretch of river had its resident and dominant bird. At one point only I saw three of them together and wondered if they were fighting it out for territory or a mate. Mostly though you see them doing that exquisite looping and hovering movement as they hunt along by the river bank then perhaps fly away low, six inches off the surface across the river. Though there are other birds on the river, sea gulls, within a hundred miles of Cairo, moorhens, a grey, nondescript wader, sparrows and swallows, occasional hawks hanging above the fields just far enough to be inland of kingfisher territory, the white and black Nile Kingfisher

142

and the pure white Mock Ibis are the aristocrats of the river.

I had hoped we would be able to reach Nag Hammadi and even get through the barrage in daylight, but in the end we tied up short of it. This, I found, was so that Rushdie could go ashore and get a shot for his kidney ailment at the Clinic which was fair enough. Once more, then, we spent the early evening waiting, the late evening in darkness and the night feeling only just warm enough. I found I had been bitten irritatingly by a mosquito and that must have happened in the Old Winter Palace, which seeing how exposed we had been in the boat was remarkable. My bites, if nothing else, kept me awake. I tried the amateur and perhaps foolish way of dispersing the poison by making a deep cross on the bites with a sharp fingernail, but it didn't seem to work. It was another night when I did not get much sleep and had plenty of time for contemplation. What, I asked myself as I tried to refrain from scratching, had I seen that could be called real and significant? The inside of a very few fellaheen houses? A village or two? What more could I do? See more villages, more houses? How could I generalize from what I had once known and what I now knew? That things took too long to complete?

I scratched myself. 'They' said that malaria had re-entered Egypt by way of Lake Nasser. That, I thought, was all that was wanted; to go to Egypt trying to find out something without knowing what it was and bring back nothing but a disease! Well, a disease was some sort of knowledge; and Egyptian health *did* seem to be improving, by way of clean water.

To say that Egyptians were slothful was a half truth. Just under the surface were the tensions which gave way every now and then to let out spurts, eruptions of that appalling energy in violence. The riots between Muslims and Copts, the sudden, animal reactions to foreign interference that had resulted in the hideous cruelties in Cairo during the fifties. Most of the Egyptian population has been helpless for thousands of years, exploited, tortured, worked to death when not disease-ridden. Small wonder that when they get the chance they repay as much of those thousands of years as they can by smashing the nearest object. No wonder their psychological spectrum stretches from indolence to hysteria. I had, that day, seen a woman demonstrate it, using a week's precious energy in her frantic leap, screaming curses, hurling a stone then jerking and jerking her arm afterwards as if she could re-create the stone and hurl a stream of them! And we, passing close, insulting her land with our wash from

143

what must have looked like a sumptuous toy, had been the last straw in her endurance of all the rich, foreign traffic of tourism on the river.

The energy could be channelled, given time and will. Driving illegally by the Suez Canal I had seen the result of one of Egypt's modern military operations. On the other side of the water the sand of the bank had been washed away to make a breach through which shock-troops might attack. Egyptians had gone in there, under fire, and washed away the bank with hoses. They had suffered heavy casualties but kept on, wave after wave, until there was a way for the mass of infantry, then tanks. In the sad annals of military heroism and devotion that action stands high. Given necessity – in this case of belief – all the generalizations came apart into a mess of particulars.

The clear night sky continued to draw the last degree of acceptable warmth from the cabin. It was cold. I huddled close, careful to keep the area of mosquito bites at once covered by material yet not so much that there was no soothing coolness on the skin. Somewhere, sketched on the darkness, was the faintest of faint sounds, rising and falling, a muezzin somewhere, in Nag Hammadi perhaps, able now to distinguish a white thread from a black one. Oh come, all ye faithful! It went on and on, seeming to my waking ears as it always did, particularly long on a given morning as if on that day, which was emerging from night, there was a festival to be prepared for, though I knew it was not Friday and the Prophet's Birthday was past. The distant sound came to us fitfully by courtesy of the north wind so that when I was certain it had stopped it began again. Then just when I was certain it would go on it stopped and compelled my ears to attend to the silence in expectation. Well, after all it was supposed to keep the faithful awake and was I not the faithful of some sort or other? A good question! The too-successful muezzin had gone back to his bed when chillily I rose from my bunk, visited our inadequate loo then set myself to dress and not scratch. Silently I stole on deck to be greeted by yet more chill. I hugged myself and stared over the stern. The fog was close and damp this time, no dust about it. I found an angle of the upperworks where the cold seemed less penetrating and set myself to watch. There was the 'plop' of a fish rising somewhere. Now the fog was more a mist and about as white as the muezzin's thread. A dark shape came drifting slowly by, a rowing boat with a black figure huddled in the stern, even its head concealed by the robe, a smaller huddle in the bows where the boat's boy was sleeping. Had they broken adrift so deeply asleep that they did not notice? Or

144

was this a local custom, row up river all day and drift all night with the current? Our boat gave a grunt as Shasli started the engine.

It was still sugar country but more and more built up. Shasli was pushing us on. We reached the Nag Hammadi barrage and lock by half past seven, by which time the air was warm under a bright sun. There were huge rafts of Nile Roses trapped against the barrage and the lock gates. Shasli put us to wait alongside a tram which was carrying a load of the ultimate product of the sugar cane when it has not been used as fuel to further its own distillation. This was raw material for paper making and resembled sheets of crumpled and unsized cardboard. I found I had come to a positive respect for the sugar cane, which seemed as vital to Egypt as the olive to Greece. I also tried my hand at a description before it slipped away. That morning when the mist drew back far enough, as we moved down river, there had been degrees of shadow so that the eastern cliffs were graded right back to the desert and the fringe of palms at the water's edge was black against the rest. All this was mirrored in old silver.

Nag Hammadi lock is ancient, large and hand operated. It dates back to the mid-nineteenth century. Each leaf of the gates has its own capstan with four bars to move it, the sort of thing round which sailors used to sing shanties while the fiddler sat on top. Each gate has four hatches with screw wheels to lift them. This sounds more complicated than the mechanism is. Eight men were assigned to the job of opening and closing the gates but only two did anything that could be called work. These moved the capstan that controlled the gate by which we should enter. One pushed one bar while man number two leaned against another bar and let it take him round with it. Man number two was the boss of man number one. Meanwhile the other six sat in the sun, scratched themselves, unwound and wound up turbans, smoked, spat, lounged off on projects of their own or composed themselves to meditation. When half of one gate was open the two openers strolled right round the lock to the other capstan of the other leaf of the gate, watched idly by the six who were lying close by it. Here the two men opened the second leaf and we moved into the lock while behind us the whole thing was repeated by one man and his boss but in reverse order. The same two men, one of them now glistening with sweat, opened the hatches of the downstream gate, one by one. When the waters were level there was a flurry of activity. The man sitting down stood up. The man lying down waved. The two others actually joined the one man and his boss at

145

the downstream capstan and leaned against the bars. The one man turned the capstan, the sweat now dripping off him. At last we moved out of the lock while the dauntless eight returned to their meditations. Time for getting through one lock: an hour and three quarters.

We found ourselves once more in a wider and I think, fishier Nile. For either the kingfishers were getting gregarious, which I did not believe of such a solitary bird, or they needed shorter stretches of water than further up stream. We saw as many as four at a time and it looked as if they were hunting small insects the way swallows do, for they would skim the water at full speed for a quarter of a mile, rising, falling, swerving, as if they were flying through clouds of gnats and midges. If that was not what they were doing (and certainly no gnats or midges were visible) then we were driven to the unscientific supposition that they were rejoicing in their speed, skill and beauty.

Now the crew fished a number of instruments out of the sternsheets stowage and when they had assembled them it appeared the result would produce *kebab* for a midday meal. This was exotic, naked flames in a wooden boat among floating robes! However no harm was done and the kebab, if not up to Charlotte Street standards, was as good as the lamb's meat would allow it to be. The performance – it was that – took all morning and most of the afternoon and our best profit was to learn to like Arab bread more than the tasteless imitation of European bread. Like most bread from poor countries it was very good.

Then just when I thought we were all set to do a record day's run we came to El Maragha and tied up. When I asked why, I was informed that north of this point the 'pirate' waters began. Those waters had shifted a bit. The time was only ten past four and we could have moved on for another two hours! When I protested this Shasli said there were no towns within reach where we could tie up and we should have to moor in the dark! So there we were, moored against the beach below the corniche of El Maragha. The crew put out a gangplank that sloped at an angle of forty-five degrees and just reached dry land, or dry mud, rather. The stone-and-concrete apron fronting the corniche was so old it was cracked everywhere and full of holes. There was a low wall at the top and a proportion of the population of El Maragha lined this to watch the show. I found it *was* Friday after all so they had a holiday. Perhaps Friday falls on a different day in each province. Or it may be that Friday comes when

146

you want it or when the Secretary General says that it is Friday. If this was not sufficiently surprising I got an even bigger surprise when the foreshore began to exhibit its fauna. Once the noise of our arrival had ended the rats came out of the holes in the apron and soon the corniche and the beach was crawling with them. When I saw the first few I thought it would be better to risk the 'pirates' but I couldn't get anyone to agree with me except Ann. Moreover 'crawling', I now saw, was the wrong word. They were well-fed high-spirited animals. When they were accustomed to our presence they played in the open as energetically as kittens but with less charm. Their agility was alarming and I kept a nervous eye on the gangplank. I had seen enough rats in dockland here and there and knew they could run along a hawser and nip into a ship before you could scream. I explained all this to Alaa who promised that the crew would Do something.

In the event old Saïd appeared, creeping out of the fo'c'sle as in a dream. He went slowly and carefully and lowered himself down at last to sit astride the gangplank just where it was fastened at its inboard end to the boat. All this time the crowd along the corniche watched the performance in silence. When Saïd finally settled down they let out their breath in one huge 'aah!'. I photographed the crowd and this appeared to please them, which was strange. A man of some portly dignity appeared among them and shouted at me. I asked Saïd what the man meant and Saïd told me the man wanted me to take another photograph.

Then I thought it was time I tried out my Arabic in public.

'Good day,' I said.

'Good day,' they said.

There was a long pause.

'Does anyone speak English?' I said.

'No,' they said.

There was another long pause.

'Goodbye,' I said. 'Goodbye,' they said.

So I went below again. Shasli of all people was urging Ann to go ashore! He was, said Alaa, proud of his two captive westerners. In his tourist boats he had had little to do with the passengers and was concerned solely with steering the boat. Meanwhile old Saïd drowsed on the gangplank and the rats (grey ones) jumped and gambolled and played on the mud beach. The crowd still watched the boat and were as indifferent to the rats as the rats were to the people above them. Descent of the corniche would be a laborious affair. Live and let live appeared to be the rule between rat and man.

Rushdie had really gone sick again. I suggested that we should put him on a train for Cairo, where he could get as proper treatment as was possible in Egypt. But he didn't want to go – just wanted to sleep. To my way of thinking the danger was that since there was no town between us and Asyut, eighty miles down river, he was taking a chance in staying aboard. However, he was an adult and I had no authority to shift him. I dropped the question of our sick list and took up the question of rats. Saïd couldn't sit on the gangplank all night and to leave the gangplank unattended was asking for much trouble. Alaa, who was preparing to go ashore himself, said once more that they would 'Do something'. They did indeed. They shifted the gangplank so that there was now a stretch of perhaps six inches of water between the end of the plank and the beach. The rats could have stepped across.

Defeated once more I returned to the cabin, where it was now necessary to switch on the light. We had supper, prepared by Akhmet and partly by Faroz. It was goat's cheese or perhaps sheep's cheese, I'm still not sure which, with Arab bread and *loukoumi*: all washed down, as they say, with mineral water. I personally couldn't have asked for a better meal, except for the mineral water, which of course was cold. So we read our books and listened for rats and tried to believe with the crew that no rat would get aboard. We heard a noise and started up, but it was only Alaa going ashore. Somehow or other I could not concentrate on my reading. I was now eager to cut my losses, get back to Cairo and do various trips that I had designed as a kind of appendix to this trip by water; a visit to the Fayoum; interviews with people, and a bit of a wander in the Delta.

Ann put down her book. I turned off the light and lay in the dark. Well, not the complete dark, of course, for there were street lights along the top of the corniche. Egypt is not badly off for electricity what with the dam and a few power-stations. That's not what she lacks. I searched back in my intentions and remembered that 'inclusive' view of 'my' Egypt which I had intended; a view taking in geology and archeology and astronomy and theology and papyrology and sociology and any other ology that might come to hand. I tried in my own mind to remember the different scales of Time, the riddles, mysteries and the problems, the histories and novels from Gautier's *Roman de la Momie* right down to the latest recreative

148

blockbuster. I tried to hold the immense canyon over which we hung in my mind together with the as-ancient (on one scale) suggestions of civilization in the pre-dynastic period. It was impossible, of course, and my mind went numb: but it proved an excellent method of getting to sleep.

That was how one sleepless night caught up with me and I slept very deeply indeed. True, I was subliminally aware of voices in the night but must have supposed it was yet another muezzin with his wailings and incomprehensible cries. So only minimally awake, reaching awareness as a dolphin reaches oxygen I dived down again away from it all, only to be jerked right up to the surface by the sound of the engine! I lurched up on my bunk. The night was pitch black. We had never had the engine on at such an hour. They had brought in the gangplank with an appalling thump. Under us the propeller began to spin faster and faster. It was preposterous. I pulled curtains, peered out of our windows and could just make out – was it Faroz? – hurrying round the deck. This was no 'Rhythm of the Nile'. Had the rats invaded us? had we fallen out with the River Police? I remembered the pirates. That was it. We were escaping. Or perhaps we were going full ahead to get through pirate waters before they were awake or so fast they couldn't catch up with us.

But Shasli, the fool, was pushing us faster and faster. I was trying to dress but the vibration made even that mechanical job difficult. When at last I had managed to drag my clothes on and tried to make a note of these events in my journal the pen danced so that I could not do it. The propeller was no longer banging but chattering in agony. It seemed to me the boat would come apart at any minute. Now there was the quick Egyptian dawn outside in the sky and I could see the bank rushing past us faster than ever before. There was a great cry from the other end of the boat. I went to the door but could not open it – something soft and heavy moved away from it on the other side. I got it open; and there was Saïd in the middle area, getting up floorboards!

'Saïd! What is it?'

The engine stopped between one revolution and the next. The hideous silence broken only by the lap, lap of decreasing momentum struck me wordless. On deck there was the sudden noise of activity. In the brightening dawn I could see the banks swinging every which way as the boat turned helplessly in the current.

150

'Saïd! Motor kaput?'

'La. Benzine mafish.'

I shut the door and sat on my bunk.

'They've run out of gas.'

'Right in the middle of pirate waters.'

The boat seemed to swing round faster and faster as the current swept it along. As I looked out of the window I could see here and there in the river the tell-tale marks of shoals. These were the diagonal lines like tide rips and some of them were in midstream. The boat by, as it were, an innate sense of hydrodynamics avoided the first three while the deck above our heads was loud with the thumps and scurries of the crew. In the mid-section Saïd had the boards up and was pawing idiotically at the engine as if he could invent fuel or push the propeller shaft round. There was yelling from on deck. All those components of awareness of the Egyptian Thing which I had tried to fuse a few hours before into a single state of comprehension! It had not included this kind of modern idiocy.

'It must have been Shasli,' said Ann. 'He was trying to get somewhere before the fuel ran out.'

'I just don't understand it.'

'Difficult.'

'I give up.'

'Really,' said Ann, trying to look interested only and not worried. 'How are you going to do that?'

It was a good question: and a shoal mark – a tide rip – was right on us. A moment later we struck so hard that the boat lurched sideways then came upright as we swung once more. There was yelling from the deck. Through a side window I could see Akhmet pushing at the bottom of the river with our solitary boat hook. There *was* danger. We could catch on a shoal and then the current could push us over, capsize us into the hole on the other side of it.

'I think that perhaps we had better. . . .'

We bumped and dragged over what felt and sounded like a rock. Then we were out in the current once more.

'Saïd! Saïd! Tell them to use that bloody grapnel!'

That was a method of using a current as old as seamanship. They call it 'Danning'. You can see it in the Thames when barges come up on the tide with no engine at all. You lower the crown of the anchor to the river bed and its drag gives sufficient differential to enable you to steer. It was a method that had been used on the Nile since those pre-dynastic times which had soothed me to sleep only an hour or two before – well, seven or eight hours before. Alaa did not appear to be on deck. We struck again and lurched but came upright. We were being carried towards the west bank, and there, among the reeds was a pirate squatting in his rowing boat and looking interested. I could see a tram coming upstream. There was a loud series of screams from our siren, shouts from the crew, more wild and uncoordinated activity. The tram slowed and hung in the current but we were in water which was too shallow for it. Now the pirate was heaving at his clumsy oars. He caught a rope from our bow and ferried it dextrously to the tram where it was made fast. He hauled off, waving.

I shouted at the top of my voice.

'Thank you! Thank you very much! *Shockran gazeelan* !'

The pirate was smiling sleepily back at the boats. His mouth opened and shut. I could not hear but knew what he said.

'*Afwaen.*'

He waved us a cheerful goodbye.

We swung alongside the tram with a crunch. We made fast bow to stern like two horses in a field. The crew started to leap about again. Once more it appeared we were in the market for fuel. Well, had not the Secretary General said we were guests of the government? It seemed only a few minutes before the engine started again and we went full speed down the river. We had the biggest yet, the fattest, longest, densest trail of smoke behind us. The screw was rattling like a castanet. The table at which we sat jumped up and down. The noise was like the inside of a sugar factory. Then just when I was sure the screaming engine would explode, we slowed down.

It was Abu Tig. Astonished, I watched a writhing Rushdie carried ashore. There was a long pause. I went into the centre cabin where the floorboards had been put back and gathered up bits of bread, some cheese and a new bottle of mineral water.

Presently the crew returned and Alaa told us the story. He was astonished, as I suppose he might well be, that we had not understood what was happening earlier. The strange noises that had reached me where I lay sunk deep in sleep were the screams of poor Rushdie, who had been taken desperately ill with his kidney complaint. The nearest clinic or hospital was Abu Tig. It was that or nothing so they had pushed on regardless, hoping to reach Abu Tig before the fuel ran out; but it had done so a few kilometres above the town. If it had not been for the convenient tram and the pirate. . . .

152

Rushdie was now sedated and under observation, said Alaa. Alaa himself seemed very upset and I guessed at awful arguments and decisions. Even his perfect English seemed to get a bit confused. He said how they had carried Rushdie ashore and looked for a taxi to take him to the hospital, found one at last and had put him in it but then found that it was standing outside the hospital. They had been very worried and not thought or had time to tell us what was the matter.

I asked why they had not tried El Maragha for help, but El Maragha, well as a matter of fact, El Maragha was Hicksville.

Peace had descended on the boat. We wrapped up and went on deck; but we had moved, it seemed, out of the fringes of the tropics and the north wind was very cold so we came down again. We had to clamber through the centre cabin because Akhmet and Saïd had now taken all the floor up once more. It was remarkable how that floor came up and down. We tended to notice, as it was the only way out of our cabin. The two of them were replacing the jury-rigged tiller line with the flexible steel wire which Saïd had brought down from Aswan. It was an all too familiar 'messing about in boats' scene. Faroz, deftly balanced on a deck beam, was cooking. There was nothing for it but to return to our cabin and wait for whatever happened.

Later, Rushdie came back or was brought back. He had been given powerful shots. Rather than be left behind at Abu Tig he had elected to hold out until we reached Minya. There he had friends who would drive him to Cairo.

So we read good bad books and presently the engine started to take us downstream with the pint or two of fuel we had begged or borrowed or stolen from the convenient tram. It was now a very sedate progress. We stopped south of Asyut but in sight of the barrage to get filled up with fuel. It was a busy place with about an acre of trams moored, much stone and brick being landed along the customary bouncing planks with their customary processions of heavily laden men. There were privileged persons wandering over the trams, one whose job it was apparently to open and shut small deck hatches to see if it was possible. He was an odd man because although he wore nothing but a loincloth and turban he looked in every way to be a European. At once we consulted our dim memories of *The Four Feathers* and decided it was young 'Carruthers', if that was the name: so time stretching itself too easily we passed some of it inventing dialogue. The fact was that the fuel was slow in coming because they could not take cash. They very kindly rushed our cash downtown, and brought back a credit slip. When these difficulties had settled themselves, delivery of fuel by means of a large hose took less than a minute.

We moved on and moored alongside another police station. It was early. I came to the conclusion that there was a kind of fluvial Parkinson's Law in operation. The various exigencies of river life would expand inexorably to fill whatever time we had left. The best I could do was to try to see that they did not overflow it. Ann decided that Egyptians worked in a different rhythm. We work at set hours and do not expect to touch work at all in the others. Egyptians do not make this distinction but expect to work or rest at any time. So the crew did odd jobs about the boat – Faroz, for example, might appear outside the window at any hour, just giving it a quick wipe over – without demanding time and a half. On the other hand the crew was just as likely to lie in their bunks all morning if there was nothing particular to do and they felt like it. They, the crew that is, didn't know what we expected, nor we they. Women work all day from dawn to dusk and beyond at both ends, work as gently as they can with intermissions for gossip and rest. They do not distinguish.

However, there were other jobs in which wretched men were caught, one was in operation outside the window. Cement was being carried ashore from a tram in large bags. Each was what one man could manage to carry, no less. The bags came out of the hold of the tram on the shoulders of a procession. Those going up the corniche had the courtesy of the plank, went up slowly, reduced to nothing but ambulant bags of cement powder. Those who were coming back did so as best they could, slipping in the dust. At any time there were six bags of cement powder going up the corniche with legs attached to them. It was ant work. I saw one heavy man with his heavy bag of cement fall off the bouncing plank. He must have hurt himself and cynically I expected him and his hurt to be ignored – but no. The whole operation stopped, the man was helped into the tram and presumably made to lie down on someone's bunk. It was a curious mixture of solicitude and brutality for in any case the work was inhuman.

Alaa came down and said that the police promised us a visit from 'the officer' who would turn up at the boat at 'half past seven'. We expected him to conform to Egyptian custom and turn up at half past eight, but in the event he turned up at twenty-five minutes past seven, sent for our passports ashore then came aboard and presented himself as the General Commanding the River Police of the Province of Asyut. He explained that this meant his patch extended all the way from Sohag to Minya. He was smartly dressed in khaki and he had a bone-cracking handshake. He was cheerful and ingenious with what English he knew. He spoke with great determination, helped out now and then with a word from Alaa. It is a good method if you are bold and also have someone to help you. I felt bitterly my own linguistic deficiencies with their attendant humiliations – being rung up from France, engaged in Franglais conversation and then finding that I was broadcasting live. Without a gift for languages to attain the capacity for minimal conversation is such a desperate plod! It is like one of those chemical equations that are written out as working both ways. Even if you reach the state of speaking the language it was no guarantee that you had reached the even more necessary point of being able to understand it when it was spoken. It is noteworthy that all the cleverest advertisements for language courses stress that you will soon *be able to make yourself understood* and play down the other necessity of understanding the language when it is spoken! However, here was our General of River Police chatting away with great success. He was a figure of authority and the crew was bent double with respect. I had the feeling that none of them was accustomed to social intercourse with policemen other than the ragged recruits with their shining guns. Now here was a general in creaky boots and leather straps only a foot or two away. He was insistent that he would do anything for us. At that point the only thing to say was that his visit was in itself a gift and would he take tea with us? This he agreed to do, the tea being prepared by Faroz, who slopped the liquid nervously, I thought. It was wickedly entertaining to guess that each of the crew – except perhaps Saïd – was inspecting his life hurriedly for moments they were accustomed normally to forget. Fortunately as visitors from Mars we passengers were watertight, pure in thought and deed. I debated taking him at his word and raising the question of the engine bearings, but as I was thinking of it he put down his teacup, shook me by the hand, crack, crack and went away. The crew began to babble and laugh like when teacher is out of the room.

We went back into our cabin to read again, when at 9 o'clock, Alaa presented himself and said would we come to his birthday party? We went back into the middle cabin and there in the centre of a low table

155

was a splendid cake with twenty-six candles on it! The Egyptian custom is slightly different from ours apparently, for we all had to link hands and blow, producing a gale that would have blown any smaller cake overboard. After that there was a cutting of the cake and distributing of it and eating it together with sweetmeats of sugar, fat and coconut with spices, Seven-Up and Egyptian beer. Somehow we had acquired another three or four crew members and Rushdie was present also, pallid but restored. It was quite a scrum. Unless Egyptian beer is frozen solid it is not a drink to be recommended. Nevertheless the crew showed surprisingly few inhibitions against this immoral consumption of alcohol. Quite soon, for I believe they all had a low threshold of tolerance, the scene became what nineteenth-century guide books call 'animated'. Alaa told us of the time when the government suddenly produced a decree that all alcoholic drinks were now forbidden by law and must be taken out of shop windows and destroyed. Nothing happened at all. There was much laughter and a general agreement that no one took any notice of the government. The police? Ah, that was a different matter! The laughter was rueful.

Rushdie began to show us card tricks. Some of our visitors did the same. One tried me with Find the Lady, at which I lost several notional Egyptian pounds. Then Rushdie that man of many talents and sicknesses, sang and played the lute, making – I was told – extempory verses about the company. These were skolia! I should like to know what he said about me but couldn't very well ask; and in those cases the truth is impossible. After that, just as elders do when the older children hold a party we thanked Alaa and everybody else and withdrew into our cabin. The ship's generator continued to run, the laughter became louder and louder long into the night; but it was a happy, warm sound and I thought it was a pity Alaa had not had a birthday at the beginning of our boat trip rather than towards the end of it. If I had had any wit I should have had one myself. So I lay in my bunk, considering the visit of the General of River Police and the way his departure had liberated the spirits of the crew so that they reacted as the grass does when you take the roller off it. The noise seemed so unlike the Nile of Egypt, the Bahr el Nil, that slow, really rather sleepy river and its indolent servants! But there was after all a long history of parties on the Nile – water parties, from the little skiff *à deux*, a noble with his wife holding on to his leg as he wacked his throwing stick at rising geese, right up to full-blown ceremonial occasions with royal barges and full pomp. There was the one which some wise man recommended as a cure for low spirits to some pharaoh or other. He told him to – no. That was on Pharaoh's ornamental lake, which wouldn't count as a Nile party, a pity because it's such a good story. Alexander the Great will have had parties sure enough, he being a partying sort of person, but there was no proof that he had ever been up the Nile further than Memphis. He seems just to have marched through the Delta then gone inland to Siwa. Cleopatra now, she was the one who gave Antony a party and drank those two pearls in vinegar just to show. The really famous party which she gave when her barge 'burnt on the waters' and the 'poop was beaten gold' and so on didn't actually happen in Egypt at all but somewhere up in Asia Minor. Hadrian now, he came all the way up to Luxor and will have given many a party on the way up for Antinous, though he was a lonely man and not at all party-minded on the way down. For the slow, sleepy Nile drowned his favourite for him, or his favourite drowned himself, nobody knows the truth of it as is the way with drownings. Wouldn't Julius Caesar give some notable parties? They weren't recorded though. Augustus Caesar would have been the only party-pooper though he too knew little of Egypt but Alexandria right down on the coast. At the best of the parties someone would sing skolia the way Rushdie had done, so we were in a very ancient tradition. Out in the middle cabin it certainly sounded as if one or two people's tongues were splitting what they spoke. But it was all laughter – and one of the most innocent parties of all that long history! There was Saïd as I had seen him, refusing beer and sticking to Seven-Up but grinning amiably at everyone and squatting gently on his heels and rocking. His skolion had seemed to amuse him for he had split from ear to ear at the end of it.

I must have drifted off at some point for I came to more or less in silence as well as darkness. The generator was off and . . . no it was not entirely night for there was a trace of dawn in the sky. For the first time in the boat I heard a not unfamiliar sound. In the middle cabin someone gave a huge snore. Far away in the depths of Asyut the muezzins began to call the faithful to prayer. In our boat I believe the call went unheeded.

Between seven and eight in the morning the boat got under way a bit sleepily I thought. Perhaps the boat really *was* still warm from the birthday party. As for the crew, there was no doubt about their level of tolerance – they seemed distinctly the worse for wear. Faroz, though willing to work, had a green look about him and Akhmet when he saw me grinned piteously and held his head. But there was a bit of wind and a job to do as we went through the lock. The hundred sluice gates were shut, with huge rafts of Nile Roses built up against them. When we came out of the lock on the downriver side, therefore, the current was minimal. The north wind was quite strong and kicking up a bit of a lop through which we slapped pettishly as though the boat had a headache too. Yet it appeared that Shasli now expected to get us to Beni Suef by the end of the day and to Cairo the day after. Shasli had got up late, hence the late start, though he had not had more beer than might be expected of a man content with a mere two wives and thus thoroughly in control of his appetites. His greeting to me had been a little wry. As for me, I felt the virtue of a man who among all these topers had been unable to stomach more than half a bottle of the sweet, sticky Egyptian beer. However, the north wind blew the fumes out of the boat, taking the warmth with it, and out of the crew as well. By midday Akhmet was asking for the engine to be stopped while he changed a filter and Faroz was as busy as ever, cleaning round the boat.

We had the Eastern Desert with us again, the cliffs sidling in towards the river. We were back in that stretch of the country where the cliffs are the main interest with their scatter of strange, black holes. It was difficult to account for the white scratches that led up to some of them. Animals might account for some, rolling stones for others and, of course, men for more. With little to look forward to now as far as the river was concerned I meditated them. It was in this area – or rather the one we had passed through frantically finding a clinic for Rushdie – that some Arabs had discovered the apocryphal gospels of St Thomas. The word was somewhere floating about in the back of my mind. I could see a process but not remember the word, it was foreign and difficult. The book was one I had not seen for many years. It was one of those books on Egypt which had sold me the place while I was still a boy and. . . .

Sebakh!

That was the word, the thing. That was an Arabic word so I had known an Arabic word all along without reckoning it in my scanty store – had a word from way back when Egypt then had seemed as far away as the moon does now. Those Arabs who discovered the Gospels according to St Thomas – of all things they had been looking for soil. It was a trade, an industry. Now I was staring at the black holes and their dependent scratches, their almost inaccessible positions, I saw the picture clearly. All those holes had been inhabited by men of one sort or another for hundreds, perhaps thousands, of years. Was it not the perfect lair for thieves, hanging over the valley, eager to snatch a living from the wretched peasants who scratched theirs from the fringes of the sown? Later it was men of this religion or that, this sect or that, monks, ascetics, hermits, saints some of them it may be, madmen too, fakirs of Christianity. So each of those holes through the centuries would acquire a thick deposit of refuse, dung, which in time would rot down to soil, very rich and desirable in the infertile desert. To think that so many years of holy poverty and desperate asceticism should end up as manure! It was an odd thought and inaccurate, violating Time. Whatever the holy or would-be holy men had done, it was for *then*. The manure was for now. But to perch year after year like a seabird on a rock, and producing guano! The thought sent me straight back to the uniqueness of Egypt. Generation after generation there had been a craft, not in the digging of relics and treasure but of what they called *sebakh*. It is the sort of word a boy would remember, the Arabic word or one Arabic word for 'night oil', dust rich in nitrogen and therefore useful as an artificial fertilizer.

The Arabs, the Egyptians who dug for it, were thought to be the lowest of the low and their name showed it for they were called the *sebakhin*, dung-diggers. Of course they were not much interested in anything else that the cave held, old bones and pots. Nor was it at all a question of caves only. In the rainless – or nearly rainless – climate of Egypt, wherever there had been humans living there would be rich layers of *sebakh*, villages, towns, cities, caves, single farms, the stuff was everywhere, and the *sebakhin* dug it. Sometimes they dug legally with a paper from the government to protect them; but as often as not, they dug illegally and then whatever treasure they found as well as *sebakh* would turn up later on the market. Early on they did untold damage to the literature of Egypt, for when they came on a papyrus scroll they tore it into pieces, since selling each separately was more profitable than offering the document intact. That was what the white scratches up to the holes in the rock signified, not animals but man, and not holy man but a dung-digger on the lookout for his peculiar loot.

It is lofty to prefer a tattered scrap of papyrus to a pot of gold. But since the *sebakhin* were commonly digging round the sites of abandoned cities in the fringes of the desert it is not surprising that most of the voices recovered from Egypt have come to us that way. Much must have been wasted – perhaps ninety per cent but there is one sense in which what we have left is more than enough. There are tens of thousands of papyrus scraps that have not been published because they are not worth the trouble, but they are, nevertheless, too valuable to throw away. Perhaps it is the thought that by some statistical freak, one day they may repair a hole in another document not yet extant.

This side of archeology appealed to my boyhood's mind as much and more than the other, the discovered pot of gold. The name was 'Oxyrhynchus'. It was the site of a city, lay on the fringe of the Western Desert, was now ten miles from the main stream of the Nile. I had wanted earnestly to visit it during the last half century or so and I had already passed it three times without doing so. On the way upstream only a few weeks before we had spent the night at a place as near the site as the river went; but there was darkness, a wilderness of canals and crops and fellaheen who would strike out at the stranger in the night with a flail and ask questions afterwards. That impassable countryside stretched for ten miles between me and the desert, too far to walk, too late to walk, too dangerous, and in a word, folly. The other two times I had passed nearer in a car, but fleeing from the bakshish boys and not really coping with a number of pressures. Now we were about to go near again. Oxyrhynchus had perched on the edge of the desert looking down on the ancient Bahr Yusuf. The Egyptians called it Behneseh. It was anciently the capital of a nome or governate. In 1897 Messrs Grenfell and Hunt, scholars and archeologists, started work there. It was not a site from which to expect jewels and gold, but they had not been at work more than a few days when they reached treasures that blazed, though in the mind's eye. For whatever reason the ancient Oxyrhynchites had thrown out old books, or scrolls, or sheets or notes with the rest of the rubbish. Mounds of paper – papyrus – were dumped, sometimes thrown out of wickerwork baskets, and sometimes thrown basket and all from the edge of the 'tell' of *sebakh* that grew higher and higher and swallowed up what paper was not already covered by drifts of sand. That was another reason why one part of my mind, and that the sensible one, told me that a visit would be pointless. The site had nothing to show now but a few grey and brown lines of wall. Of all the sites in Egypt of such importance it was probably the least

PREVIOUS PAGE: Faroz. 'We thought he would be excellently cast as Aladdin.'

LEFT: 'Alaa and Rushdie descended into the stern sheets and played music. In Arab music if you have a good thing you don't let go of it. The first three notes of *Three Blind Mice* but in the minor mode lasted them for rather more than half an hour.'

BELOW: The lock at Asyut.

ABOVE: Rushdie. 'The rhythm of the Nile is the art of doing nothing. It is a good way of life if you can accommodate yourself to it.'

BELOW: 'The whole scene, river and shore, was wholly unlike the Nile of further north where we had seen the kilns and brickyards. Here all was rock and water.'

ABOVE LEFT: 'On the way we found that the camel drove had been, as i were, tapped all along the road. Here and there were trucks still loading camels, their owners having forestalled the Esna camel market further north.'

LEFT: A herd of camels being driven north from Esna. 'They had made one of the longest herding treks in the world – all the way through the desert from south of Khartoum. The escorts were a number of genuine-seeming Sons of the Desert.'

BELOW: Esna cattle market. 'Hundreds of camels were being sold, some for work but most for slaughter. There were trucks waiting from as far away as Cairo and Alexandria.'

RIGHT: A young boy with donkeys.
'It seemed odd to see a donkey
doing what it liked and not laden
to death.'

BELOW: Papyrus plants stacked on a
truck. 'The Ministry of Culture has
caused papyrus plants to be
reintroduced into gardens near
Cairo so that the stems may be
made into papyrus, following
exactly the ancient methods.'

ABOVE: The Colossi of Memnon.

LEFT: A poor fellah's house. 'It was not so much dirty as untidy, for who minds a bit of dried cowdung and dried straw about the place.'

ABOVE: Hassan Fathy's New Gourna. 'It is signed all over by Fathy's particular vision. There is everywhere the sophisticated use of mud brick, use of the vault and the dome. There is a sense of grace and fitness.'

BELOW: Kalabsha. 'The houses were simple. The walls were rendered so I was not able to find out what was underneath but they didn't seem to be built of mud brick.'

ABOVE LEFT: 'There were many trams under way with lighters full of cane made fast to them.'

ABOVE RIGHT: A 'gaggle' of feluccas.

LEFT: The Nile Kingfisher.

OPPOSITE: Near Giza.

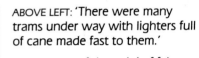

BELOW: 'Once again we were in time to see that curious moment when the trance of the night turned into the slow movements of dawn.'

OPPOSITE TOP: 'In El Fayoum itself a more interesting sight and sound is the multiple waterwheel. It consists of several undershot waterwheels placed side by side and linked.'

OPPOSITE BOTTOM: 'The noise seems always on the very verge of concord or even melody as if, given just one tiny further impetus, one last heave, it would manage against all the odds of the universe to sing.'

BELOW: The waterwheel which is still used for irrigation throughout Egypt.

OPPOSITE: Cairo. 'So we set out with Alaa into deepest Cairo much as an English botanist – an amateur one at that – would enter a Sussex woodland and hope to find a species of plant that nobody had ever noticed before. We went straight to the most touristy bit of all, the bazaar.'

RIGHT: The Mosque Al-Azhar, Cairo.

BELOW: 'Outside the gate we passed at once from medieval to modern with traffic to be dodged and crowds hurrying to catch buses.'

ABOVE: 'An aspect of any Egyptian town that is bound to surprise a westerner is how the children swarm everywhere. They seemed healthy enough to me as did the population generally.'

ABOVE: Near the Well of Umm Fawakhir. 'The boy declared we must go further on then further. Instead of gold mines and huts we were now to inspect graffiti which were not what I had set out to see.'

RIGHT: Graffiti by a desert road.

OVERLEAF: Dusk on the Nile.

spectacular to the outward eye.

I remember during World War II there was a mountain of books collected for the troops and it could not be found storage space. It lay by the Great Western Railway and rotted in the rain, a sad sight. But Oxyrhynchus had the sun. Nothing rotted or decayed. When the two scholars first walked over the sand they actually found they could detect papyrus underground by the elasticity of the sand under their feet! The baskets with their loads of official and unofficial rubbish were still in place. Here and there they had only to scuff with their boots to turn up a layer of papyrus. This was a city of educated men, of administrators who spoke and worked in the language of diplomacy and business – Coptic for the locals, Greek for the outer world, and later, Latin for the *orbis terrarum*.

What is there about Greek that makes it so immediately attractive? Is it the fact that even if we have not studied it most of the letters are the ones we are accustomed to use in our own alphabet? Has propaganda affected us? Are the huge names sold to us so early, Homer, Plato, Aeschylus, Thucydides, that we are conditioned to bowing down as it were before the altar of an unknown god? For one small boy it was so; and I cannot have been much more than ten when I read my first bit of Greek and was hooked. The phrase is carved above the Pump Room at Bath and you can see it now if you choose. It is, though I did not know this, a phrase from Pindar, *Ariston men hudor*. Well I knew about aristocrats and I was precociously familiar with hydrogen and hydrates and hydroxides so I saw it meant 'Water is best' and an Ancient Greek had spoken to me in his own tongue.

It was Greek mostly that turned up at Oxyrhynchus. Somehow in my mind's eye the scraps of papyrus, ripped in two most of them, as if it was not enough merely to throw away a book but you had to 'kill' it too, just as they 'killed' pots in pyramids by breaking them, the papyrus scraps had acquired an extravagant power as if some form of magic inhered in them; or as if that grace which informs Egyptian goldwork was to be found in next-to-indecipherable ink! Sometimes a scrap of paper was a whole sunburst. It might be Sappho:

Some say the fairest thing on the black earth is a host of horsemen, others of foot, others of ships: but I say the fairest sight of all is the one you love.

And,

161

I remember Anactoria now, far away; whose gracious step and radiant glance I would rather see than the advance of the Lydians and the charge of mounted men in armour.

I was therefore, you may say, in the habit or under the compulsion of remembering a place I had never seen, a kind of Adlesthrop of the mind, haloed Oxyrhynchus. It seemed an instrument through which one could gaze directly back through time.

Yet there is what one might call an inherent absurdity about the place. For the name means 'Sharp-nose', or 'Pike'. When Typhon, whom the Egyptians had called 'Set', had killed Osiris he cut up his body and threw it in the Nile, the grey green river down which we were now moving with our clattering screw. The great religious centres all down the Nile were each organized round a shrine containing a piece of the body. At least this was so in thirteen of the fourteen of the shrines. However, the exotic and complex nature of Egyptian belief is shown in a further detail, for Oxyrhynchus was the fourteenth place and it did not contain a piece of the body, everyone agreed, for the fourteenth piece was the penis of Osiris and a pike had swallowed it! This is why, of course, the place was called 'Pike' and the whole story must have been true because no priest in Oxyrhynchus would eat of the pike, which had become divinely unclean! I had often wondered what the early Christians made of it. There must have been zealots and bigots among them, people willing to cross the river to the eastern cliffs and live in holes in the rock. For them, in the passion of a new belief everything else must have been swept away. For them there would be no elaborate exegesis of the Osiris story. It would be dismissed as a string of pagan obscenities.

There were other Christians about the place as well only they were not zealots and did not live in holes in the rock. We know about them because their traces are to be read in the papyri. It has been said that Christianity was watered by the blood of the martyrs, those who refused to conform. What uneasy people they must have been to have about in that indolent land, people stubborn, anguished, heroic and maddeningly incomprehensible to those who said: 'But *look* ! All you have to do is drop a pinch of incense on the altar of the Divine Augustus! It's really a political gesture – you don't have to *believe* anything!'

It must have been horribly magnificent and sordid. We read on the papyri the other side of the story – read the words of those whose

162

belief was not perfect, those who could not wholly believe they would step through the stroke of the sword or the jaws of the wild beast into paradise. For in the days of the persecutions, when to sacrifice to the Divine Emperor was no more than a way of saying you would obey the law, those suspected of Christianity had to attest their loyalty. We have their attestations from Oxyrhynchus where the pike swallowed the penis.

> To those chosen to superintend the sacrifices at the village of Alexander-Island, from Aurelius Diogenes, the son of Sabatus of the village of Alexander-Island (being about seventy-two years old, a scar on the right eyebrow). It has always been my custom to sacrifice to the gods and now in your presence in accordance with the decrees I have sacrificed and poured libations and tasted the offerings and I request you to counter-sign my statement. May good fortune attend you. I Aurelius Diogenes have made this request.

Then there is the official confirmation and signature below.
'I, Aurelius Syrus, as a participant have certified Diogenes as sacrificing with us.'

Those bleak documents were not all. There are moments recorded from the adventures – one can call it no less – of Messrs Grenfell and Hunt which are brilliantly exciting. One such occurred only on the second day of their excavations. Dr Hunt was the lucky man. He was examining a crumpled piece of papyrus that had been dug out the day before. It contained only a few scarcely legible words. One of them was the Greek word 'karphos' and when he saw it I think he must have begun to tremble from the feet up. For he knew that here was treasure. 'Karphos' is a very rare Greek word and it means a 'mote'. He made out the sentence and though the beginning is lost it read '. . . and then shalt thou see clearly to cast out the mote which is in thy brother's eye.'

It was, as all the world knows now, a part of the *Logia Christou*, (Sayings of Christ) and a document older by hundreds of years than any other New Testament extant. It was thought at the time that these 'Sayings' were extracted from copies of testaments now lost; but modern scholarship inclines to the view that the four gospels were themselves worked up from such collections of 'sayings'.

But whatever the truth of the matter – Egypt must hold many a yet-undiscovered manuscript – these sayings were a prime example for me of the imagined instrument by which I could stare backwards into Time. For I thought, however mistakenly, that the 'Sayings' predated the whole paraphernalia of theological debate, of heresy-hunting, of furious bigotry on one side and cynical dismissiveness on the other. In discussing poetry there is an ultimate argument you can use in defence of a particular poet.

'All the same,' you say, 'he has a voice.'

That is it, then, sounding like the still small voice after the tempest, the unmistakable voice of the man who was supreme poet and teacher, whatever else he may or may not have been.

'Raise the stone and there shalt thou find me, cleave the wood and there am I also.'

The sameness of these two river banks gave me little to do but think. Was this to be fourth time lucky? For the point has to be made again that at the site itself there was nothing to see. The site existed on the map. It was over there to the west, on the fringe of the desert. It would be covered now with drifted sand, the old quarry-like holes of excavation smoothed in with all the rest. My boyhood's dream – ridiculous, ridiculous! – was of walking there and finding a mound which was elastic to the foot, then drawing forth from beneath the sand a full basket and bringing the basket back to 'my' boat and then sorting through. . . .

The things I have found in that basket! At one time it had been the lost works of Sappho and a *mélange* of Greek lyric poets generally. Later still it had been Euripides. A statelier dream had been that of finding what has never been found and probably never will be – a native Egyptian History – since history as we understand the word was invented at a much later date. Sometimes it must be confessed, the manuscripts concerned the first few years of Christianity and these oscillated according to the various states of my belief in that matter. For why should there not be an account of the lost years (Jesus in Egypt) as there might be of the lost years of Shakespeare in Italy or the Low Countries? Why should the boy not journey up from Alexandria – I made him study at the university – looking for a wise man as Socrates had wandered in Greece? What did he think of the pyramids, all gleaming white and smooth, then? Did he ever get as far as the City of the Pike? If he did then I thought he would have eaten fish deliberately as he did later in Palestine. In Cairo you can still be shown the crypt of the synagogue in which the Holy Family sheltered, let alone the two different places in which Moses was drawn from the bulrushes! How far up did he go? Did he walk or ride a donkey? Or did he sail up all the way to Luxor then to Aswan and the beginning of the unknown? So I used to wonder about all the unknown years of that short and unique life. Sometimes, when the whole cycle of Christianity had seemed simply too implausible, a fantasy and a ridiculous one from Adam onwards, in a glum way I would unearth documents which proved him no more than a man or perhaps not even that but only a compilation. What a river it was down which I dreamed my way in the ill-defined boat which had no engine to make it shake! What sights there were, what statuary, what buildings, what Haggardesque temples, what dreadful tombs!

I remember coming to Memphis thousands of years ago in the area opposite where Cairo would be but was yet undreamed of, and for miles the streets were lit with a soft light; and like Odysseus out of sheer curiosity I stole ashore and walked, skin pricking, in the city; for before every door was a small pottery lamp lit so that the whole place shone. But there was no one about. For this was All Souls' night when the dead walk, and the boy who had gone adventurously forth with his bronze sword in his hand fled screaming back to his boat with the terror of the dead around him.

And now we were slapping down a quite different river through a bit of a lop and leaving a long smear of dirty smoke behind us. I brooded for a long time through that chilly afternoon as we moved up on the Oxyrhynchus I knew now I should never see.

15

Once more Shasli got us moving next morning before 6 o'clock. This was not an emergency. It was sheer eagerness on his part to get back to Cairo and find out when his tourist boat would be ready for him. It was evident that he had not found the crew to his liking and his accommodation aboard our small craft had been unsatisfactory to a man of his dignity. Poor man, that same dignity had not allowed him to share the fo'c'sle with the rest of the crew so he had found a variety of sleeping places, a tram perhaps, or the guest room in a village. Once or twice he had slept in the wheelhouse which was shorter from one side to the other than his length and must have been a kind of 'little ease' for him. That could not have helped. Even at Alaa's 'birthday party' he had veered from lofty isolation to ingratiation. He was, after all, in control of the crew to some extent and he was not the sort of man who could be matey one moment and give orders or rebukes the next. It was not really surprising that he wanted the voyage done with as soon as possible. Now, from south of Minya he was aiming at what may be called our home port, the Yacht Club of Ma'adi, south of Cairo but still in the suburbs. We passengers were happy in the thought of baths and that product of western high tech, beautiful loos. I spent the morning jotting down odd scraps of information that I had forgotten to put in my journal. I recorded how during one of our breakdowns, when moored by a reedy bank, a fellah had risen, as it commonly seems they do, out of the earth and shown me one of the reeds saying it was papyrus, but it was not. I had seen papyrus growing in botanical gardens, and, for example, in the Fountain of Arethusa, Syracuse, Sicily. I suppose 'papyrus' has become the common Egyptian word for any riverside reed. It is odd how after nearly two thousand years of complete indifference to any Egyptian history that predated the founding of Islam, a common adjective now known to all was 'pharoni'. In fact anything old at all was now called 'pharoni', even a particularly inadequate wine, which must have been matured for a week or two until it was considered dynastic.

There was no doubt that the closing of the barrages was having an effect. As we sped down the river on our last lap I noticed here and

166

there coigns of the bank which I remembered from passing them on the way up. Here I could see that in mimicry of the old seasonal flood the water was indeed rising. Mud beaches had disappeared. Grass was now sticking out of shallow water. Water buffaloes were half-walking, half-swimming to higher ground. It was a reminder of what Egypt had once been, the river's seasonal orgasm of fertility, now not to be seen again until silt has filled Lake Nasser and men, if there are any left, witness the next 'geological event'. There were small events, too, that had occurred in the apparently eventless countryside. In one area the place seemed served by no animals other than milk-white asses. These, perhaps being frisky by nature, had their forelegs hobbled when not in use; I had seen one being loaded with the usual huge bale together with a medium-sized fellah. Meanwhile his woman held the creature's head. When all was arranged she bent down and unhobbled the forelegs. The ass flung himself free with a single bound and broke into a wild gallop. The woman went base over apex in one direction, the bale and the fellah flew off in the other. The milk-white ass galloped into a field of beans and disappeared. Then, as so often, though our progress had seemed slow before, now it seemed too fast and before we could see what had happened we were past and gone.

I added a note to my cherished understanding of the river and its traffic. In this rainless area since the air is dry there is less weight in the wind for a given speed. That is why sailing boats on the Nile can set a larger area of sail than would be possible for the same waterlength in a wetter climate. I thought it possible that the extraordinarily tattered old mainsails they wore were not a sign of poverty so much as frugality. Why use a good sail in light airs when you can make do with a worn out one? I thought that possibly after we left and the summer advanced, with the hot *Khamsin* really blasting from the southwest, the traffic would not stop but set new white sails that would hold the wind without splitting. Then there would be high jinks and white bow-waves on the river and those ferries would need more than an inch of freeboard!

The generally held view of the Nile – *no* – *my* preconception of the Nile had given it a muddy bottom. How should it not be after those ages of seasonal silt? I had been wrong. Wherever I saw boatmen poling their boats along as they sometimes did not only close to the bank but out in midstream they had been shoving against something harder than mud. Once, when we had been swept on to a reef, our engine dead for lack of fuel, I had seen a lightish-coloured bottom rise nastily to within a foot or so of the surface. Indeed, with the soupy Nile water and the then light, I could not have seen it at all through more than a foot of water. Again, as we knew from bitter experience, a boat going aground in the Nile does not slither to a stop. She hits with a jarring crash and if she does so after that, does so in a series of bumps. It may be that in days when each year brought down inches of silt the river did in fact have a muddy bottom. But even if the silt did still come down, the current, now kept to a relatively narrow channel by the control exercised on it by the high dam, has scoured it clean. The Nile seems to have some kind of hard pan down there. It cannot be rock, so high in the canyon! It must be rafts of gravel, or sand, or boulders, all now concreted and rock hard. It would not be easy to anchor in midstream and we had never seen it done. The grapnel that Shasli had begged from a tourist boat had been used to make a shoreline fast, had been dug into a mud beach or bank and never dropped in the water. After all, the bank is always within half a mile at most and if you break down, what with the interplay of wind and current let alone the assistance of a passing tram and pirate you don't need to.

It was a mixed morning. When I could no longer remember things for odd jottings I tended to brood on the difference between anticipation and actuality. Common sense told me that if the two had been identical I need not have undertaken this journey at all but could have written the whole thing comfortably at home. On the other hand it was arguable that I had imprisoned myself in a boat rather than set myself free to do whatever I wanted wherever I wanted, had crawled hundreds of miles along this ditch in both directions with most of Egypt reduced to two banks so high you could rarely see over them. By not taking the trouble to learn more than a fraction of the language I had condemned myself to receive processed and filtered information. True, my forehead was minimally more brazen. I did dare to ask questions. I could now look the crew in the eye instead of smiling uneasily in their direction out of a sense of the false position I had put myself in by having no authority; or been put in. Perhaps, I thought, now I am about to return to a car – the westerner's natural home – things will be different!

We were back in red brick country where every few hundred yards the chimneys of kilns smoked away and the red brick came down to and tumbled into the river where the sandals waited. It was depressing to realize how much good earth was being hardened irretrievably into brick and how the rash of building with all the wrong angles would continue to spread. I suspected now that I had identified Egypt's prime difficulty. It was indifference, *malesh*, don't bother to complete a job because it is impossible to complete it and in any case it doesn't matter.

I suspected that the Secretary General's 'bricks' not yet built but *remaining to be built* out of desert sand were a mirage. As for the mud brick arches for the fellaheen, no one would use them, for when you got down to it, except for the rare bird like Hassan Fathy – were there any others? – no one would bother.

It was just about then that I received the news that the crew's loo had packed up finally which was why we were moving towards the western bank. We made fast, of course, in a brickyard. Out went the gangplank, down tramped all the crew. With the exception of Shasli they were dressed western style, ready for the sophisticated living of the metropolis. They wandered about, looking for cover. Shasli simply beamed in the general direction of the boat, spread his skirts, was tented and contented. It occurred to me that I was not helping the rest by staring at the brickyard out of our window. I withdrew abruptly and struck my head, hit the base of my skull. Ann made soothing noises while I swore.

'Base of the skull?' said Ann. 'That's where people are always being struck by a blunt instrument. You do it with a boat.'

I was reminded of something else. Oxyrhynchus now lay behind us. Did it matter? *Malesh*.

The crew returned much more cheerful than their expedition would seem to warrant. I canvassed the centre cabin for breakfast, a meal which I was gradually discovering is a very late importation into Egyptian comprehension. Saïd was in the kitchen area. What would I like then?

I knew that to ask for eggs and bacon was asking for the moon. I managed in my kitchen Arabic to ask if we could have coffee and bread and butter and marmalade. There was, however, no marmalade. It had been popular with the crew. There was no jam. I did not know the word for honey. I therefore stuck my thumbs in my ears, and waggled my fingers as fast as I could, meanwhile making a buzzing noise. Saïd looked staggered for a moment or two, then he burst. He became a real Nubian who has found a joke. He took it into his body and soul. He howled with laughter until the tears streamed down his black face. I returned to our cabin wondering what would happen next. Presently there was a tap at the door. It was Saïd with our breakfast. He was still grinning; but miraculously standing among the pile of Arab bread, was a small pot of honey.

So with coffee and bread and honey we slid past the gleaming quarry of Tura and watched the awful suburbs of Cairo with its high-rises for workmen come inexorably nearer. It was desirable but not really welcome. It was welcome but not really desirable.

I learned *why* we had missed Oxyrhynchus again. The nearest town to the site is Beni Mazar, ten miles from it on the river. The ten miles did not matter for we could have hired a taxi, there being a road. But Alaa, to whom I had not confided my inexplicable desire to see a place where there was nothing to see, had asked Shasli to moor us away from the river police! So, somehow all things had not come together. *Malesh, malesh* better that basket of the mind.

Ann and I busied ourselves packing. We loaded the waste-paper bag with good bad books and a couple of bad bad books. I took the ugly pottery heads we had bought from the tourist kiosk in El Minya and shoved them in among the litter of bottles and tins in the galley. I did not like to throw them in the Nile but they were too heavy to take home by air. We were badly enough off as it was, for luggage space.

We got into Ma'adi at about midday. I went round, giving the crew presents of money since we were not in a position to give them anything else. They seemed friendly and regretful, told us that they would willingly come with us again 'next time'. Saïd, wise and happy old man, grasped both my hands in his and said with profound seriousness:

'English troubles all long time away.'

We waited for the owner of the boat, Dr Hamdi. When he came I gave him a rundown of the virtues and vices of the boat, which must have been useful. The way to find out what needs doing to a boat is to give it plenty of exercise and we had certainly done that. Then transport was provided for us by Alaa's extended family. We drove to our hotel through Cairo rush-hour traffic, which has not much to do with the rhythm of the Nile or any other kind of rhythm. In Cairo the only way to stay alive in traffic is to be just as crazy as everyone else.

Anyone who has ever unpacked after a month or two in a boat will know what a mess we were in. Indeed, one of the troubles when you have lived out of suitcases is not so much to identify laundry and get it done as to identify the few things that don't seem to be dirty. You end, generally, by bundling the lot irrespective into a laundry bag and hoping what you have on will last you until the rest comes back. Of course in Egypt laundry does not take long. If the practitioners of the ancient art of washing clothes knew what possibilities of delay are inherent in the transaction I have no doubt they would perform exquisite delicacies of procrastination but fortunately they don't. The sun is always there so washing-by-return seems as natural to them as provision of umbrellas to us. Even so, the larger hotels, mindful of their international status, have managed to extend the period artificially and a fellah and wife will do the job faster in the country than a steam laundry in the city. I have always been faintly suprised to find myself how pleasant cleanliness is, for the detailed cleanliness which civilization has come to demand is not only boringly repetitive but is also unnatural. I would not go so far as to stand up and be counted with Dr Johnson, who declared that he had no great love of clean linen, but I am, for example, unable to see why advertisements can talk about restoring the natural oils to a body after insisting that you wash off your own. In any case the human body and any other body is such a continent of warring tribes, of infestations and defenders, of symbiotic creatures that go unheeded because they are so small they go unnoticed, of near-autonomous congregations all working on our behalf by a self-regarding benefaction there seems little point in demanding a physical purity which at best is notional. So I at least, as far as my own crumpled linen was concerned was content to be led by the nose and continued to regard clothes as wearable so long as I could not smell them. This set us free to elaborate the transition from ship to shore. It seemed reasonable to do this by treating Cairo itself as if it were some place to be investigated – we had, after all, landed there. We would spend the rest of the day – one foot still at sea, one foot on shore – trying to find some observations that might be regarded as new, interesting and helpful to the traveller. In this respect, unfortunately for me, Cairo has been worked over year by year and inch by inch. So we set out with Alaa into deepest Cairo much as an English botanist, an amateur one at that, would enter a Sussex woodland and hope to find a species of plant that nobody had ever noticed before. We went straight to the most touristy bit of all, the bazaar. We had tea in an alley which every tourist will remember because it is what you expect. The difference was that we were the only tourists present and listened as we waited to an extraordinary old woman talking to some

171

dozen or so young Egyptian men, who were enthralled. They grinned or laughed every now and then. The old woman wore the costume of the country but her face was uncovered.

I whispered to Alaa.

'What's it all about?'

He was looking embarrassed. I felt certain we had stumbled on some revolutionary activity or its equivalent in Egypt, overt feminism.

'Come on, Alaa! Is she attacking the government?'

'I don't understand it!'

'That's Arabic, isn't it?'

Frowning and unwilling, he answered me.

'She is telling dirty stories.'

The young men burst into loud laughter then listened eagerly again. I watched this incomprehensible Scheherazade. She was, I suppose, in her sixties. She wore much jewellery, rings and bracelets and anklets. Earrings depended beneath the veil, which did not cover her hair. If that jewellery was not costume jewellery then it was very expensive indeed. It was only the second time in Egypt that I had seen a woman wear anklets. Presently she got up and walked away. The young men dispersed.

'Explanations, please.'

'It's too complicated.'

We drank tea. Except for us, this tourist area was deserted. I suggested that a simple thing to do would be to get out of the tourist area by drawing a beeline towards a poor quarter and sticking to it, for what does he know of Cairo who only the bazaar knows? Alaa agreed and took us into a side alley only a few yards from the first one and lighted by no more than a crack of sky. It was a cobbled alley with no sidewalks and lined mostly with blank wall. The few openings seemed to lead into small cellar-like spaces where equally small businesses were being carried on. In one a man was filing a piece of metal. In another two men were working over a pile of camel skin. In yet another a man was mending a small lathe. As we passed, each man spoke to Alaa. When we reached the end of the alley at a T-junction I asked him what they said.

'In general they told me I should not have brought you down here. I am – how would you put it – letting down the image of Cairo. I should have kept you in the other alley.'

'Where the old woman was.'

'Yes.'

'But I like this better than the other alley!'

Alaa nodded, glumly, I thought.

'I guessed as much.'

We walked back into the tourist area, crossed it and emerged on the other side. Somewhere or other I remembered I had read that archeologists had decided, perhaps in the sort of 'fun' which might be expected from them, that just as you can identify various eras of civilization by the type of pottery which turns up in an excavation, so now in England you can identify the Victorian Age by the blue-and-white willow-pattern fragments of china.

'Alaa, if you ever undertake again the job of bear-leading the ignorant round this city, or if it comes to that any other city in Egypt I give you for free a piece of information which will interest them and what is more make them feel you have lifted one corner of the veil that protects the tourist from real life. Wherever you see the head of Nefertiti that is a tourist area. Where you don't it isn't. What is more you can suggest to the tourist that if he can find one of those heads that includes her diseased eye you – or perhaps I – will present a ten pound note to the next person who looks as if he could do with it.'

'In the mean time,' said Ann, 'have neither of you noticed the real difference between the city and the tourist area? It's staring you in the face.'

I looked round. Alaa looked round. It was obvious that the people weren't tourists, but that was all.

'I pass.'

'How many Egyptian women did you see in the tourist area?'

It was true. We had seen just the one old woman. Otherwise there had not been a woman in sight. But here, not a hundred yards away there were more women than men. We really were gathering genuine information, though useless. We have, I said to myself, and then out loud to the others in a suitable jargon, 'We have identified an interface.'

How about that for splendour of language, precision, penetration, abstraction, and objectivity? We stood on the street corner, laughing at the ingenuity and particularity of words which by happenstance can illuminate a situation and at the same time ensure it is given the precise degree of importance of which it is worthy. We were so happy with our interface! *There* the olive-skinned men lounged in western suits. *Here*, the wrapped women bargained, cheapened cloth, bought and sold, were busy – busier by far than those caryatid and leisurely figures we had seen so often pacing down to the river under a clay or flashing pot. Nor were their clothes as colourful, but brown and black or sometimes a dull green. Here and there, though, young or youngish women threaded their way through the crowd in a very slight modification of western dress. Their skirts would be calf-length. Their faces would be uncovered but void of visible make-up, even the eyes. They wore as a veil some filmy stuff that covered but did not hide their hair. It seemed a gesture in the direction of something.

I asked Alaa. He nodded.

'That is true. It means they accept Islam but in an Egyptian way, which is very modified.'

We came then to a gate. I wouldn't know it again if I heard its name. There was an elegant building just inside, disused now. This was a water station. In the days when Cairo had existed only inside these gates the building had been set up just inside the gate so that travellers entering there could stop and drink. It was another sign of the civilization which had had so much to offer Europe had it not been for those miserable clashes of interest and belief. There was a mosque at the gate and we took off our shoes and went in, to stare up at the inside of a magnificent tower where the pendentives of the squinches hung like tree moss in a tropical forest. We examined the gate itself but declined an invitation to climb on the wall.

Outside the gate we passed at once from medieval to modern with traffic to be dodged and crowds hurrying to catch buses. We plunged then into a kind of high tunnel between wooden-walled houses where the ground floors were occupied by small, open shops. It was dark and uncrowded, casual, a good place to take the weight off one's feet. Ann went into a shop where men were making cushion covers. I wandered off while she watched this handicraft. Near the end of the tunnel I found a blanket hung up outside a shop that did in fact have a rather grotesque version of the head of Nefertiti appliquéd to it. I persuaded myself that it was a sport, the exception that proved the rule, an example of cultural back-breeding.

We wanted a loo so Alaa found us what was appropriate in a third class hotel. According to tourist lore it should have been unbearably dirty but it wasn't. Or at least it was no dirtier than a third-class hotel anywhere else. The only drawback was that damned Egyptian utility music, now turned expertly into Musak, the curse of our electronic society. Moreover Egyptians like any noise as loud as possible and of course Musak lends itself to sheer exhibitionism in the matter of decibels. Still, quiet is the most modern of luxuries and you can't get it except at vast expense. In Cairo you can get something approximating to quiet in a mosque; but what a world in which to listen to silence you have to take your boots off!

Alaa, shouting through the Musak, told us there was another interface which we had not experienced: the ultimate drabness of the concrete city, high-rise after high-rise, piled-up tenements where the people gained nothing. They lost the group-living which is so precious to Egyptians where each person finds his identity, even when he does not like it. I replied that by and by we would experience this interface for the security of knowing what we were talking about in Cairene terms though really it wasn't necessary. Any big city would show the same.

There was another part of the city that I did not much want to see because I had done so years before and once was enough. The massive flooding of fellaheen into the city has swollen the population beyond the capacity even of the tenements to absorb it. So in their tens of thousands the migrating people had taken over and now lived in the vast Muslim cemetery, as if the squatters of our own country should set up houses in Highgate Cemetery. But when I put this point Alaa told me it was nowhere as bad as I thought, though it was bad enough. I had thought, when I saw the children playing football among the tombs where their parents lived, that the decaying bodies must be part of a hideous township, but it was not so. Every vault was securely underground since the bodies of the faithful, whether it be king or commoner must be buried wrapped but uncoffined in the earth: 'Then shall the dust return to the earth as it was. . . .'

The buildings, therefore, which the squatters have turned into undesirable residences of a township, are those set up for the guardians; small houses for those who tended and prayed at the graves. I thought we could do without a second visit, or might drive through it swiftly by car.

Then after a little more wandering we went to a restaurant, the name of which is familiar to every expatriate though I have forgotten it myself. It appears to be constructed entirely of bamboo, if that is sufficient for purposes of identification. I chose a vegetable casserole, supposing this to be a dish without meat, toying meanwhile with what the Greeks would call 'mezethes', I don't know the Arabic.

When the casserole came it proved to be fifty per cent meat, which defeated me. Still, the place was cheerful and cosmopolitan even by Cairene standards.

I ought to add that Cairo resembles an Egyptian village in at least one way. It subscribes to the higher untidiness. I don't mean litter (though there is much of that) and I don't mean dirt. I mean that the narrow street that joins two broader ones is likely to be heaped with rubble as though a house has collapsed; and you may find on inquiry that that is precisely what has happened. You have to inquire, for the fall of a house, as in ancient Rome, is so common an occurrence that it passes unnoticed except by those personally interested. You come across heaps of wall-plaster, old boarding, a few tiles, cardboard boxes and anonymous bits of material which give the whole mass an aspect of dirt which it does not deserve. It isn't dirt. It's débris and that is different. For the dirt of Cairo is specific. It is a direct result of a defect unknown in the villages. They have no drainage system, Cairo has. It is so old and designed for so much smaller a city that it has collapsed. In any street you are likely enough to see the broad, wet patch which is nothing more or less than sewage.

Lacking a sewerage system, employment of a simple pit dug in porous soil keeps the untidy villages clean. Employment of an inadequate sewerage system keeps Cairo, untidy at the best of times, subject to explosive disasters of dirt. The stories – and let us hope they are apocryphal – are hideous.

Meditating on all this with the hardihood of a man who has spent something like a month in a boat with an inadequate loo, I toyed with my meat and ate what vegetables I could find.

And then it was time for bed.

16

We set off early next morning in Alaa's car, which was better than Bassem's but not much better. Nevertheless, we did not propose to misuse it so drastically. We were to make an expedition to the Fayoum, which is not quite an oasis but very nearly. On the map the Fayoum looks simple enough; a green bulge hanging on the side of the green snake which is the Nile Valley. There is a lake in the Fayoum, natural in origin perhaps but site of the vast reservoir which the early pharaohs had constructed there. It is possible that the Bahr Yusuf runs in the bed of an early river which cannot be counted as one of the Niles because the beds are different. It may have been a river that flowed into the Qattara Depression; or perhaps there was a river joining all the oases of the Western Desert and this was a tributary; so that in effect, Joseph's Canal was an improvement on nature in the sense that a river was turned into a canal of controllable water. Even now, Bahr Yusuf leaves the main river more than a hundred miles south, between Mallawi and Minya and wanders along by the Western Desert to end in the Fayoum at Birket Qarun, the ancient reservoir. You can approach the Fayoum from the south and stay among green fields all the way; but we proposed to go north about, through the desert. That road goes from Giza, leads past the pyramids and strikes out into the howling wilderness. It is the Sahara and it looks flatter than the Eastern Desert because you are only able to see about one-thousandth of the way across, there being three thousand or more miles of rock and sand between where the pyramids are and the shore of the Atlantic Ocean. So to say whether it is flatter than the Eastern Desert or not is a bit of sheer local impertinence; but it looks flatter and as far as the Fayoum is concerned remains that way. So we drove then into this flat or flattish area of sun and sand, orangey white and brown, where power lines looped from pylon to pylon endlessly and the desert was marked or pock-marked all over with purposes of an ineluctable kind with here and there evidence more interpretable of men. There were disturbed sites on the horizon. Alaa said they were desert cities and intended to syphon off the surplus population from the green valley. But once again the government was at a stand because no one would

177

go. Nor, I thought, would I! If ever there were places built for the damned these are they. It seemed so demonstrably fatuous to expect to settle there without compulsion or enormous bribery, that knowing now their propensity to shift whole populations without a by-your-leave, I had instant suspicions of the government. But if to force people into such a position would be criminal, to invite them there would be ridiculous. It was a puzzle.

Then we came to a camp among the pylons and it looked occupied.

'What is it? A prison?'

'I think,' said Alaa carefully, 'it is a camp for police.'

'But there's nothing out here *to* police!'

'Training. Training special police. You know. For riots.'

'Riot police?'

'On the French pattern. All very civilized.'

We dropped the topic. Now a dark line appeared on the horizon. It was the descent to the shallow Fayoum and its green fields. Here and there in the desert were buildings and a set of ruins that might have been of archeological interest in a country not over supplied, as Egypt is, with archeological sites. Then there was a trickle of water running through the desert towards the Fayoum but interrupted before it got there. There were greenhouses. It was, we saw, the *Institute for the Multiplication of Mango and Olive Trees*. It consisted of four greenhouses and one small wooden office. The trickle of water ran close by it, one of the few trickles that arise in the desert. We stopped and went in, I walking behind my new brazen forehead. The place was run by a European, a Doctor of Science, a botanist. He had an Egyptian graduate assistant. They seemed surprised that anyone should be interested. They showed us around. We inspected thousands of seedlings, all rigidly controlled and all healthy. It was one of those modern establishments where, as they say, plants are not so much grown as manufactured. Here they were using the latest method of multiplication, 'meristemming', which relies on the apparently magical capacity of a single cell from the growing tip of a seedling to divide and grow into the complete organism in the right conditions. At one point, the individual cells have to 'tumble' in a solution of nutrient otherwise the whole process doesn't work.

It was impressive and I said so.

The doctor spoke abruptly.

'All the same. I'm leaving next week.'

178

'You sound as if you mean "leaving for good".'
'That's right.'
'Who will take your place?'
'Nobody. Him. My Egyptian assistant.'
The young graduate assistant spoke.
'Egypt needs one million olive trees. There is ground everywhere on the edges of cultivation which is suitable for olives.'
The doctor nodded.
'Yes. The land is there all right. Nothing simpler.'
'And he will grow them? This young man? You?'
The assistant shook his head.
'I do not think so.'
The doctor took up the explanation.
'The science side is okay. It can be done. Could be done. And the minister – *he*'s all right. He wants me to have a free hand – wanted me to. He believes in this place. He wants Egypt to have her million olive trees – think of it! An industry as big and bigger, healthier, more valuable than sugar!'
'Well, why not?'
'You don't know Egypt, do you?'
'No.'
'The bureaucracy. It's . . . a pyramid, as old and as immovable. No matter what the minister says or tries to do, somewhere in the pyramid the order dies, is lost. I am quite simply giving up. After years and years, I am giving up and going home.'
'What will happen to the institute?'
'This young man will try to run it, God help him.'
The Egyptian assistant shook his head. He spoke in his careful English.
'It will be too much for me. When the doctor goes, I shall go.'
'Where?'
He shrugged. The doctor took up the conversation.
'It's beaten me. The country I mean, I came full of enthusiasm. To help. A Third World country – It would be *so* simple! Nature, you see? It's a kind of stagnation.'
'And the Institute?'
'Are you familiar with the desert?'
'No.'
'There are relics everywhere. Dry. Weathered. Sand-blasted. *Malesh. Mafish. Afwaen.*'

179

'I. . . .'

'You see it's how you get to feel.'

'Well. . . .'

It seemed silly to wish anyone good luck or pay compliments to the obvious dedication that had set up and maintained this plant factory in the desert. In the end we did a lot of shrugging at each other and came away.

'Motoring up the Nile by water, driving up the bloody Nile by road, driving out into the desert to have a look round, seeing a temple or two, being whimsical, making a book full of pretty pictures with a load of irrelevant writing. . . .'

'There, there. Calm down. What did you expect? And you know, the Nubians just *might* get their road.'

'And their olive trees, I don't think!'

'I,' said Ann in a positive way, 'shall let this whole business of the olive trees get an airing.'

'You?'

'I. Me.'

'This,' said Alaa, 'I long to hear.'

The Fayoum is bigger than it looks on the map. It is the size of an average English county. You do actually go down into it from the desert; you approach first a grey-green line which broadens, unfolds, becomes a brighter green and then you are quite suddenly in a land that seems even more fertile than the Nile Valley. Our ancient friend the Bahr Yusuf ends here and the Birket Qarun is a sizeable lake lying up against some low hills to the northwest. I had wanted to identify yet another site where papyri had been found, El Hammam on the south shore of the lake, so we drove slowly along to the west, skirting the water. There were rowing boats drawn up in rows or moored just offshore and these were brilliantly painted like the rowing boats of Upper Egypt rather than the Delta or Middle Egypt. They made a pretty picture in the sun, but no one seemed to be using them. Perhaps the fishing had to wait for new water to be led down the canal and into the lake. The land did not seem to have more than a general relationship to the map. We looked for a bay where there was only a straight line of shore. Where there had been, according to the map, something of a headland with El Hammam on it, there was a group of buildings set back against a straight line of shore. The truth dawned on us. The lake has shrunk year by year, land has been reclaimed and El Hammam, once on the shore of the lake was now well inland. Not that it mattered as far as I was concerned after all. I was as capable of talking about Fayoum papyri after a non-visit as before it. That is to say, I should, like everybody else at some point, discourse on the extraordinary insight into daily life, the vivid immediacy of the words that emerged from sand and soil, the contracts, love letters, business, lust, love, household minutiae, ignorance and learning, law, war, childhood. . . .

> Theon to Theon his Father greeting. That was a fine trick you played, not taking me to Alexandria! If you refuse to take me along with you to Alexandria I won't write you a letter or speak to you or wish you health. Mummy said to Archelaus 'The boy gets on my nerves – take him away!' So send for me, please, please! If you don't send I won't eat, won't drink. So there! I pray for your health.

You can quote from them endlessly, letter to a man in debt, letter of expostulation, invitation to a party, to a festival, to a funeral, deed of divorce, marriage contract. . . . There is a letter of consolation, pre-Christian and bleak:

> Irene to Taonnophris greetings. I was as much grieved and wept over the dead as ever I did over Didymus. I did everything that was fitting and so did all who were with me. But truly there is nothing anyone can do in the face of such things. So do you comfort one another. Farewell.

Pre-Christian? Modern, perhaps. Post-Christian?

Come to think of it that one was actually from Oxyrhynchus, but what of it? You need a Sir Thomas Browne to deal mellowly with these very partial resurrections, and seeing that the *Institute for the Multiplication of Mango and Olive Trees* is laying down a correspondence every bit as human and vital and illuminating one need not make too much of the fact that the ancients suffered as much as we. The day-to-day material from the rubbish baskets of ancient Egypt seems to speak most clearly the trite observation that all men must die. To contemplate the spectrum of literacy that emerges from the sands of Egypt – from a census return, through a play by Euripides to a lyric by Sappho – is to discover in oneself a new respect for literature and a new evaluation of its purpose as life-proclaiming and life-enhancing.

North of El Hammam at the limit of the reclaimed land was a pile of buildings that looked like a fort with a lighthouse on top. We found some of our old acquaintances the river police here, silted up as it were at this 'lonely outpost'. They were even raggeder than their fellows of the main stream, on duty at the furthest end of the Bahr Yusuf, where pirates were to seek and one supposed that no one ever came. Even their rifles were silted up and should have been in a museum. I swear they dated from the nineteenth century and had not been cleaned for some years, probably for fear that they would fall to pieces. If fired, I judged they would be dangerous fore and aft. So we turned away, left them guarding nothing in particular and drove into the richly fertile countryside. But before we got there we crossed an intermediate area, either just dried out or officially reclaimed, and this area was so thick with salt it was glitteringly white. Salt is the bane of Egypt and rises from deep down. There is a method, if your engineers are good enough, of so draining the land that salt is flushed out of it. Indeed, during the best years of Egyptian irrigation all the Nile water that flowed into the Mediterranean was salt-flushed into low ditches mile by mile and drained away so that the fields had nothing given them but sweet water while the sea, which could cope with it, took the salt. For the salt is rising everywhere since the high dam was built and the whole land not so amply flushed. It is eating, to take an example, at the lower stones of the Temple of Luxor and making a bad joke of reclamation. The archeologists of Chicago House are working against time to keep a record of the temple before the salt eats it.

All the same, the Fayoum seems to be a favoured area of Egypt, bar some small stretches such as we had seen by the shore of Birket Qarun. It does not seem to have the profound and muddy squalor of life just inland from the Mediterranean nor the confined and overspecific life of the narrower valley. It is ample, spreads. Ann was the first to notice that uniquely (for Egypt) in the Fayoum the inhabitants have space to give to flowers. There is a degree of dignity in the housing which speaks of lives long established in relative comfort rather than lived hand-to-mouth for generation after generation. There is substance in the buildings. We visited some famous springs round which a 'pleasaunce' has been organized – I can think of no other word since it is not a park. You pay for admission and though prettily enough arranged it is very small. The day we were there the place was crowded with students. The girls seized on our Minder and demanded to be photographed with him for reasons which may have been sufficient to them but which escaped me. The standard of health and dress seemed to be higher here than anywhere else in Egypt. There were many villas. It was in some sense *bougainvillaea* country with all the marker implies. *They say* that bilharziasis has been eradicated from the Fayoum which implies even more for the province than *bougainvillaea*. The whole area is densely populated but so bursting with greenery the people are hidden by it.

We came to the city of El Fayoum itself, which was once sacred to the crocodile god Sobek so the Greeks called it Crocodilopolis. It was here, I seem to remember, that other tourist – a bit of a VIP – fed cakes to crocodiles. He was a Roman senator and we have the letter ordering preparations to be made for his reception. He was coming through to see the sights so guest chambers must be got ready, he must be met with gifts – a custom that has endured – and provided with scraps to feed to the sacred crocodiles. Perhaps after all he wasn't a tourist but a prospective ruler.

El Fayoum is a busy city with road, water and rail connections to the main valley of Egypt. It seemed to me to be less heaped with débris than Cairo and less dreary than Asyut. Tourists don't go there since Sobek has gone. In El Fayoum itself a more interesting sight and sound is the multiple waterwheel. A tiny park has been constructed round this at the centre of the city. It consists of four undershot waterwheels placed side by side and linked. They deal with some of the water which enters the province by way of Joseph's Canal. Since the city lies in the centre of the great depression, or more accurately on a small rise or *tell* at the centre of it, the wheel lies just below street level. There is much noisy traffic in the complex of streets round the wheel, which is a pity since the most curious thing about the machine is the sound it makes. It – or should I say 'they?' – they, then, revolve slowly. Silver skeins of water drop down through their elaborate mechanism and it may be that these chime on themselves or the metal of the structure, but they are not heard. The wheels, however, exhibit what can only be called the capacity for just being able to move, as one might suppose Heracles only just managed to hold the sky up for a bit. As they do so they make a complication of sound as if each wheel bears its individual part. It is a groaning, whining, creaking, whistling, screeching discord which would be horrible if that were all. But it is not. The noise seems always on the very verge of concord or even melody as if, given just

one tiny further impetus, one last heave, it would manage against all
the odds of the universe to sing. The sound, close up to your ear, yet
distant, contradicting your experience because distancing itself,
gives you the impression that this is not something happening here,
close by, but out there where there are stars and things and this is a
suggestion of their music. Meanwhile the silver skeins waver and
drop and the parping traffic drowns out just that last resolution into
concord so that you never hear it. This, oddly enough, seems the
richness of water dripping and splattering as the great wheels groan
and gasp and do I cannot tell what – produce electricity or grind corn
or perhaps do nothing but just succeed in getting their own unoiled
weight to revolve like the cloudless heavens. But we drove away and
left it, still groaning and wailing; which I suppose it is doing as you
read this.

We drove on south towards the narrow entrance/exit of the
depression. We passed the guarding pyramids of Hawara and El
Lahun and the desert came in on both sides. We crossed Joseph's
Canal, that great work which became complex with all kinds of weir
and barrage and bridge just where it entered the province, and I at
least said goodbye to it with some regret, supposing I should not see
it again. I am convinced it is in fact Joseph's Canal, a great work
worthy of a pharaoh and worthy of one with the good sense to make
Joseph his vizier. Going up and down Egypt you come more and
more to a feeling for the logic of that canal, feeding the vast reservoir
of the Fayoum as it did in days when men had hardly got over the
cultural shock of Writing.

So, having traversed the Fayoum from north to south we turned
north again along the main stream of the Nile. On this road you have
the Nile on your right and the desert on your left; and for between
twenty and thirty miles the edge of the desert exhibits a series of
pyramids. For us it was a strange contrast; the days we had taken in
the boat, pushing south against the current, lucky to make four or
five miles an hour over the ground, and now, doing the same stretch
at fifty miles an hour.

Our next designed stop was to be the pyramid of El Meidum. It
had been an object I had wanted to see from close by because you
could say it is the only pyramid to have suffered a disaster and quite
possibly been improved by it. According to received opinion, most of
the pyramid collapsed in one go. The result is that it is no longer
pyramid-shaped but resembles the pedestal for a statue. Of course, it

would not be possible to construct a colossus to the same scale, at least one free-standing. I suppose the Sphinx might well crouch up there out of cannon shot and so stare from a bearded and unblemished face clean across the Nile to the Eastern Desert? But unstatued, the thing is more impressive for my money than any other pyramid. Perhaps it speaks to me because I am a child of my generation and century and we no longer hope for the whole truth. It is the informing movement, the brave attempt, the suggestion, the remnant that moves us. So the pyramid of El Meidum, huge even by the scale of Giza yet heaped round by its own ruins, is more to our taste and a surer invitation to our curiosity.

We turned off on a side road, then, when the vast shape invited. We drove twisting along a banked-up road until we reached the desert. There seemed to be a track over the sand so we took it. We passed holes that had held prehistoric 'crouched' burials. There were modern Islamic or Christian tombs; and after that a great area of flat sand and black flakes of shale about half a mile from the pyramid. It was clear that something unusual was up. On the southwest corner of the monument the débris from the early collapse had been peeled down, newly revealing many courses of crudely shaped limestone. Forty or fifty Egyptians – fellaheen with a *Reis* controlling them – were scraping away and hurrying the sand down to reveal yet more which no one had seen for the last few thousand years. Evidently massive archeology was come to Meidum. However, the human figures gave us a scale and, of course, inevitably, we found that the figures looked like ants. You can't say anything else.

But how beautiful the building is! The layers that fell away have revealed what I suppose must be called the core of the pyramid. But this core has sides more nearly vertical than is commonly thought to be a pyramid angle. *That* work is clean and clearcut as a crystal. Indeed, you feel as you look that the layers that fell were some kind of husk or integument or wrapping which at a given and surely significant signal had collapsed all together. How the dust must have gone storming up! How the falling rock must have thundered! For sure, a god would keep that apparent catastrophe for a great occasion! Staring across at it and fiddling incompetently with my camera I thought that it seemed like a moment of myth made visible. Moses should have stretched out his staff towards it; or when a god was so intolerant and cruel as to slay every firstborn throughout Egypt, the layers should have fallen in disgust and despair. Then, when the thunder had rolled away towards Sinai and the dust had sifted down, the last trickle of fragments ceased among the fallen stone, the crystal had stood there, perfect and not a shape anyone had expected, like a newly discovered and eternal fact.

As far as I know, the pyramid of Meidum – built it is now decided for Pharaoh Huni – is the only pyramid to have *done* anything other than weather slowly. After all, objects of that size and shape have little enough capacity for spontaneous action. There is a certain even tenor, an uneventful sameness about the long existence of a pyramid that makes Meidum and its evident catastrophe even more remarkable. Apart from that, the whole structure, rose-red brick core, off-white limestone on a foundation of desert colour against a pale blue sky is eminently satisfying. Man made the phenomenon. But nature, gravity, temperature change, rain, time and desuetude took over. The result is subtler in simple beauty than anything that ever came from a brush. At last I had seen in Egypt an ancient monument which not merely met my expectations and anticipations but surpassed them.

So having looked too little and photographed too much in the modern manner we climbed back into Alaa's car and drove towards the pyramid across the sand and black shale. Before we got close we were intercepted by a 'guardian' and a tourist policeman, who angrily forbade us to take the photographs that were now in our cameras. They explained that any photograph of the pyramid was forbidden – any photograph!

It was odd. We supposed the archeologists had declared that pictures of their discoveries were forbidden and the ignorant tourist police had interpreted this prohibition more widely than had been intended. For the pyramid is visible for ten miles in every direction, the dig itself for two or three miles and there is no way in which you can be prevented from photographing that object, impressive even when it is on the horizon. So we came away, defiantly photographing and descended to the valley again. Then we drove towards Cairo, the various pyramids revealing themselves to us in the car and on the highroad as they had not done when we were at low water level in the boat. There is one pyramid which may show a reaction to Meidum's sudden outburst (I don't *want* to be a pyramid – I want to be a pedestal!). This is the 'bent' pyramid, in which the angle changes on the way up so that the whole shape is rhomboidal. One theory is that this pyramid, built for the successor to Huni, was under construction when the pyramid of Meidum shed its covering. It may have been taken as a hint and the angle of the bent pyramid changed as a result, to make the thing more stable. What a row of monuments they are – even the ruined and destroyed ones! They hung over the ancient city of Memphis – named from them – like palaces of the next world. They must have entered popular tradition in a thousand ways now lost to us. Nor, it seems, were they the ruinous burdens that it might appear. They may have been a form of relief work during the flood season when people had little to do but sit the time out, twiddling their thumbs. Certainly the greatest of them all, the pyramid of Cheops is anonymous in the sense that there is no inscription giving it to him. In fact his name only occurs on a block of stone tucked away in the body of the building and it seems to have been a workman's scrawl. Truly, the various pyramids must remain a source of controversy and conjecture, not just because there is a lack of hard evidence about them but because we cannot put ourselves back into the states of mind of those people so distant in time from us, either ruling or ruled.

So we came back to Cairo and its modern traffic, Alaa exhausted by driving and we exhausted by a very full day's seeing. The business of getting anything down in my journal seemed next to impossible. The traffic of Cairo seemed more dangerous than before and its noise more exacerbating to the nerves. I began to worry over trivial things, like the possibility of having trouble getting visas extended.

I had assumed that the hotel could do it for me, but no. It appeared that we should have to spend time again in Cairo on that chore when we seemed to have done so little. It would be infuriating to spend time in an office, queuing; and now we should have to go to the British Embassy, which, I here record for the information of other travellers, shuts at one. We were tired indeed and the future seemed to have burdens in it that were . . . pyramidal. We drifted down to the basement of the hotel, where there was a twenty-four-hour restaurant and we lingered long over a meal, not eating much but not saying much either. It was difficult to get the drumming of the car out of our bodies.

That night once more I couldn't sleep. In the end I got up, switched on the smallest of the lights and set about putting various things in my journal. It made me feel better. Writing things down is therapeutic.

After breakfast we braced ourselves and set off to extend our visas. By an odd irony we got the job done in seconds and at once the tragedies of the night became silly. We were now stuck with additional time when we had not expected to be free. As we were in the right area we went to the Museum of Egyptology, that very odd building with its, of all things, Latin inscriptions on the front. I had to do this because I proposed to write at least a thousand words on the muddle the museum was in, having been shocked and disappointed the last time we visited it. Any writer, or perhaps I should say any journalist, will understand my irritation when I say that in the years between my visits the display had been entirely reorganized and was now as accessible and reasonable as most other museums. My thousand words (already composed in my head) went straight down the drain.

Of course the museum shows too much for the available space. But what else can it do? The needs of the scholar, the casual amateur and the tourist all conflict. The first needs to know everything, the second something and the last nothing. The inevitable crowding of sculpture together, while it is convenient for a scholar more concerned with comparison of details, does remove any possibility of aesthetic enjoyment. You cannot concentrate on one piece of sculpture when your eye is jostled, so to speak, by a crowd of others. However, aesthetic enjoyment is a modern addition to whatever those carvings were about so perhaps it is no great loss. You could even argue that the splendidly enjoyable *objets* so lovingly exhibited in the Luxor Museum is some sort of falsification; but of what?

They say there is or was a mummy room in the museum, but I have never seen it. The craft of the Egyptologist is too often mortuary for my comfort and I think that mummies are at once disgusting and pitiable. Once the experts have done their jobs of examination, from an assessment of how many threads to the inch in the bandages, through a numbering and photographing of the amulets to the final belated medical examination of the patient the remnants should be burned. There was good sense in the custom of using mummies for fuel in the earliest Egyptian railways. It got out of the way objects that had already lasted too long. So if there *is* a mummy room we did not see it.

What we did see was first the collection from the tomb of Tutankhamun. The collection is, as all the world knows, an extraordinary assemblage of furniture of one sort or another. It is as if when the young man died the whole contents of his house had been swept together by the removal men and dumped in the tomb. It's difficult to think that he would really need all those bows in the next world. Someone (a removal man) scooped them out of the bow chest or bow rack or bow cupboard and dumped them. As for the famous shrines that guarded the mummy they seem tinselly. The celebrated goddesses who stand round the shrine and spread their arms protectively are often published as if they were life size but in fact they are only about eighteen inches high and doll-like. It is not really easy to feel with Howard Carter that they are 'moving symbols of love and compassion'. Sheer numbers in the case of this exhibition defeat their own end. I guess that an Egyptologist would trade most of the heaped-up duplicates for one written document! It is difficult not to feel irritated with the ancient priests who packed away rolls and rolls of papyrus in the tomb – all of them blank.

We also went to the carefully guarded jewel room, where only a certain number of people are admitted at a time. Here again it is difficult not to carp. The truth is that jewellery dies if it isn't worn. There is a curious dullness that comes over gold in a showcase as if it knows it's in the wrong place. *They say* that gold doesn't tarnish. What, then, accounts for the obvious difference between the gold of your wife's wedding ring and the stale pieces of yellow metal exhibited in museums? Is it microscopic dust? Is it dirt? Does the gleam of gold when worn derive from the 'natural oils of the body?' If so, then there should be a stately ball given once every so often for curators and their wives or girlfriends or husbands or boyfriends (we have to be *so* careful!) at which that ancient stuff is given an airing and a chance to resume its former splendour. There is, alas, a proviso. The jewellery is for men as well as women and in both cases you have to be dark brown. Anyone who has ever seen a 'white man' on the stage masquerading as an ancient Egyptian will know what I mean.

The question of rarity value is interesting. Silver was more precious than gold, steel rarer than either. Yet there must have been masses of meteoritic iron lying about the place though we have only one dagger blade to show for it. What happened to all the rest? In any case, precious stones do not seem to have been gathered for intrinsic value because where possible the jewellers used glass. The splendid pectorals which Tutankhamun wore were once thought to be full of precious stones but not a bit of it. The object of the pectoral was to be colourful and splendid, not glittering and precious. In any case the repertory of precious stones should be called rather of 'semi-precious stones'. They used quartz and obsidian for the eyes of statues – obsidian probably from Lipari on the north side of Sicily. Turquoise they found in Sinai. Lapis lazuli probably came all the way from Afghanistan! Gold came from Nubia by the ton. The nearest source of silver was Anatolia and they very rarely used it. They found amethyst and green feldspar in the desert. Also yellow jasper. But though they would use stones when they were pretty (rose-quartz is an example) they were happy with coloured glass and may have regarded it as just as valuable. Their most precious stone by our reckoning was emerald. The sight of all that jewellery set me wondering how 'value' came about. I don't mean 'value' as it applied by the time the Lydians invented money. I mean how the concept of value arose in the very beginning when even the idea of 'mine' and 'thine' must have been no more than hazily formulated. There must have been a time when the man-creature liked not just to pick up the pretty pieces of yellow stone from streams or sandy plains but to keep them; and then, oh most destructive and aweful moment, swapped them, this one for that or this one for a lick of your marrow bone or this white stone for that yellow stone. Ignoring as we should the authoritative declarations of professional economists can we not see a mystery in the way the ancient Egyptians mingled what we should call 'costume jewellery' with the occasionally 'genuinely precious' stones? Certainly they were not at all interested in sparkle, for their jewels were never faceted except by accident as in crystals. Their only cut was flat or cabochon. Then, too, they carved rock crystal into smooth rounded surfaces with no apparent delight in the exquisite geometry of nature. It is impossible to put oneself back there in the position of people so stripped of our assumptions, or perhaps it is better to say innocent of them. We are so furred up with the growth of needs and complications and laborious knowledge.

Here and there are the objects that would delight any age but suffer where they are from museum dullness and surrounding competition. The outer, gold sarcophagus of Tutankhamun lies at one end of the room; and with a feeling for the symbolic nature of gold rather than its rarity, its financial value, even its beauty as an exhibit, the makers have covered it thickly with coloured inlay – enamel I think – which disguises the metal. Perhaps in the jewel room more than anywhere else you find a denial of the facile idea that they were 'just like us'. We find on the contrary that they were very, very different.

Here, in the museum, I suffered once again that simple trip-up by circumstances which can make long-laid plans come foolishly to nothing. I wanted to see the diorite statue of Chephren but simply could not find it. I wandered round and consulted the plan and then the museum shut. That was that.

However, seeing the museum at all was a bonus, a visit snatched from time laid aside for renewing visas and therefore a sheer gain. Reeling with sleeplessness and too many exhibits we got ourselves taxied to the hotel and slept away the afternoon. This was necessary because our day was only just begun. Time was now short and endurance almost at an end. I needed to make up for several nights I had lost. I fell so deeply asleep that when I was woken up I had no idea at all where I was.

Alaa called for us and drove us to an exhibition of modern paintings by the modern Egyptian artist Salah 'Enany which we had wanted to see. It is one thing to go mulling round among ancient leftovers but what is Egypt if not its young people? So we went, looked and were impressed. They were oils mostly. They were, and this seemed strange to me at first, pervaded by gloom. I mean that though the interiors were shaded reasonably enough and the figures in shadow, even street scenes were dimmed by the same atmosphere of shadow as if a total darkness were waiting in the corners and would at some future time well out from them and submerge the whole. Yet the pictures had compassion and satire in equal quantities. It could not be satire of a very overt nature. Egypt is not the kind of country where it would be tolerated. The pictures, if they satirize anything, strike out at city life and bourgeois life at that. All the characters are seen to be busy doing things and staring at emptiness. They are not even puzzled by the worthlessness of their own lives. Sexual encounters seem either a desperate grabbing at something which must of its very nature get away, or the juxtaposition of people who

191

are really attending to something else. You feel all the time that apparently normal groups of people are beginning to attend to something, listen for something that is expected and will prove to be an unpaintable horror. Yet that horror will be vacuity. The artist in question had a long training as a caricaturist on a daily paper. He painted the whole of this exhibition, some forty or fifty canvases, in a violent burst of passionate creativity. I asked him why the pervading tone of the pictures was dark in a land of such brilliant light? He replied that Egypt may seem so to foreigners. But, said he, smiling, you may if you like believe that since the city Egyptian spends his life in shadowy rooms the darkness of the picture is not in any sense a social criticism!

This was the tip of something. What is more, the job of unearthing the rest of the mountain or political structure, whatever it may be, will be left for someone else. I cannot do it. Why was there a fattish man in a dark red *tarbush* standing on a barrel and surrounded by a small crowd in a narrow, dark street where all the figures were dark? Why was that 'extended family' seated round a table, all withdrawn, all silent, all preoccupied with the contemplation of something not painted? Did I overreact, and was this nothing more than a brilliant perception of boredom? I do not think so. There was in this painting evidence of that trite bit of criticism 'more than meets the eye', and talent getting less attention than it deserved because to draw overmuch attention to it might get the artist or the critic into trouble. It was all as enigmatic as the old woman who was loaded with jewellery and telling dirty stories.

We returned late that night to the hotel and ate a silent meal in the downstairs restaurant, which only came properly alive after midnight. Then sleepily into the night or morning I scribbled notes of the crowded day before I went to sleep. It was not possible to leave them till later in the week, for in the morning I was booked to take a kind of dive into the Delta. It is after all the place where the man who wants to know about Egypt should start, rather than end. It was all proving to be – to have been – a messy, upside-down journey.

'Tomorrow the Delta. I don't want to and am seriously considering having a headache or something. I learn too much; or less and less.'

We were fourteen storeys up on the west side of the Nile again. The traffic was still swarming and glittering and parping down the corniche.

The morning hummed with sleep-lessness. Alaa called for me in his car and I had not the energy to resist. There was a third person in the car. I shall call him 'the doctor'. He was tall, very thin and elegant. He was connected with a university, perhaps as a medical adviser, and he was willing to talk but had little English. He wore a dark suit, very sharp, with flared bottoms to his trousers. I was reminded of Akhmet returning to 'his' village though this was a more expensive suit. It is high fashion in Cairo. We drove off north down the river then across by the most northerly of the Cairene bridges. There were miles of city then more miles of advertisements, Esso, Mobil, Michelin, food, clothes, restaurants, all advertising in two scripts which started from opposite poles and never seemed to achieve an absolute transliteration. Then, as the billboards became fewer and we could see open country, there were pyramids of oranges and tangerines for sale by the road, stacked on the ground, lit brilliantly by the sun . . . heaped richly for miles. We reached Berket el Sab a considerable city or at least a centre of dense population since this now was un-tourist Egypt with a vengeance, very crowded and beautiful when we turned off the main road on to a narrower one. Almost at once we turned again but on to a wider road made of heaped-up earth. It ran straight for miles and its builders seemed to have been indifferent to the boundaries of the fields through which it ran. The doctor told me it was 'a treaty road'. When the British – us, if you like – withdrew to the Canal Zone, a condition was that the Egyptian Government should build these roads to make British troop movements easy. Those 'treaty roads', once an inconvenience and imposition on the fellaheen, were now tree-lined and useful, with grateful shade and a wide, dirt surface for pack or draught animals, for flocks and herds, the occasional truck and bicyclists. The fellaheen call the bicycle 'the iron donkey'. They have taken it to their hearts in a way they never did their donkeys. The machines are tended but the animals scruffy.

We turned off into a yet smaller road by which a yoke of a cow and a buffalo, both blindfolded, were turning a new metal waterwheel. We passed several more of these. I couldn't believe that they were drawing water from the narrow canal. It must have come from boreholes. The Delta is the most diseased area of Egypt though the people here looked as healthy as in Upper and Middle Egypt. We turned off again and were in the village where the doctor was born. There was the usual village mess, usual uninspiring untidiness, straw, sticks, reeds, dung, dust and a narrow, soupy canal that trees hung over. There were palms, acacias and figs. Crops were high and dense, green, dark green, heavy. We were met by the doctor's cousin, a good-looking young man, not dressed like the doctor but in a grey galabia and turban. At once he got Alaa to tell us that he was home on holiday, which was why he was dressed in this manner. He had been working in Iraq as a driver and would go back at the end of the month. He was energetic. He rushed us to his house, where we met his father, a white-bearded old gentleman who had known the *Koran* by heart by the time he was twelve. He was holy and had lips which were far too red and full for perfect beauty. We had tea, served by one woman while others peeped. The *Koran* provided him with a quotation for any eventuality. He asked me if I spoke Arabic. When I said that regrettably I did not he replied at such length that Alaa had to translate. 'It is much to the glory of God that he creates men of different kinds and natures and languages.'

After delivering this apothegm he bowed round the company as *Reis* Shasli had bowed when talking about his two wives and children. We drank our tea in silence. At length the cousin led us off to see the house opposite, his own house, which he was having built with money he had earned in Iraq. It was yet another example of that drift away from the land to where there is good living to be had, money to be made and an eventual return of the native to local wealth and dignity. The house was three storeys high and just like his father's house had not a single exact right angle. Everything was slightly *off*. It was all made of concrete. We stood with the proud owner on the concrete roof and gazed at what seemed acres of yard for storing junk. I asked to have this explained. Well, it was a vista over the roofs of the village. You have wooden rafters, then bamboos at right angles, then a layer of straw, then a layer of earth. After that you use the flat roof to store fuel – maize stalks, sugar cane, branches of cotton with a few white bols still adhering, reeds, straw, farm junk, cow dung. It all made sense when you understood it, for this was a way of not using the valuable land that came up to the very walls of the houses in exquisitely neat fields of wheat, bean, clover.

There was a woman working below us in the fields. She carried a basket and was tossing not seed but fertilizer between the rows of vegetables. Once it might have been unnecessary before the various dams were built; then after that, it might have been *sebakh* but now it was phosphates from the Eastern Desert – from the factories I had seen on the Red Sea coast or on the road to Kom Ombo. Today, the soil of Egypt, once famous for its inexhaustible fertility needs artificial fertilizer. So the high dam gives and takes. I found that the doctor's cousin had a diploma in agriculture and was quite aware of what was going on. It was hyperphosphate the woman was spreading and yes, it came from the Eastern Desert. Later she would spread fungicide and after that insecticide. I asked, in as matter-of-fact a way as possible, about sanitation. Well, the soil pits were only cleaned out after several years. The soil is so porous it absorbs and neutralizes the night soil. They do not use the night soil as manure after it is dug out. I was not clear what happened to it.

We came down from the roof and the doctor led us away. We went down the alley past a snorting mill, which was grinding flour for the village. It was co-operatively owned. It was crowded with women, all with baskets or sacks of grain to be ground. Probing, I found that the mill had once belonged to 'a rich man, a landlord'. But after the revolution. . . .

What had happened to the landlord? Well, the landlord was still about. Yes, he still has some land, not much.

We came away and the landlord was pointed out to me. He glanced our way then walked sideways into a thicket and disappeared. The doctor led us onwards to a large stable with barred windows and a big, rickety wooden door. Only, of course, it was no stable but the house of the doctor's father. He tapped the door then opened it. His mother appeared, tiny in black, with wrinkled, yellow face. She welcomed us to the usual complex of haphazard walls and screes of rubble. She was sharing the kitchen with a goat. She showed us a door at the top of two steps. We went up into the main room.

On our left that end of the room was occupied by a vast bed, the fabrics of which seemed not to have been touched for years. There was a couch opposite us, then another on our left under the iron-barred windows. On the couch opposite us was what I first took to be a pile of rags. But then I saw a cap and shawl with an aquiline and emaciated face between them. This was the doctor's father, Mustapha. The doctor bent down and kissed him on both cheeks. He was ancient and sick. He held out a lean hand to me and Alaa in turn, then relapsed into a drawn preoccupation with his own sufferings. I sat under the window with Alaa. At first the doctor sat on the couch by his father but his mother brought him a chair. The cousin came in and took the place the doctor had left. Alaa began to murmur in my ear. 'The old man is Mustapha. He is seventy-six. He farms two acres and deals in corn.' It was strange. Once more, what is dirt? I had ceased to know, except in the starkest terms of filth and decay. In this room there seemed to be no more than dust and a worn, desolate look about every object among the customary untidiness. Already the doctor's sharp, black suit was affected. The dust of the place, the cobwebs pendent from the high ceiling, the oily patterns of the cement walls had modified his startling otherness, his city slickness, and made him part of the rest. Suddenly there was loud discussion. Father Mustapha was shouting. 'No! No! No!'

I turned to Alaa who murmured again.

'They are talking about Mustapha's granddaughter. She is – how would you say – our doctor's niece.'

The old man went on crying out. There was now another woman in the room. She was the doctor's sister and the niece was her daughter. She was the daughter of Mustapha and the old woman. She looked the same age as her mother, wrinkled, drawn, yellow-faced in black. Indeed, there was no more than fourteen years between them.

The doctor talked soothingly to his father. The two women went away to prepare a meal. What would I like, meat or vegetables? Oh, vegetables for sure! So very soon the meal came, bread, old cheese, and new cheese, and huge, hot pizza-like cakes on a vast tray of pewter. We used our right hands to eat with in the traditional manner, delicately keeping our left hands hidden except for an occasional furtive shove at a recalcitrant piece. It was an excellent meal. The old cheese was good but fierce. The doctor went on talking to his father between bites. The old man ate nothing and answered grumpily.

Alaa murmured again.

'The price of corn is going down. The doctor knows corn merchants in the city – big men. They say Mustapha should hold on. But the old man is pessimistic and wants to sell now, even if he loses money.'

'What are they all saying about a girl?'

196

'That's the granddaughter, the doctor's niece.'

I soon saw that Alaa had killed two birds with one stone. I needed to have a glimpse of the Delta and the doctor needed to see his family. The girl was in trouble sure enough. She was at the university. She had sat or was about to sit on a committee of protest at student conditions. There had been no violence or illegality or even protest, so far. The president of the university had agreed to meet the committee and had appointed a day for it. The matter was wholly internal to the university. Nevertheless, a few days before the police had called on the doctor's brother-in-law, had brow-beaten him, an ordinary peasant farmer – a fellah. 'You have bad children,' they said. 'You should be careful. You don't know what trouble you may get your family into, not controlling a girl like that. We want you to order your daughter to come home so that she is in the care of her parents. What does a girl want with a university?'

I exclaimed at this as in duty bound, my liberal habits of thought, if not conviction, outraged.

Alaa murmured reminders. After the Ultras murdered Sadat there was trouble throughout Egypt which never got into the papers. The Ultras had stormed the police stations at Asyut – oh, our ragged river police with their shining guns! They had killed the policemen and taken their weapons. They held Asyut for three days until the government dropped paratroops on them. Did I not remember the new camps for training a 'sort of police'? After Sadat's murder there had been shooting in Cairo for weeks. The cost in lives would never be known, the truth never told. Now the government was still scared of the least breath of criticism and at the first hint of it, would send in the police.

The talking had become fierce again. This time the doctor's sister, who, of course, was the girl's mother, was doing the shouting. I could just make out the tenor.

'It'll be a scandal! I won't have it! She will go to prison and the family will be ruined! Scandal! Scandal!'

The doctor's little mother chipped in. Alaa swore that his translation was exact.

'We shouldn't make too much of a fuss about it. It's really rather honourable to take part in a protest.'

At this, the heap of old clothes erupted. Thin arms shot out of it and shook fists in the air.

'No! No! I won't have it! Consider *me*! The price of corn is going

197

down, my piles are torturing me and now the police – what have I done to get this wretched girl as a trouble on top of everything else? Bring her to me here, and I'll kill her!'

The master had spoken it seemed and there was silence for a while. Then the doctor began to talk again, quietly, soothingly. No one else said anything. This was what it was all about, evidently. The doctor would go and see his brother-in-law and together they would consider what should be done. After all, he himself knew the university. There were good men in the university after all. So he would leave us for fifteen minutes.

Water was brought and poured over our hands into a bowl. The doctor stood up and went off for his fifteen minutes. The father of the cousin – the old man with the full, red lips who had known the *Koran* by heart when he was twelve – came in, bowing to all. He sat down by the heap of rags and the yellow, aquiline face, which I could now see had a touch of the doctor's profile in it. The grandfather withdrew into his preoccupation with corn and piles and granddaughters and piles again. The father of the cousin talked soothingly with his full, red lips. He was quoting from the *Koran* it seemed.

The old man's eyes shut. Fifteen minutes passed, thirty, forty-five. An hour. There was silence except for the bee-murmur of the *Koran*.

The doctor returned. There was talk. He had advised his brother-in-law to wait – to do nothing for ten days. It might well be no more than a scare. To bring the girl home would be to admit that the family had done wrong. Everyone should wait and see. Simpler all round to wait and see. Probably nothing would happen, nothing at all.

It was time to go. The show was over and I should never find out what did in fact happen. We stood up and said our thanks. It had all been dramatic. But the question of the corn was not settled, the piles a little worse and the girl – there was no conclusion. It had been dramatic but it was not a drama.

In the car on the way back along the dirt road the doctor turned to me.

'How would it have been in England?'

The differences were so vast I couldn't even think where to begin.

'The police wouldn't . . . no. Let me think.'

Presently the basic difference appeared to me.

'In England the family involvement would not be so widespread. It would be – nuclear, if you see what I mean!'

'I understand.'

'Only if the girl was very young would it be seen as a matter for her parents.'

'Ah!'

'Uncles and aunts, grandparents – they wouldn't be brought into the picture at all.'

'Not ever?'

'They wouldn't expect it.'

The doctor nodded.

'Well,' he said. 'Now you have had a glimpse of what the books mean when they talk about the Third World and the extended family.'

'I'd always thought of the extended family as rather a good thing, in itself.'

Alaa and the doctor laughed together but said nothing.

So we came back along the treaty road, then along tarmac between the heaps of unsold oranges in the hot sun. It had all been depressing in some ways but I had asked to move a little closer to Egyptian life, particularly the life of the fellah and there it was, wide of family, narrow of outlook. The patriarch and his piles, a grandfather wounded in his self-esteem by his granddaughter! The mother more bitter than anxious, the father no more concerned than the others, the educated son, smoothing things down and persuading everyone to do nothing.

But things had improved for them. The doctor was a doctor, the cousin who was a driver in Iraq had a diploma of agriculture.

'Alaa – the cousin's diploma – what will he do when he comes back?'

'He proposes to buy taxis and start a firm.'

'What about his land?'

'Who knows?'

They had piped water from the city, their few beasts had looked healthy and the old man had surplus corn to sell.

'Alaa – how much money was involved in the corn deal that didn't come off?'

'About two thousand pounds.'

The grandfather was a top fellah, then, a *Kulak*. The cousin will first drive a taxi then manage taxis, then be a 'Big Man'. What will happen to the neat little fields that lap around the ill-angled house? The granddaughter – I imagined her as one of the round-faced girls you see in western dress with calf-length skirt and a handkerchief hiding her hair – she will be given in marriage; or if she stays the course and gets a degree she will join the serried ranks of the graduate unemployed. I remembered the cousin telling funny stories of how the Iranians attacked and how the Iraqis dealt with them. It was, he implied, really very amusing.

So it was back to the hotel again and an attempt on my part to pull things together. We had done most of the things we had set out to do but really very inadequately. This was, I now saw, inherent in our situation. I had resisted that realization for months but had now to accept that whatever I wrote would not be about Egypt, it would be about me, or if you like, us middleclass English from a peaceful bit of England, wandering more or less at will through infinite complexity, not even looking for anything specific but hoping that the lucky thing would turn up. It was not that there were so many Egypts, it was that there were so many Egypts in me, none of them conflicting but none of them connected. The canyon filled with the débris of ten million years, the long line of pyramids so recently erected, Muslim and Copt, Arab and Jew, the ankh in the apse of the Catholic church – I was trying to do in effect what the Egyptians themselves were trying to do with their adjective 'Pharoni'. It was a pretence of unity throughout time where there was, and had been, none.

The traffic was a noisy river beneath the window. We could never be more than favoured tourists, seeing occasional strangenesses but unable to bring them into coherence. Even if I could bear to come back to Egypt I could only add to my own confusion rather than simplify an attitude. There was the country round Sinai to be seen, the oases to visit, Nubia to examine where it lay along the lake above its drowned villages. Even outside the window of our hotel the modern city was ineluctable. How to describe the high-rises that make this stretch of the Nile look like anywhere else? They look a little papery, those high-rises, the way Egyptian temples look like brown cardboard. Both types *look* like that but there's no connection. There's a bit of the insect's nest about a high rise in the hot sun, they are not like honeycombs though but combs for the hair, set upright. They look like fitments for an electronic system where you slot bits in. The papery balconies give them the look of a corncob that has been gnawed all the way down so you have the core left and attachments where the seeds were. Or if their metal and concrete seems more solid than papery, then you feel that if you ran your thumbnail down them you would make a note, more or less. Colour? Biscuit, light brown, dark brown, ugly. They are deliberately ugly you'd say, ugly without compromise, a disease of the city, a formal deformity and unconscious insolence. In fact, of course, they are none of these things but neutral. In theory they should be a stack of homes in which inhabitants make a bit their own, slot a unit into the system but the attempts are invisible if they exist and the human sign is likely to be a scrap of paper floating down past empty balconies and sheets of glass, blank, blank, blank, until it lands in the river, where it does not move; and the stillness of the water in a river that once ran and spread is an emblem. It is the same shape and size and colour, that river, as the Thames.

We had meant to see Nubia but had seen Kalabsha. We had hoped to see poor fellaheen but for the most part had met prosperous ones and craftsmen. Either we had been steered deliberately in paths thought most suitable for us – which knowing Alaa now I did not believe – or Egyptian health and wealth, by the new supply of clean water and the mysterious non-operation of economic 'laws', had improved out of recognition. I had only seen one poor devil of a boy who was skeletal and surely dying. It had been said that a Nubian from Upper Egypt could do the work of ten Egyptians from the Delta. If that had ever been true, it was true no longer, of that I was certain, yet the proper person to report on this would be a medical statistician, a doctor.

I was tired. Tired I went to bed and endured a confusion of dreams and tired I woke to a day that in prospect seemed as long as the river. This was the day on which (as cultural objects) we were to be presented to the Minister for Cultural Affairs. I braced myself to ask questions. I think Ann had an idea that given an opening she would put in a word for the research station that was trying to produce a million olive trees and stop it from being closed down. On the other hand she had come to an understanding of what a wife should be in Egypt: at least one step behind her husband and not speaking until spoken to, if then. To me, who knew her so well, the conflict was perceptible.

We were called for after breakfast by a ministerial side-kick and driven to the appropriate ministry. It was not much like the house we had been in the day before. It was a mansion that would not have been out of place in the Champs-Élysées. Ann, Alaa and I went in and were seated. The minister was surrounded by aides but proved to be a very large Egyptian gentleman, dressed by Savile Row and speaking excellent English. He had that extraordinary air of sheer happiness and good nature, an enjoyment in the act of living which I had come mistakenly to believe was inseparable from the good luck of being Nubian. Evidently you could have it and be Egyptian too. We began to talk, Alaa now silent, because unneeded. Everything was amiability. I was not asking questions, I was being asked them! After a certain number of queries as to our health and comfort, the ministerial penny dropped. It was conceived that as a cultural object I might have some influence with those two rock like institutions the British Museum and the British Government! This was flattering but unnerving. I did manage to mention Kalabsha and the plea for a road back into Nubia; and once I saw Ann open her mouth then shut it again. It seems, though, that roads are not really cultural. Certain objects in the British Museum undoubtedly are. It was all, said the minister, very difficult. Undeniably the Sphinx's beard, then held in the vaults of the British Museum was useless to the museum and essential to the Sphinx. But there are rules – such rules! And so on. What could I do? Eventually I promised to exercise the Englishman's inalienable if useless resource and write to *The Times* about it. We then stood up to go but had to be given our presents, that invariable Egyptian custom which I find so embarrassing because with air travel one cannot take a supply of presents to give in return and I did not think that passing presents on (Minya to Cairo) would be appropriate.

We were also given a present of quite another kind and I found it very valuable. The minister, explaining the work of the ministry, told us that they had already shifted 50,000 tons of rubble out of Cairo and would 'soon' get rid of the rest, which was essential if the architecture of the city was to be seen at its best. When they had cleared the side-streets Cairo would be as clean as a western city. More than that, his department had given its approval to and was overseeing the plan to restore the ancient mosques of the city. Had we seen this work?

No, we had not.

In that case he would send Mr So-and-so (Mr So-and-so leapt smartly to his feet) with us and we should be given a chance to see what the Ministry of Culture was doing to preserve and protect Egypt's Muslim heritage. So, with expressions of mutual esteem we left, Ann never having had a chance to have her say about olive trees.

'But I *will*, I promise you!'

'You'll have to lobby the Minister of Agriculture.'

We drove off through the city, slowly as necessary – one mile an hour is good going in Cairo. You sit in a jam, or stoppage – a '*Sudd*'. In between you do sixty miles an hour.

The mosque was enormous. It was fourteenth century and built right round a great square. It had been a school, too, or contained one – a university perhaps, but now the only people allowed in were the restorers. They were astonishing. At once, at a blow, we were given an insight into what Alaa, in his more committed moments, called the 'Islamic Revival'. It was not so much the work of restoration itself as the attitude of the restorers. There must have been fifty of them. They were quiet and concentrated but they radiated a happiness, quieter than a Nubian's but to be felt. They wore western dress, some of the young women not even covering their hair. Here and there they had set up trestle tables and plans were spread on these and objects, stone elements of a carving it might be, photographs or ink drawings to scale. Everywhere round these tables people were examining and talking in low tones to each other about the work in hand. Here and there young people, mere children, were busy with rough work; cleaning the surface of stone, picking dirt out of intricate carvings. These, too, seemed to be doing their humble work with the dedication of a lay brother in the monastic vegetable patch. It was all so quiet. Mr So-and-so from the ministry introduced us to the director, who took us round, first from table to table. In one part cooks were preparing food for the workers. In another a few experts were carving stone to replace what had worn or weathered away. At yet another table paints were being mixed, the strong, assertive colours of Islam and the Arab world.

We went into the mosque itself. The dominant colours were brilliant blue and gold. Typically you would see a quotation from the *Koran* in gold leaf against brilliant blue. I was told how beautiful the calligraphy was, but of course saw it with the blank stare of incomprehension. To me the interlaced patterns were agreeable, nothing more; but I accepted what I was told.

The mosque had stained-glass windows and here we felt on firmer ground. For western and, better still, medieval western stained glass sets a standard which can be equalled but not surpassed. The Arab – Egyptian? Nubian? – genius expresses itself in colour combinations that we should call garish, when they put pieces of stained glass together. It is usually, though not invariably, a mosaic of geometrical patterns and I cannot say, even in this mosque that the glass was particularly good. It had, like all southern glass, a slight touch of the conservatory or even the bathroom about it. Nevertheless, like everything else in the mosque it was being restored painstakingly by glass specialists among the young people.

A notable point about these windows and one which delighted me (since I have always thought of stained glass as a method of keeping unwanted light out of a building rather than letting it in) was that these windows were accepted as means of keeping out the light of the sun – and the moon! They were known as 'Sun and Moon windows'. The name was suggestive of a southern full moon, such as the moon we had seen rise in dustless, cloudless brilliance over the Eastern Desert, a moon you could read by and which could well try the eyes, not by forcing them to strain after the curled script but by making the whiteness of the paper intolerable.

We walked round in this collegiate rectangle, enjoying the near-silence, which was only modified by the murmur of consultation, the gentle tap, tap of a mallet and the occasional sound of a heavy blow from up on scaffolding where great blocks of stone were being shifted. It was a most moving atmosphere of health and sanity in which you knew all intolerance and hysteria had been put aside and what was being done was for the greater glory of God. So there is that strand too in the 'Islamic Revival'. It is a thing to remember among all the horrors of terrorism.

But we had yet another appointment. We went by car in the direction of the citadel, turned off to the left then climbed again to the region that I believe is called Darbel Habbena. We were going to call at last on Mr Hassan Fathy. He lives on the top floor of an ancient Mameluke palace. We climbed to it by way of a winding stair, which I felt would have been more appropriate to the tower of a cathedral. He received us with gentle courtesy. This at first was made a little difficult by the behaviour of his seven cats. They exhibited every half-minute or so their feline capacity for instant combat with yells and thumps. Mr Fathy would expostulate each time mildly with an admonitory 'Oh pussy, pussy!' He sat in what was either a smoking or dressing gown behind a table with a few papers on it. We had come to pay our respects, nothing else, but this was difficult while the cats were at war. Finally his housekeeper, a large Egyptian lady in traditional costume, tempted the flock, herd, group – what can one say as a collective noun of creatures so solitary by nature? – by means of food out of the room and shut the door behind them and herself.

Hassan Fathy is in his eighties and is said sometimes to be a little abstracted in manner, but we did not find him so. I wished to pay him the respect due to a man who has conceived, promulgated and tried to carry out a great social idea. He murmured that it had all been a failure – in Egypt at least. He had tried and tried again but each time it had all come to nothing. I suggested diffidently that the mosque and the houses he had built at New Gourna were there for all to see. If only the tourists who thronged round the Colossi of Memnon could be induced to walk a couple of hundred yards. . . .

No, no, he said. That would do no good. It was the fellaheen – they were the people who should be reached, and after that, well, there was the government, that solid immovable rock. It had been a *complete* failure. Gentle old soul, he seemed to cherish the failure for its own sake.

Then he brightened.

'All the same, I have been in Mexico – New Mexico. I was there for twenty-three days and – do you know? They took to it at once! They have adobe, of course, and when I introduced the idea of the mud brick arch to them they took to it at once! Think of that! Forty years I have tried in Egypt without achieving anything! Then in New Mexico in only twenty-three days I achieve a success! Even my book – they read it. My book is now a text book in America and France.'

We stayed a little longer, trying to convey respect and admiration without being too fulsome. Finally we stood up and Mr Fathy said how kind we were and so on – all the courtesies. We went away down the winding stair and into the night.

'Actually,' said Alaa, 'I did not tell you, but he is a prince.'

'Officially?'

'Of course. But since the revolution. . . .'

We drove away across the city to spend the evening with a friend of Alaa's who was a film producer and made documentaries of the Egyptian countryside. They spoke for themselves those films, making audible what we had seen. There was a worker in a mud brickyard endlessly setting out the pats of mud. He was grateful for pathetic small mercies, as well he might be. There was a refugee from Suez, a mother with small children, who simply talked about them and her animals, not really distinguishing one from the other. There was a portrait of a village. The work and play – play of children at

205

least – broke off at a certain moment; and then you found they were all flocking to a level crossing and waiting for the train. It was the great event of the day. The train trundled through slowly and the children waved and people looked at the faces in the window, infinitely distant from them. The film was called, *The Village Where The Train Does Not Stop*. She showed us the video film of a festival of Arab music which took me straight back to the boat, with Alaa and Rushdie or *Reis* Shasli switching on the tape of Arab utility music. But she was very kind to show us so much about Egyptian life and we were duly grateful. We were in fact getting the insights we might well have started with. Then we drove back to the hotel and fell into bed. The night disappeared without trace and in a flash and we had interviews in the morning so got up at dawn more or less and packed. Ann was interviewed first and was shown the picture in the morning papers of our interview with the Minister for Culture. Emboldened, she appealed to the women of Egypt to rescue the *Institute for the Multiplication of Mango and Olive Trees*. Surely any Egyptian male worth his salt would give his wife an olive tree? Were Egyptian women not capable of seeing the beauty of this idea? A million olive trees! Then I was interviewed and answered the usual questions. The hotel suddenly became very respectful and presented our bill almost with an air of apology. We drove to the airport, said an emotional farewell to Alaa, went through the airport as in a dream, were lifted into the air where we both fell fast asleep. Sleeping we flew out over the choked canyon, then the sea, Greece, Yugoslavia, Austria, Germany . . . and woke with the plane commencing its long descent across the North Sea. It had been a dream really.

What I have tried to describe and what these sixty pictures show is a touristic commonplace, the *fact* that Egypt is a land of wonderful beauty. Perhaps I have been able to contribute a rider to that fact – if a fact can have a rider – call it a proposition – that proposition: namely that Egypt suffers from the indifference of its inhabitants to that beauty; and that those with power and influence in the land have missed a golden opportunity of counteracting the drab and dangerous ugliness of its domestic buildings. Perhaps the omission has been deliberate on the part of what is commonly called 'vested interests'. I do not say that Hassan Fathy's mud brick vaults are a complete solution to the problem, but at the very least they would restore to Egypt what it has so sadly lost, a belief that buildings other than ruins are worth thought and care.

In our defended wanderings we have been forced into a deliberate mistake, that of trying to look at everything and having an opinion on everything. Of course the result is that you end with opinions on nothing. It must remain then an expanded journal in which I have been able, by consulting my notes, to put back to some extent what I felt and more often what I was thinking. The reader may here and there find sufficient description to enable him to some extent to share the irritations and excitements of our absurd journey. There is a sense in which any journey is absurd. If he finds himself now and then lying on his back in my bunk and staring upwards through a deck and two miles of superincumbent rock now worn away and aware at the same time that he is suspended over an invisible canyon two miles deep, he will perhaps have added to his experience a way of imagining things that will be unfamiliar. If he feels he would have made better use of the journey, come to more informed opinions and written a better book about it all, he may well be right and I would recommend him to stick to the one hundred pictures. It was, after all, a kind of challenge to see what would arise in an unusual juxtaposition of two cultures and two wildly differing sets of experience. As the scrap of papyrus says in the original Greek set out as epigraph to this volume:

> Sailors who skim deep waters, Tritons of the salt sea, and you
> Riders of the Nile who sail in happy course upon the smiling
> waters, tell us, friends, the comparison of the ocean with the
> fruitful Nile.

But an ampler summation of the experience in all its strange and nonsensical complexity can only be achieved by nonsense at the highest level: and as we returned at last to our own country a bit of nonsense from its literature seems an appropriate explanation and conclusion:

> the dram of eale
> doth all the noble substance of a doubt
> to his own scandal.

Illustration Acknowledgments

All photographs in the book are by William Golding except for the following:

Between pages 96–7 (i–xvi)

Brian T. North: p iv (top and bottom); p v (top); p xi (top)

Rainbird Archives: p vii (bottom)

Alaa Swafe: p viii (below)

Between pages 160–1 (xvii–xxxii)

J. Allan Cash: p xxx

Bruce Coleman: p xxiv (centre)

Douglas Dickens: p xxvii

Brian T. North: p xxi (top and bottom); p xxv; p xxviii; p xxix (top and bottom)

Roger Viollet: p xxiii (top)